CW00867542

The

Broadly Christian

ASSEMBLY BOOK

100 FURTHER READINGS FOR ASSEMBLY

EDITED BY DAVID SELF

Heinemann Educational Publishers
Halley Court, Jordan Hill, Oxford OX2 8EJ
a division of Reed Educational & Professional Publishing Ltd

OXFORD FLORENCE PRAGUE MADRID ATHENS
MELBOURNE AUCKLAND KUALA LUMPUR SINGAPORE
TOKYO IBADAN NAIROBI KAMPALA JOHANNESBURG
GABORONE PORTSMOUTH NH (USA) CHICAGO
MEXICO CITY SÃO PAULO

First published 1996

00 99 98 97 96 10 9 8 7 6 5 4 3 2 1

British Library Cataloguing in Publication Data
A catalogue record for this book is available from the British Library

ISBN 0 435 30247 7

Designed by Mike Brain
Typeset by Books Unlimited (Nottm) NG19 7QZ
Printed and bound in Great Britain by Clays Ltd, St Ives plc.

Acknowledgements
Copyright acknowledgements appear on page 339.

Contents

Introduction   *vii*

Festivals of Faith

1   Michaelmas (29 September)   *2*
2   Divali   *5*
3   All Saints' and All Souls' (1–2 November)   *10*
4   Remembrance   *13*
5   Thanksgiving (fourth Thursday in November)   *15*
6   Hanukkah   *18*
7   Maryam and the Miraculous Baby   *21*
8   The Road to Bethlehem   *26*
9   Epiphany (6 January)   *29*
10   Martin Luther King Day (third Monday in January)   *33*
11   Mardi Gras   *36*
12   Lent   *40*
13   Holi   *43*
14   St Patrick's Day (17 March)   *46*
15   The Annunciation (25 March)   *49*
16   Miss Mary Magdala   *55*
17   Wesak   *61*
18   Whitsun   *64*
19   Midsummer Fire (24 June)   *68*
20   Ramadan and Id-ul-Fitr   *71*

Stories, Parables and Legends

21   The Gift of Fire   *76*
22   The Happiest Man in the World   *80*

23   Parables Jesus Told   *83*

24   Take Up Thy Bed   *86*

25   The Talkative Turtle   *89*

26   The Baal Shem-Tov   *92*

27   Bubblefoot   *96*

28   Three Parables   *101*

29   The Blessing of El-ahrairah   *104*

30   The Peaceable Mongoose   *108*

31   The Man Who Planted Trees   *110*

32   The Mystery of the *Marie-Celeste*   *115*

33   Learn the Lesson   *117*

34   The Bricklayer   *119*

35   Nothing to be Done?   *121*

36   Blackout   *125*

37   Being Accepted   *128*

38   A Walk in the Woods   *132*

39   Four Eyes   *136*

40   Red the Bully   *139*

Saints Are Sinners Who Keep on Trying

41   Legion and Jairus   *144*

42   Pontius Pilate   *147*

43   The Young Prophet   *151*

44   The Prophet's Escape   *155*

45   Guru Nanak and the Banquet   *158*

46   John Wesley   *162*

47   No Schooling   *164*

48   Florence Nightingale   *168*

49   Don Bosco   *172*

50   William Booth   *176*

51   Lilian Westall: Housemaid   *180*

52   The Small Woman   *184*

53 'Jumbo' Wilson and Changi Jail *187*
54 Auschwitz, 1944 *191*
55 'Chesh' and the Cheshire Homes *195*
56 Sherpa Tenzing *199*
57 Another Country: Nelson Mandela
    and Willem de Klerk *202*
58 Rock On, Bobby *206*
59 The Princess *209*
60 Parents *212*

Thoughts for a Day

61 When the Curtain Goes Up... *216*
62 Our Doubts Are Traitors *217*
63 Oh Well *220*
64 Love is the Solution *222*
65 Prayer for Today *225*
66 What a Piece of Work *228*
67 Meditations *231*
68 The Incomplete World *235*
69 Keeping an Open Mind *237*
70 The Incredible Exploits of Nothing *240*
71 One God *244*
72 Accident or Purpose? *246*
73 The Gambler's Argument *249*
74 The First Mover *252*
75 Something In It? *255*
76 Bronze Heads *257*
77 No Pain, No Death *260*
78 Sure and Certain Hope *263*
79 Doomsday *266*
80 Something After Death? *269*

Love Thy Neighbour as Thyself

81 Tiny Tim: a Terror *274*
82 Temper, Temper *278*
83 Too Tall or Too Short? *281*
84 You're Just Immature... *284*
85 Streetwise *287*
86 Childhood 100 Years Ago *290*
87 Why Do We Go to School? *294*
88 The Problem with Food *298*
89 A Counter-blast to Tobacco *301*
90 Position Vacant *304*
91 The Bad Samaritan *306*
92 Human Rights *310*
93 The Automotive Nightmare *313*
94 Death Penalty *315*
95 Belsen: a Glimpse into Hell *317*
96 Hiroshima *319*
97 Urgent: Crisis in Africa *322*
98 Prisoner Abroad *326*
99 Facts of Life *330*
100 Dying ... and Death *332*

Calendar *335*

Author Source Index *336*

Acknowledgements *339*

Introduction

One of the regular performers on the original wartime *Brains Trust* on BBC Radio was the philosopher Professor C E M Joad. He quickly established his catchphrase: 'It all depends on what you mean...' It does, of course, all depend on what you mean by 'broadly'.

The 1988 Education Reform Act with its injunction to hold daily 'acts of collective worship' is not exactly helpful when it stresses that these acts should be 'wholly or mainly of a broadly Christian character'. No wonder the Act has caused confusion, uncertainty and even anger. What is meant by 'mainly'? How broad is 'broad'? And how can you make someone (especially a truculent teenager) 'worship'? After all, school 'worship' is not like, say, church worship if only because those present have not chosen to be there. If we are realistic, we must agree that a school act of worship (at its best) can do no more than provide an *opportunity* for worship. Whatever some politicians might like to believe, worship (which is a state of mind, not simply a posture) cannot be enforced. Other specific problems and questions of conscience arise in predominantly multi-cultural schools.

Over all, what can be said is that (as a result of the 1988 Act and subsequent circulars) more assemblies are now being held than was once the case, and that there are many more assembly leaders urgently in need of inspiration or at least of practical help. For it seems that schools *are* observing the new Act rather more closely than they did the 1944 one. This does not, however, mean that the whole school (or even years) are coming together for regular daily acts of worship or even assemblies. As Circular 3/89 issued by the then Department of Education and Science stated, daily collective worship may be organized for separate groups of pupils at any time during the school day – which allows for 'assembly' being part of a class registration period, conducted by a form teacher. In some schools a whole year may come together on certain days for a more conventional assembly while whole years may combine – as may houses and other groupings.

Many teachers have taken heart from one reading of the Act which suggests that so long as a majority of assemblies are Christian, then the Act is being observed. Increasingly (and with the support of some senior church leaders) it is being argued that the law contains within itself considerable flexibility: schools can use it to develop collective 'spiritual' acts which, in their broadness, leave space for all pupils to 'explore their own beliefs'.

But teachers (and OFSTED) are also aware that assemblies (the word is more comfortable than the phrase 'act of worship'!) 'must reflect the broad traditions of Christian belief to an extent and in a way which gives them a Christian character'.

It is for all these circumstances that this *Broadly Christian Assembly Book* has been compiled. So it includes passages about the other world faiths – but offers more Christian passages than might have been found in a comparable anthology published fifteen years ago. Like its companion *100 Readings for Assembly*, this is not a book for those whose creed is 'Just stick to God, most people believe in him – but don't bring his Son into it.'

It must also be remembered that it is only a resource, not a course of ready-made assemblies. The appropriate atmosphere (in which, for example, stillness and quietness have their place) cannot be created by a mere book. Nor is it suggested that any assembly leader work steadily through this collection, day by day or week by week. Nor will every passage be suitable in every context. As the Act reminds us, any materials must be 'appropriate having regard to the family background, ages and aptitudes of the pupils involved'. Nor do I imagine that every user of the book will wish to endorse (and consequently read) every passage it contains. However, I have not included anything I would be embarrassed to stand up and read aloud myself and I hope that whoever uses this anthology will find plenty of passages which engage those who hear them.

I have chosen passages which have an immediate aural appeal and which 'come off the page' easily. (The unsigned passages are adapted from scripts I wrote myself for broadcasting: they are 'spoken word texts' rather than written essays.) I hope I have included pieces which will entertain, stimulate and even provoke. Most, I trust, will be new to even the experienced assembly leader. Where there may appear to be gaps, it is often because that festival or topic is well provided for in the companion *100 Readings for Assembly* and I did not wish to duplicate material for those who may be using both books.

I have usually resisted the temptation to label individual passages as being particularly suitable for given age groups. That would, I feel, merely patronize the user of the book. He or she is the best judge of the 'sophistication' or maturity of those to whom he or she will be reading. And, after all, what works well one year with, say, Year 9 may seem inappropriate for their successors twelve months later or for their contemporaries in another school.

The hundred passages have been presented in five sections. The first twenty seasonal readings are arranged chronologically through a school year and the majority (but not all) are probably more suited to the younger end of the secondary age range. A calendar (page 336) includes dates for the seasonal use of these and other passages in this book.

The second group of readings (Stories, Parables and Legends) all have a strong narrative thread and again are aimed at younger pupils. The following twenty readings about 'good people' are presented in historical order and should appeal over a wide age range. The 'Thoughts for a Day' will, it is hoped, encourage experiential exploration of religious and philosophical ideas as well as explaining the beliefs of others.

The final section is partly concerned with social and moral issues: 'loving thy neighbour' is, after all, a religious injunction. Other passages in this section have been chosen because I believe they emphasize the holiness of life. And both of the last two sections include passages that raise uncomfortable and difficult topics. Some are deliberately provocative. Several are included in the hope they will generate a feeling that 'something must be done'. Most are more suitable for older pupils and these sections include readings which may be useful to those who, since the 1988 Act, have been surprised to find themselves leading sixth form assemblies.

Rehearsal is advised before any reading, and (where relevant) some thought might be given as to who is the best available reader (or readers) for any particular passage. No matter how much at home you feel reading to the assembly, remember that even a professional actor or reader prefers to have time to rehearse; that is, to check that he or she understands the meaning of what is to be read, to absorb its mood and tone, to appreciate the writer's viewpoint and to note where pauses and changes of pace are necessary.

Two introductions have been provided for almost every passage. The first is a background note for the assembly leader's information. The second will serve as a ready-made introduction which can simply be read aloud to introduce the passage to the assembly when time does not permit the devising of a more locally relevant introduction.

The gathering together of a number of people for assembly places a heavy responsibility on those who lead that assembly. I hope this collection will lighten the load a little and help the arrangement of assemblies or even acts of worship which nurture an awareness of the transcendent and the needs of others; which develop a sense of community and of what it means to be religious; and which create a feeling of wonder, mystery, joy and (especially) idealism.

DAVID SELF

FESTIVALS OF FAITH

'Don't ask for watermelon in the middle of winter'
GREEK PROVERB

'Everything must wait its turn… peach blossoms for the second month and chrysanthemums for the ninth'
JAPANESE PROVERB

1

Michaelmas (29 September)

In the Christian calendar 29 September is the Feast of St Michael and All Angels. Tradition has it that St Michael was one of the seven archangels who defeated Lucifer when he rebelled against God. In art he is depicted as a winged warrior.

Marks & Spencer chose his name as a trademark partly because its founder was Michael Marks but also because St Michael is the guardian angel and patron of Jewish people. Michaelmas Day is also one of the four 'quarter days' when quarterly accounts were traditionally settled.

29 September is St Michael's Day. That does *not* mean it's a day for thinking about underwear. It's named after the angel Michael. Some Christians believe he acts as a kind of messenger between God and humans and that he protects people at the time of their death. His day is also known as Michaelmas Day.

◆

WITH THE DAYS 'drawing in', and chilly, misty, autumn mornings, our ancestors' thoughts turned naturally to the approaching winter and all it might bring. Inevitably they were reminded of death and doom. They feared that as the sun declined, evil spirits might be on the prowl again. There is still an old country saying that you should not pick blackberries after Michaelmas Day because the devil has spat on them. In fact, maggots and early frosts may well have made them unfit to eat.

St Michael, the protector of all men, particularly 'at the hour of death', seemed a good person to have around at the onset of winter. In the year 486, 20 September was designated St Michael's Day, or, as it is better known, Michaelmas Day. ☞

St Michael is not the usual kind of saint. He is not a martyr, nor a Doctor of the Church, nor a great religious leader. He is not even a real person. He is an angel – one of a band of spiritual beings who act as messengers between God and mankind. Michael (from the Hebrew meaning 'who is like the Lord') is a top-ranking angel – one of the seven archangels, and their leader in battle against the devil and 'the powers of the air'. He is appropriately the patron of high places, and many hill churches are dedicated to him. He is generally depicted with huge wings, armour and a flaming sword. You could confuse him with St George if it were not for his wings.

St Michael has a flower named after him – the Michaelmas Daisy. But perhaps he is best known nowadays as the trade-name of Marks & Spencer. The first manufacturing firm linked with Mark & Spencer had as its trade-name 'St Margaret's', because its factory was near St Margaret's church, Leicester. In 1928 Marks & Spencer registered their own brand-name for goods manufactured to their orders.

A number of saints' names were considered to go along with 'St Margaret', but eventually 'St Michael' was chosen, partly after the founder of the firm, Michael Marks, but also because St Michael is the guardian angel and patron of Jewish people as well as Christians, and Marks & Spencer is, of course, a Jewish firm.

In Britain, for practical and business reasons, the year is divided by law into four quarter-days and four terms. Michaelmas appears in both lists.

Quarter-days are the days when rent, paid 'quarterly' or four times a year, becomes due, and when tenancies on properties begin and end. In England and Ireland these quarter-days are: ☛

Lady Day, 25 March; Midsummer Day, 24 June; Michaelmas, 29 September; Christmas Day, 25 December.

The four terms, which now only apply to Law Sittings, but which formerly applied also to universities, are Hilary, Easter, Trinity, and Michaelmas. For convenience' sake universities cut their terms down to three per year of about nine weeks each, and schools followed suit. Oxford University's terms are called Hilary. Trinity and Michaelmas; at Cambridge they are Lent, Easter and Michaelmas. The Michaelmas term is the start of the academic year in universities and schools.

Michaelmas is a major landmark in the farmer's year. Not only is it the great season for the sale of livestock, but most farm tenancies run from one Michaelmas to the next. With the harvest gathered in and animals disposed of, it is the obvious time for making a move, starting afresh – or giving up altogether! ◆

PETER WATKINS AND ERICA HUGHES

2

Divali

Divali is a Hindu festival which (depending on the date of the New Moon) is celebrated in either late October or early November. The word 'Divali' means 'row of lights'.

Hindus believe in one great power called Brahman. The aim of every Hindu is to become so good that he or she becomes part of Brahman. He or she is helped to do this by the gods and goddesses of Hinduism. Two of these are connected with Divali: Lakshmi and Vishnu.

At this time of year, followers of the Hindu religion celebrate the festival of Divali. They believe this is when Lakshmi, the goddess of wealth, visits every home where she sees a row of lights burning – and brings good luck to that family.

Hindus also believe in Vishnu, the god who protects people from danger and who once came to earth as Rama, a warrior and king.

◆

PRINCE RAMA LIVED in a city called Ayodhya and was the king's eldest son. When his father died, his enemies prevented him from becoming king, and forced him to leave the city and live for fourteen years in a forest. He didn't go alone: his wife Sita chose to go with him, and so too did his brother Lakshmana.

For many years, they lived in the forest where they faced much danger – because, within that forest, there also lived many demons. The king of the demons, Ravana, had the power to turn himself into any shape he wished. He knew that Rama and Sita were living in what he called 'his' forest and he had seen that Sita was very beautiful indeed. He very much wanted her for his own and so he began to plot. How could he seize her and take her where Rama could never reach her?

At last he thought of a plan. He waited until Rama had gone hunting for food. Then he changed himself into a golden-coloured deer and followed him. In this shape, he got close enough to Rama for the prince to glimpse him through the undergrowth.

Rama began to track what he thought was a deer. Before long, they were in the thickest part of the forest. Rama then realized he had been so keen to catch the deer he had not marked the way he had come – and so there he was, lost in the forest, not knowing quite what to do. But Ravana knew exactly what to do. He gave a great shout of 'Help!' – only in Rama's voice. And he used his evil powers to make the shout travel back through the trees to where Sita and Lakshmana were waiting.

'It's Rama. He needs help,' begged Sita. For a moment, Lakshmana hesitated. Should he stay and protect Sita – or should he rescue Rama?

'Please!' cried Sita again. 'Please go!'

So he did.

As soon as Lakshmana was out of the way, Ravana magicked himself back to the hut that Rama had built for himself and Sita to live in. He was looking forward to his next trick. This time, he changed himself into an old beggar. As soon as Sita saw him, she wanted to help.

'Surely,' she thought, 'there can be no danger in helping a weak old man such as this?' So she called out, 'What do you want, Old Man?'

And in the tired voice of a very old man, Ravana croaked, 'Will you help a holy man? Just a little water, if it please you...'

As soon as she had invited him into the hut, he changed himself back into his demon shape, seized her, dragged her to a chariot he had hidden nearby and drove off – far, far away to a palace he had on an island called Lanka (which we now call Sri Lanka).

When Rama and Lakshmana eventually returned to the hut, of course they couldn't find Sita. Rama was heartbroken that he had been tempted to go so far in his hunt for the golden deer. But help was at hand.

During their time in the forest, Rama and Sita had made friends with many animals – including a monkey called Hanuman. Hanuman was the powerful leader of a troupe of monkeys and he now summoned them together to search for Sita.

At last, they met an eagle who had seen Ravana taking Sita across the ocean to Lanka. So Rama, Lakshmana and Hanuman set off, south towards the sea.

When they got to the coast, Rama stood staring out across the water. He had no boat. It was too far to swim. It was here that Hanuman used his magic powers. He stood for a moment catching his breath and then, with one leap, jumped across the sea to land on the island of Lanka. Quickly, he began his search for Sita. It was not long before he found her, inside Ravana's palace, in a courtyard, surrounded by high walls.

Hanuman began to tell her what had happened and how Rama would rescue her – but he was soon interrupted. For a demon can smell out a monkey and Ravana was quickly on the scene. Hanuman was not afraid. Boldly, he told Ravana that if he did not let Sita go free, Rama would bring an army to fight against him.

Ravana roared with laughter. 'Take this foolish monkey outside,' he told his guards. 'And to teach him a lesson, set his tail on fire.'

The men did as they were ordered but Hanuman (who felt no pain) simply ran up a palm tree in the palace garden, setting it on fire as he climbed. From the top of that tree, he leapt to another – and to another, setting each alight. And so in all the smoke and confusion, Hanuman was able to escape, back to the edge of the sea. With a second huge jump, he landed back on the mainland at the feet of Rama.

A great army of forest animals now came to their aid. Using the stones and pebbles from the beach, they built a roadway across the sea towards Lanka, and thus were able to reach the island.

There was a fierce battle. On one side was Rama, Lakshmana, Hanuman and the forest animal army; and on the other side, Ravana's demon guards. The fighting continued for days until Rama decided he must use his holy power. Saying a prayer, he took a special arrow from his side, fitted it to his bow and took aim. Through the sky it flew, and hit Ravana in the heart.

The demon fell – and there he died.

In a second, Rama was in the palace; in another second he was in the courtyard; in a third, Sita was in his arms. Without delay, they crossed the sea and made their way back towards the beautiful city of Ayodhya – for now, the fourteen years had passed and Rama was free to come home as king, with Sita as his queen.

As they reached the outskirts of Ayodhya, it was getting dark – but one woman saw them coming and lit a lamp. She placed it in her window to celebrate their return and so that they ☛

might see their way. Her neighbour lit another lamp. A third, a fourth, a fifth – they all placed lamps in their windows and soon the way was bright with flickering lights, celebrating the return of good King Rama.

And every year at Divali, Hindus light lamps and candles to remember how Rama and his good friend Hanuman triumphed over evil and brought Sita safely home to Ayodhya – and to attract the goddess Lakshmi to their homes. ◆

3

All Saints' and All Souls' (1–2 November)

In recent years Hallowe'en (31 October) has become a controversial festival – partly because of its commercialization and partly because some believe it encourages an unhealthy interest in the occult. It is interesting to note that its origins lie in the pagan feast of Samhain which Christianity converted into All Hallows Eve: the eve of 'All Hallows' or All Saints' Day. Some might say that, with the decline of the Church's influence, its pagan roots are again dominant.

All Saints' is a day for thankful remembrance of the lives of all forgotten, unknown and unrecognized 'saints'. All Souls' Day is when Christians, especially Catholics, pray for the souls of the departed – particularly those close or dear to them.

For many people, this time of year is a time for playing Trick or Treat or for dressing up as witches. For Christians, it is a time for remembering the dead. On 1 November, they give thanks for the lives of all the people who have done good in their lives. That's All Saints' Day. On 2 November Catholics remember relatives and friends who have died. Many visit the graves of these people. In Italy, people do this on 1 November, which is a national holiday. This passage, written by a Roman Catholic priest, describes what happens.

◆

IT WAS OBVIOUS, even from a distance, that I had stumbled on some kind of carnival. Millions of flowers, banked high along half a mile of road, were the focal point towards which thousands of people were converging – on foot and cycle, by car or public transport. The day was hot and bright with sunshine and so, having nothing else to do, I joined the crowd to discover what was happening. As I approached the gates of the park I realised that I was also witnessing the biggest traffic jam I had ever seen or hoped to experience.

Whole families were there, from great-grandma down to the tiniest carry-cotter. There were groups of schoolgirls; soldiers, sailors, policemen. And everyone was carrying a bunch of flowers and making a blaze of moving colour – red and yellow, white and orange. Even the teenagers in their tight jeans and their long hair did not look strange with their bunches of flowers. In fact, it was I, flowerless, who seemed glaringly obvious. The flower vendors tried to make me buy their roses, their dahlias, their chrysanthemums. Uncertain still, I refused, and passed guiltily through the gate without my passport of flowers.

Only then did I realise what it was all about. I had just entered Rome's largest cemetery. It was 1 November, a national holiday, on which all Rome goes to honour its dead. It was a feast of colour and life, full of the gaiety of the living mourning their dead with affectionate joy. Perhaps this somewhat flamboyant expression of family devotion might seem exuberant to us, but I did feel it expressed a Christian hope. The dead were not completely gone from their families. These people clearly thought of their dead as still alive – to be remembered with joy on All Saints' Day.

For Catholics, November is traditionally the month to remember the dead. I suppose one reason is that autumn is the season when nature dies – the leaves fall and the earth is barren. But Spring and new life are not far away. So too with human death. Catholics pray for their dead. Some people find this hard to accept, but for me it is a beautiful, consoling idea. The Bible reminds us that nothing imperfect can enter God's Kingdom. Many of my friends have died, but few of them were perfect. Few of us will be perfect at death, but surely few of us ☛

will be so bad as to be permanently excluded from God's Kingdom. Look at it this way – most of us do not at once welcome an unexpected visitor late at night. We have to tidy-up a bit before opening the door. I suspect that when death catches us we shall need to tidy-up before opening to God.

We call this process purgatory – but thoughts like intensity or duration are meaningless. Death is only a stage in the journey to God. God is there to welcome us, but we pause a little at the threshold before going to the complete joy beyond.

Those Roman flowers were a sign of love of the dead, or encouragement to those tidying-up, of congratulation to those in the full joy of God. They were a sign of faith in a life to come, and a recognition that death is, after all, but a very thin veil. ◆

FR ROBERT MANLEY

Remembrance

World War I ended at the eleventh hour of the eleventh day of the eleventh month of 1918. For years this day was remembered as Armistice Day. In more recent times the dead and wounded of both world wars, and other conflicts, have been remembered on the second Sunday of November – Remembrance Day.

Wilfred Owen's poems about 'war and the pity of war' are among the most telling pictures of trench warfare in World War I.

Remembrance Day is a time to remember those who lost their lives in the two world wars and in more recent conflicts. One of the most famous poets who fought in World War I was Wilfred Owen who was killed just one week before that war ended. This is the last letter he wrote home. By the time his mother received it, he was dead.

As Company Commander (of 'A Coy' or Company), he had a 'batman' or servant.

◆

Thursday 31 October 6.15 p.m.

Dearest Mother,

I will call the place from which I'm now writing 'The Smoky Cellar of the Forester's House'. I write on the first sheet of the writing pad which came in the parcel yesterday. Luckily the parcel was small, as it reached me just before we moved off to the line. Thus only the paraffin was unwelcome in my pack. My servant and I ate the chocolate in the cold middle of last night, crouched under a draughty Tamboo [a shelter], roofed with planks. I husband the Malted Milk for tonight and tomorrow ☞

night. The handkerchief and socks are most opportune, as the ground is marshy, and I have a slight cold!

So thick is the smoke in this cellar that I can hardly see by a candle 12 inches away, and so thick are the inmates that I can hardly write for pokes, nudges and jolts. On my left the Coy. Commander snores on a bench: other officers repose on wire beds behind me. At my right hand, Kellet, a delightful servant of A Coy. in 'The Old Days' radiates joy and contentment from pink cheeks and baby eyes. He laughs with a signaller, to whose left ear is glued the Receiver; but whose eyes rolling with gaiety shows that he is listening with his right ear to a merry corporal, who appears at this distance away (some three feet) nothing [but] a gleam of white teeth and a wheeze of jokes.

Splashing my hand, an old soldier with a walrus moustache peels and drops potatoes into the pot. By him, Keyes, my cook, chops wood; another feeds the smoke with the damp wood.

It is a great life. I am more oblivious than alas! yourself, dear Mother, of the ghastly glimmering of the guns outside, and the hollow crashing of the shells.

There is no danger down here, or if any, it will be well over before you read these lines.

I hope you are as warm as I am; as serene in your room as I am here; and that you think of me never in bed as resignedly as I think of you always in bed. Of this I am certain you could not be visited by a band of friends half so fine as surround me here.

Ever

Wilfred x ◆

WILFRED OWEN

14

5

Thanksgiving (fourth Thursday in November)

Thanksgiving Day is a national holiday in the United States and was originally celebrated by the Pilgrim settlers (the 'founding fathers' of America) after their first harvest in 1621.

Thanksgiving Day is when Americans give thanks for God's blessings. It is also a reminder of some of the first Europeans to settle in America – the Pilgrim Fathers who sailed from Britain to find a new life in a part of the country called Virginia (which was then a British colony ruled by the Virginia Company). As it turned out, they were to settle in what they later called New England. One of their reasons for emigrating was because laws in Britain at that time did not allow them to worship in the way they wanted. This is the story of how the most famous group of the Pilgrim Fathers hired two ships to make the crossing of the Atlantic Ocean from London and Southampton.

◆

IT WAS JULY 1620. Two ships had been chartered: the *Speedwell*, fitted in Holland, and the *Mayflower* hired in London. The *Speedwell* joined the *Mayflower* at Southampton and between them the two boats carried about 140 passengers.

The Journey
They left Southampton about mid-August but before long the *Speedwell* sprang a leak and they were forced to put into Dartmouth for repairs. After a few more days at sea the *Speedwell* once more began to take in water and they had to return to Plymouth. It was decided to abandon the leaking ship and the remaining 102 passengers crowded aboard the *Mayflower*. ☞

After enjoying much kindness and hospitality in Plymouth, the *Mayflower* finally got under way in September.

The journey was one of great discomfort and hardship, and one passenger and four crew died *en route*. It took just over two months to reach America, and due to a navigational error the ship dropped anchor at Cape Cod; the ship's crew refused to take the Pilgrims any further – Virginia was some 200 miles to the south – and they were forced to go ashore. 'Falling on their knees they thanked ye God of heaven who had brought them over ye vast and furious ocean.' The place of anchor is today called Provincetown Harbour.

Because theVirginia Company had no rights there, and therefore no authority, it was essential to draw up some kind of constitution; such a move would also introduce a measure of law and order and prevent some of them from imagining they could do as they liked. All the male passengers on board who were of age were called into the ship's cabin to sign the *Mayflower Compact*.

This document became the basis of a democratic constitution for the new colony and signified the colonists' loyalty to King James and the Crown. It declared their intention to plant a colony (sometimes called a 'plantation') and to draw up all the necessary laws and other legal enactments for the general good and 'for the advancement of ye Christian faith, and honour of our King and Countrie'.

By now it was mid-November and winter was rapidly approaching. Food supplies were scanty and the surrounding area seemed bleak and uninviting. But the faith and courage that had brought them this far did not fail them, and they were determined to overcome the difficulties. They appointed deacon John Carver as the first governor of the provisional government and then began a survey of their new homeland. Over the next two weeks they made several excursions around the bay and finally settled at a place they called Plymouth, in honour of their last port of call. They built their first log huts and celebrated their landing with 'Forefathers' Day' (21 December).

Thanksgiving Day

Conditions over the first winter soon began to take their toll; of the forty one men who signed the Compact, only nineteen survived to Spring and fourteen out of a total of eighteen married women also died. But the Pilgrims stood firm and mastered their new surroundings; they learned agricultural skills and paid off their debt. In 1621, after they had reaped their first harvest, they held a service of thanksgiving to God and had a celebration meal that included wild turkey.

The practice was continued each year on the fourth Thursday in November and is called Thanksgiving Day.

The Pilgrim Fathers came to America to build a New England and to find a place where they could worship in freedom. But they accomplished much more: their influence in laying the foundations of the United States of America was out of proportion to their numbers, and their stand for democracy, freedom of religion, peace and standards of value is one of the nation's most precious assets. If the New World has cause to be grateful to God, then it is for such people as these who stood at the dawn of the nation's history. ◆

GEOFFREY HANKS

Hanukkah

*Hanukkah (sometimes transcribed as Chanukah) is also known as the
Feast of Lights. It is an eight-day long Jewish festival that begins on the
25th day of the month of Kislev which usually falls in December.*

For Jewish people, this is a special time of year known as
Hanukkah when parties are held, candles are lit in their
homes and everyone remembers the story of Judah
Maccabee. It happened nearly two hundred years before the
birth of Jesus. At that time, Palestine (or Judah) was part of
the Greek empire. This part of the Greek empire was ruled
by the King of Syria, a man called Antiochus Epiphanes.
Some of the Jews living in Jerusalem had started speaking
Greek and following Greek fashions. But others hated all
things Greek – they especially hated Antiochus Epiphanes
whom they nicknamed Antiochus Epimanes (which means
Antiochus the Madman). Two of those who objected most
to Antiochus were a priest called Mattathias and his son
Judah Maccabee – whose followers became known as the
Maccabees.

◆

THE HISTORICAL EVENTS which gave rise to the festival
are recorded in the books of the Maccabees (not found in the
Bible). They involve a battle ostensibly between Jews and Antiochus Epiphanes when he became King of Syria in 175 BCE.
In reality, it was a struggle on a wider and deeper scale – a clash
between Greek and Jewish values. Since the time of Alexander
the Great, Jews had been influenced by certain Greek ideas and
the contact between the two cultures had been of mutual bene- ☞

fit. But now Antiochus prohibited Jews, under penalty of death, from living Judaism. It was not primarily an antisemitic motive which prompted him but rather a desire for conformity and unquestioning obedience from all his subjects.

When Greek idols, notably that of Zeus, were placed in the Temple at Jerusalem, some Jews were so incensed at the sacrilege that they resolved to make a bold bid for freedom. The struggle of these Jews, knows as the 'Maccabees', was *not* fought to extend the border of Judea nor to the glory of the Jewish leadership.

The leader of the Jewish uprising was Mattathias. He was joined by his sons and a small number of like-minded Jews who used the deserts and mountains as bases for guerrilla attacks on Greek army units. As well as fighting the Greeks, the Maccabees were also engaged in a battle of *wits* with fellow Jews, who had been lured by the attractions of the Greek lifestyle. The Greek invasion had been with ideas as well as arms. Mattathias died after a year, and his son, Judah Maccabee, took over as leader.

The day which Judah Maccabee chose for the rededication (Hanukkah) of the Temple in 164 BCE coincided with the third anniversary of the decree by Antiochus that idolatrous sacrifices were to be offered on the Temple altar.

When the time came to rekindle the Temple's perpetual lamp, the Maccabees found a jar of oil, undefiled by their enemies, with the seal unbroken. For many, what happened next was a miracle: there was enough oil to keep the lamp burning for one day only, but in fact it lasted eight days – exactly to the point when fresh supplies of oil arrived. For others, the miracle operates on another level: the light of Jewish faith and hope ☛

might have seemed doomed to die, but it endured and burned as brightly as ever.

The central ritual of Hanukkah is the kindling of lights on eight nights. In order to 'proclaim the miracle', the Hanukkah lamp should be lit soon after sunset, ideally outside but otherwise at an open door. This should happen before anyone – even the youngest child – goes to bed, so that all may witness the event and know the miracle. The *hanukiah* [or Hanukkah lamp] should burn for at least thirty minutes: traditionally, it is of olive oil but it can also be of wax candles, gas burners or electricity.

The pattern of lighting the *hanukiah* is to kindle one light on the first night, two on the second, growing to eight on the eighth night.

Hanukkah remains a season of simple family gatherings on long winter nights. It is party time, especially for children, and an occasion to exchange gifts. ◆

ANGELA WOOD

7

Maryam and the Miraculous Baby

Jesus is revered by Muslims as Isa, one of the great prophets, but they do not believe, as Christians do, that he was divine. This Islamic account of his birth is offered as an alternative to the well-known account in the Christian Bible (as told in the early chapters of Luke's Gospel) and as a reminder that Jesus has a place in Islam. (See also passage 15.)
    This reading may be used in two parts.

You may think you have heard the story of the birth of Jesus many times. You may not have heard it the way Muslims tell it. They believe that Jesus (or Isa, as they call him) was an important prophet and teacher but they do not believe he was the Son of God, as Christians do. Maryam is their name for his mother, Mary; Allah is the Muslim word for God.

◆

MARYAM WAS NOT the boy that her parents had hoped to have, but she was the chosen one of Allah. The angel Jibril (or Gabriel) had brought her a message from Allah. 'Allah has chosen you. He has made you pure, above all other women.'

Maryam prayed, and worshipped Allah in the temple. She gave thanks for Allah's blessing and prayed to Him to help her lead a good and pure life. She knew she had been chosen to serve Allah in His temple. Only someone pure in body and soul could do this. From childhood, praise of Allah had always been on her lips and no evil spirits could touch her, nor could the devil come near her.

Maryam had grown up with her uncle, Zakaria. She was beautiful, but she did not notice her own beauty. She never forgot her duties in the temple.

☞

One day, a young man appeared before her in the temple when she was worshipping. Maryam was surprised to see him. She was a lovely young girl but she never thought about men and marriage as other girls of her age did. She backed away from the man, thinking he meant to harm her. There was nowhere to run to. She could only put her trust in Allah. Trembling, she said, 'I turn to Allah for protection against you. If you are a good man, you will fear the anger of Allah.'

The young man smiled at Maryam's words. He was not going to harm her. He told her not to be afraid.

'I have been sent by the Lord to tell you this. Allah sends you the good news of a child called the Messiah, Isa son of Maryam, who will be great in this world and the next, and will be a man of Allah.'

Now Maryam realized who the young man was. He was the angel Jibril. But still she could hardly believe his words. Full of amazement she said, 'How can I have a child? I have never been touched by any man.'

The angel Jibril replied, 'This is the truth. Allah can do whatever He wants. When He wants something to happen, He only has to say the word. This is how you were created, so will your son be created.'

Maryam took a deep breath as the angel spoke. When she released it, he had gone. She tried to tell herself to accept the will of Allah with joy. She remembered Allah's promise that she was His chosen one. Because she had been chosen by Allah, only she, of all the women in the world, would have a child without knowing a man. But it was difficult for her to accept this. What would people think and say? She knew that her people were quick to judge others and think they had done ☛

wrong. She prayed for strength and faith, then returned calmly to her family.

Her family were respected and well-liked. But would people still believe in her purity? Maryam was not happy. As the days passed her fears grew, especially when she felt the new life within her.

She left the holy town and went to a small village far away. This village was called Bait al-Lahm (Bethlehem). There she lived alone with her fears and worries. She had only the strength of her faith to support her.

Now Maryam needed all her strength to face the test Allah had given her. She thought of the baby and the gossip among her people. She thought of the questions and rumours. She had no peace as these thoughts filled her head.

She walked slowly from her lonely little house. Her hand clutched her stomach. She was sure her baby would be born very soon now. She sat alone beneath a shady tree as the pain grew stronger. There was no midwife to help her, no friend. All Maryam had was faith and courage. She closed her eyes and cold sweat ran down her forehead. Alone, using all her strength, she gave birth to her baby. Allah had said the baby was to be called the Messiah, Isa bin Maryam. The name and the bearer were blessed by Allah.

The angel Jibril had been guarding Maryam, and he wiped the body of the baby to protect it from the devil and evil spirits, as her mother had prayed at the birth of Maryam. Maryam looked at her newborn baby. Doubts and fears came into her mind.

She was so tired and in her exhaustion she thought of the sorrow and pain that lay ahead. She thought of the love that ☛

her baby needed and the cruel things that people would say. She closed her eyes as if she could not bear to see the world around her.

Allah sees and hears everything. He hears every whisper and sees the suffering in people's hearts. He sent the angel Jibril to comfort Maryam. 'Do not despair', said the angel. 'Your Lord will make water flow from under your feet...'

At the sound of a voice Maryam opened her eyes. To her amazement, from the dry ground under her feet clear water began to flow.

'Subhanallah! Subhanallah! Subhanallah!' she cried with joy.

She heard the voice speak again. 'Shake the stem of this bare palm tree and ripe fruit will fall at your feet.'

Maryam looked at the delicious fruit that fell to the ground. Slowly she tasted the clear water and the fruit and she praised Allah as she ate and drank.

The angel Jibril had not left her yet. She heard the voice again. He told her to tell no one about who she had spoken to. Then the angel went away.

Maryam felt strong and brave again. She picked up her baby and covered him carefully, then she went home to her family in the town. She went into the house without a word. The family were astonished to see her with a baby in her arms. For a moment there was silence. They were shocked and surprised. They all thought the worst of her.

'Maryam! You have done a terrible thing! We did not think that you, such a good girl, would do such a thing! What will people say if they find out? How could you, Maryam! You have shamed your family, now your whole family will suffer.' They all shouted at her at once.

Maryam listened to their cries quite calmly. She did not say a word. She knew that whatever she said, her family would not believe her. And she had promised the angel Jibril she would tell no one what had happened. Silently she pointed to the baby, as a sign that they should ask the baby, not her.

The family thought she was mad. 'How can we ask a newborn baby where he has come from?' they laughed.

But then the prophet Isa spoke.

'Truly, I am the servant of Allah', said the baby. Everyone was struck dumb with amazement. They stared at the baby's lips. They could not believe he had spoken. Then he spoke again. 'I shall be Allah's prophet. Wherever I go I have His blessing. Allah has commanded me to worship, and to give to the poor, to honour my mother and never to be proud. He was at my birth and shall be at my death when I will return to Him once more.'

Now they knew this was not just any baby. They believed the words of the prophet and accepted Maryam. They knew she was pure and without sin. ◆

ABDUL RAHMAN RUKAINI

8

The **Road** *to* **Bethlehem**

This passage provides some historical and social background to the Nativity story.

Which was Jesus's home town? No: Nazareth, not Bethlehem.

But he was *born* in Bethlehem, which is to the south of Nazareth, because that was the original home town of Joseph. He and Mary had to return there for a census for tax purposes. So what was the journey like for Joseph and his expectant wife, who was to become the mother of Jesus?

◆

EVEN BEFORE THE Romans took over Israel there was a good road system, although such roads were often no more than tracks. The best were hard-surfaced, either paved with stones or cut from rock. The worst were just dirt trails that covered travellers in dust during the summer and bogged them down in mud during the winter rains. The road from Nazareth in southern Galilee to Bethlehem in the south of Judaea was one of the country's main highways, marked out with kerb stones and repaired fairly regularly. But by our standards it would still have been narrow and quite dangerous.

The distance between Nazareth and Bethlehem is about 120 miles (190 kilometres). Mary and Joseph probably travelled by donkey, in which case they would have been lucky to cover 15 miles (25 kilometres) each day. Horses were certainly a good deal speedier and could cover about 25 miles (40 kilometres) a day, but they were only used by the Roman army and wealthy people. ☞

26

The journey would have been even slower and more uncomfortable than usual because Mary was about to have a baby and must have needed to stop and rest frequently. Few doctors would recommend a rocking, jolting ride on the back of a donkey for the health either of the mother-to-be or her unborn child. The journey may well have brought on the birth more quickly than anyone had expected; and perhaps the reason that Mary gave birth to her baby in a lowly stable was that there simply was not time to make more elaborate arrangements.

Bethlehem, which in Hebrew means 'house of bread', is 5 miles (8 kilometres) south of Jerusalem. It is quite high up – about 2500 feet (750 metres) above sea level – seated on the main ridge that runs from north to south down almost the whole length of the country that was then Palestine and is today Israel.

At the time of Jesus' birth Bethlehem was surrounded by pasture on which flocks of sheep and goats fed. There was probably more woodland around the town than there is now. As a result of over-grazing, the amount of desert has increased over the centuries and this area today is less green than it would have been when Jesus was born.

Because Bethlehem was on a main north-south trade route, many caravans of travellers would have passed through the town. The inn that sheltered these merchants was called a *khan* – a kind of motel for camels.

We feel shocked that Mary and Joseph had to stay overnight in a stable because the local inn was full. But it was not uncommon then for people to live alongside animals. In fact, it was normal in remote country areas and has remained so until the present day. The humans lived in a kind of loft while a variety of animals such as cows, chickens, and goats were accommodated below. In winter this arrangement certainly made for more warmth, even if rather smellier than most of us would like.

The 'manger' in which the baby Jesus was laid was the feeding rack for cows and horses. It was made of wood and shaped like an open basket. If it had been lined with straw and also perhaps a woollen blanket or a sheepskin it would have been very comfortable, in fact a perfect crib. ◆

MICHAEL STEPHENSON

9

Epiphany (6 January)

Note that Twelfth Night, the traditional end of the Christmas season, falls on 5 January (try counting from Christmas Day!). In the Christian calendar 6 January is the Feast of the Epiphany; that is, the 'Manifestation (or showing) of Christ to the Gentiles' which marks the coming of the wise men to the infant Jesus.

   This reading may be divided and used on two occasions.

Christians know 6 January as the Epiphany, which means 'showing'. It is a reminder of how the wise men came to visit the baby Jesus. You may think of them as the three kings but nowhere does the Bible say they were kings.

◆

THE 'WISE MEN' are mentioned only in the Gospel of St Matthew and he does not actually state that there were three. The tradition started because people assumed that since Matthew referred to three gifts – gold and frankincense and myrrh – they must have been given by three separate individuals. Although St Matthew does not call them *magi*, tradition has always given the wise men that name. The word *magus (magi* is the plural) is related to the word 'magic' and means someone who was skilled in astrology and the occult.

In the ancient world, all aspects of magic were taken very seriously. Magic was used to foretell the future, to chart a person's destiny according to heavenly signs, to decide the right time to make an important journey, or to initiate a new venture by consulting 'oracles'. In the Old Testament there are many references to the movements of the stars as signs of God's power.

Because astrology was so important, it would have been fitting that the birth of the Messiah should be heralded by what appeared to be a magical positioning of the stars. The Gospel writers would have pointed this out to their readers in order to emphasize the significance of the event.

It is also important for another reason. Matthew reported that the wise men 'fell down and worshipped Him'. This implied that they were saying to Jesus, 'You are a greater power than all the old forces of our magic. We bow down and recognize it.' In other words, the old pagan religions were giving way to the new religion called Christianity.

Exchanging gifts was, and still is, a very important ritual in the Middle East. Even today it is considered an insult, when visiting a home, not to bring a gift, which must reflect the standing of the receiver.

Each of the three gifts given to the infant Jesus by the wise men had a special meaning.

The first was gold, which represented kingship. The second was frankincense, a sweet-smelling gum from a tree that grows in Arabia, burnt during religious ceremonies and therefore associated with holiness and prayer. The third was myrrh, also a gum from an Arabian tree, used as an oil for anointing priests and kings, but also for embalming the body after death. When myrrh was mixed with wine, it could act as a drug, dulling pain. Sometimes it was given to those about to be crucified in order to ease their suffering. Indeed, it may have been such a mixture that was offered to, and rejected by, Jesus during his crucifixion. So its association with death foretold Jesus' fate on the cross.

MICHAEL STEPHENSON

Now just supposing you were in the position of the wise men, ☞

what would be the most valuable thing you could bring to the child Jesus? Possibly the most valuable thing we can all afford to give is time. To give time to other people – by helping them, listening to them and encouraging them. To give generously and without hesitation.

You may remember thinking that being expected to give up time to do something for someone else was unfair. It's your life you said. You've only got the one life; your time was precious.

Time *is* precious. Once you've spent it, you can't get it back. Nobody's going to invent a time machine for you so that you can travel back to the good times and experience them again – or travel back to the bad times so that you can change them or get your own back on other people.

The past is over. Dead.

And the future – well, in the Bible, Jesus says we should not fret about tomorrow. It may turn out good, it may not. What really matters is time present, the present moment. That's what we have to decide how to 'spend'. How we should act now.

An American poet of the last century, Henry Wadsworth Longfellow, put all this quite simply in what he called 'A Psalm of Life'.

> Trust no Future, howe'er pleasant!
> Let the dead Past bury its dead!
> Act – act in the living present!
> Heart within, and God o'erhead!
>
> Lives of great men all remind us
> We can make our lives sublime,
> And, departing, leave behind us
> Footprints on the sands of time.

It's natural at the start of a new year to start thinking about time passing. Another year has gone – and what have we achieved?

If we *are* going to leave our footprints on the sands of time by doing something worthwhile with our lives (and there's nothing wrong with hoping to do that), then there's all the more reason to use the gift of time to good effect, to put right what we can in the world around us. As St Paul says in the Bible, it's our duty to make the most of the time, or as he puts it, to redeem the times we live in.

And that may mean being prepared to give some of our precious time away to help those around us; to redeem the time – and so make our lives (and those of others) that bit better. ◆

10

Martin Luther King Day (third Monday in January)

This passage is part of Martin Luther King's 'I have a dream…' speech, delivered in front of 210,000 people at the Washington Monument on 28 August, 1963. He was awarded the Nobel Peace Prize in 1964 and assassinated in 1968. His 'day' has been observed since 1977.

In 1963, black people in America did not have equal civil rights. There had been many protests and meetings about this but one day in August 1963 over two hundred thousand people gathered for a civil rights rally in Washington. The main speaker was a black clergyman, the Reverend Martin Luther King – who believed in non-violence. Even so, he was assassinated five years later, but by then he had done much to bring about black rights. This is part of the speech he gave that day.

◆

GO BACK TO Mississippi, go back to Alabama, go back to South Carolina, go back to Georgia, go back to Louisiana, go back to the slums and ghettos of our northern cities, knowing that somehow this situation can and will be changed. Let us not wallow in the valley of despair.

I say to you today, my friends, that in spite of the difficulties and frustrations of the moment I still have a dream. It is a dream deeply rooted in the American dream.

I have a dream that one day this nation will rise up and live out the true meaning of its creed: 'We hold these truths to be self-evident; that all men are created equal.'

I have a dream that one day on the red hills of Georgia the sons of former slaves and the sons of former slave-owners will be able to sit down together at the table of brotherhood.

I have a dream that one day even the state of Mississippi, a desert state sweltering with the heat of injustice and oppression, will be transformed into an oasis of freedom and justice.

I have a dream that my four little children will one day live in a nation where they will not be judged by the colour of their skin but by the content of their character.

I have a dream today.

I have a dream that one day the state of Alabama, whose governor's lips are presently dripping with the words of interposition and nullification, will be transformed into a situation where little black boys and black girls will be able to join hands with little white boys and white girls and walk together as sisters and brothers.

I have a dream today.

I have dream that one day every valley shall be exalted, every hill and mountain shall be made low, the rough places will be made plains, and the crooked places will be made straight, and the glory of the Lord shall be revealed, and all flesh shall see it together.

This is our hope. This is the faith with which I return to the South. With this faith we will be able to hew out of the mountain of despair a stone of hope. With this faith we will be able to transform the jangling discords of our nation into a beautiful symphony of brotherhood. With this faith we will be able to work together, to pray together, to struggle together, to go to jail together, to stand up for freedom together, knowing that we will be free one day.

This will be the day when all of God's children will be able to sing with new meaning:

> My country, 'tis of thee,
> Sweet land of liberty,
>   Of thee I sing:
> Land where my fathers died,
> Land of the pilgrims' pride,
> From every mountainside
>   Let freedom ring.

And if America is to be a great nation this must become true. So let freedom ring from the prodigious hilltops of New Hampshire. Let freedom ring from the mighty mountains of New York. Let freedom ring from the heightening Alleghenies of Pennsylvania!

Let freedom ring from the snowcapped Rockies of Colorado!

Let freedom ring from the curvacious peaks of California!

But not only that; let freedom ring from Stone Mountain of Georgia!

Let freedom ring from Lookout Mountain of Tennessee!

Let freedom ring from every hill and molehill of Mississippi. From every mountainside, let freedom ring.

When we let freedom ring, when we let it ring from every village and every hamlet, from every state and every city, we will be able to speed up that day when all of God's children, black men and white men, Jews and Gentiles, Protestants and Catholics, will be able to join hands and sing in the words of the old Negro spiritual, 'Free at last! free at last! thank God almighty, we are free at last!' ◆

MARTIN LUTHER KING

11

Mardi Gras

The last day before the Christian penitential season of Lent is known in this country as Shrove Tuesday (to be shriven is to be absolved of your sins) or Pancake Day. Traditionally it was the day on which to eat up those foodstuffs that would not be needed during the Lenten fast. In France it is known as Mardi Gras (Fat Tuesday) and in many countries as Carnival, said to be derived from 'carne vale' or 'farewell to meat'.

For us, Shrove Tuesday may mean pancakes and not much else. In other parts of the world – such as the West Indies – it is far more of a festival or carnival. There it is known by its French name, Mardi Gras.

FRENCH PEOPLE SETTLED in the West Indies and carried the Mardi Gras festivities there. At first it was celebrated only by the French but it took on a local flavour when the participants began to dress up as their own slaves and servants.

This changeover of roles is a common theme in many festivals. At the Roman feast of Saturnalia master and slave would change places for the day. This also happened at the Feast of Fools in medieval England, and a remnant of the custom is still found in some British regiments where officers serve their men Christmas dinner.

Perhaps this theme is echoed in the New Testament where Jesus, before his crucifixion, is mocked as a king who is humbled and must die.

In 1833 slavery was abolished in the West Indies and so Mardi Gras became a festival of a newly freed people. At first they copied their former masters by dressing with exaggerated ☞

finery, but later festivals included figures dressed as characters from stories the slaves had brought from Africa. During the present festivities any fancy dress is acceptable and, especially in Trinidad and Tobago, the carnival has become a fantastic spectacle with thousands joining in.

In Trinidad and Tobago Mardi Gras lasts over the two days before Ash Wednesday, with Shrove Tuesday celebrations forming the climax. The carnival is very carefully timetabled and different types of fancy dress are paraded at separate times.

Everyone who wants to join in starts to plan his or her costume as soon as Christmas is over. Some costumes are cheaply made but others have become so brilliant and ingenious that they are very expensive indeed. Groups of people work together and, during the parade, are often led by a steel band. Each group has a king, queen and courtiers who must be properly dressed. Wood, wire, plastic, metal, velvet, beads and feathers are among the things used to make costumes. By the time Mardi Gras arrives there are as many as a hundred thousand people with specially made costumes.

At dawn on Carnival Monday the first sounds are heard. People taking part shout 'Jouvay', which means daybreak, and the parade begins. The streets are suddenly filled with people dressed as witches, ghosts and devils, making weird and chilling noises. These sounds are soon drowned as traditional steel bands begin to play. Their own special music, which is now familiar to people all over the world, becomes the only sound to be heard over the crowds in the streets. Steel bands playing calypsos are now as much a part of Mardi Gras as fancy dress.

As the eerie Jouvay characters flood through the streets they are immediately followed by people in traditional costumes. These costumes change little from year to year and are often ☛

37

passed down through families. Clowns, devils, cowboys and dames flow through the streets dancing to the beat of the steel bands. The devils wear bright red, close-fitting clothes with long tails. They dance around the Beast, a fantastic creature with the head of a dragon and a scaly body of metallic green and silver. The whole band is led by Satan or King Lucifer, who has a huge horned head and flowing robes.

Next in the parade comes a crowd of figures from history. The twirling, shifting mass of colour may be made up of Romans, Vikings, Egyptians, Aztecs; in fact nearly everyone in history is represented.

Next in line come the most fabulous costumes of the whole carnival. These are original costumes which are intended to display the talents of the designer. They are often the most expensive to be found. Shifting, shining colours swirl through the streets to the never-ending throb of the steel bands. St George and the Dragon, with the dragon forming part of St George's costume, leap and dance alongside the God of Paradise. Close by, the shimmering tail feathers of a Fire Bird lash out towards the King of the Sea.

From dawn to dusk this seething crowd dances and sings its way through the streets, drawing people from the watching crowd along with it. As dusk approaches, prizes are given for the finest costumes and the best steel bands. Singing and dancing continue long into the night as fireworks burst and sparkle across the sky.

On the second day, Mardi Gras proper, an even greater display takes place. This time the winning costumes are given pride of place at the head of the procession. Everyone dances and sings to the music, usually in a shuffling, stamping style of their own. Every so often, though, a special set of steps begins to ☛

emerge and fantastic characters leap and twist in the air. Mardi Gras then draws to an end with dances and picnics in the open air.

Mardi Gras in Trinidad, Tobago, New Orleans and Rio de Janeiro has become one of the most colourful ways of celebrating this festival anywhere in the world. It is easy to forget in the face of carnvival that a deeply religious side exists. This is still a time of preparation for Lent and throughout the celebrations this is remembered by all the Christian participants. ◆

MARGARET DAVIDSON

12

Lent

Lent is the period of 40 days leading up to Easter and so its dates are dictated by the date of Easter. For Christians, it is a period of penitence when they may try to set aside more time for prayer and Bible reading. Traditionally it has been marked by fasting. It also commemorates the 40 days Jesus spent in the wilderness at the start of his ministry (see Mark 1 and Luke 4).

During this period called Lent, Christians remember how Jesus went into a desert place to fast and meditate before starting his work of teaching and healing. The Bible tells us that, while he was in the desert, the devil appeared to him and tempted him in three ways: to turn stones into bread, to throw himself off the top of the temple in Jerusalem and let God have him land safely (so as to attract followers); and thirdly to worship the devil in return for power.

◆

AT FIRST READING, the temptations Jesus experienced after 40 days in the wilderness seem very moderate. At least, the first two temptations do not seem to suggest anything frightfully wicked. It scarcely seems necessary to imagine the devil appearing with horns on his head and a spike on his tail to make them.

Yet all three temptations strike at the very heart of what Jesus preached. What the devil suggested to him was a familiar excuse which everybody will instantly recognize: 'Those ideals are all very fine, but you've got to think of yourself.'

1. 'If you are the Son of God, tell this stone to turn into a loaf.'

Having fasted for 40 days and 40 nights Jesus was, not surprisingly, hungry.

'You ought to look after yourself. Go on,' you can imagine the voice urging, 'have a good feed, build yourself up. You need it. You won't be much good to anybody if your health breaks down, will you? Use your power. There's nothing wrong with having enough to eat and drink.'

But Jesus never used his power to his own advantage.

2. Next, the devil took him to Jerusalem. On the parapet of the temple he said to Jesus: 'If you are the Son of God, throw yourself down from here.'

'Those little cures and wonders you perform in small villages out there in the back of beyond are all very fine. But you've got to do something impressive. Think big. You've got to convince the people who matter, here in the big city. Get them on your side and all the others will follow. So do something really spectacular. Jump off the top of the temple and land on your feet. That'll show 'em. *Then* they'll believe you.'

But Jesus never used his power to impress people, not even to impress them with the truth of his words.

3. Finally, the devil took him to a high mountain and pointed out all the kingdoms of the world below. 'I will give you all these kingdoms, and the glory of them. Worship me and it shall be yours.'

'You are on to a good thing here. Look at all those people, the way they flock to you. They are all talking about your sermons. They think you're fantastic. If only you would organize yourself you could do such a lot of good. Take a little collection now and then, not for yourself of course, but to promote your ☞

work. You will be astonished how generous these poor people can be.

'Then you can get proper transport so you can travel the length and breadth of the country preaching your message. Think of all the people you could reach that way! You could pay people to organize your meetings and have crowds waiting for you wherever you go, properly trained people that is, not those nitwits you have collected behind you.

'And why shouldn't you have proper accommodation wherever you go, why shouldn't you enjoy yourself a little? You work hard, you need to relax, you deserve some little reward for yourself. In any case the people like to see their preachers properly looked after.'

But Jesus never sought to advance himself, either materially nor socially. He never sought anything for himself. ◆

BERNARD O'CONNOR OSA

13

Holi

Holi is a Hindu festival which occurs at the start of India's hot season in either late February or March. It celebrates the Lord Krishna's love of amorous jokes and games and is a time for carnivals, processions and dances. Barriers of caste and rank are forgotten as people throw coloured water and bright powders at each other. Students have licence to chase their teachers down the street and workers spray their employers with water. The evening is a time for visiting and exchanging of sweets and gifts. (The festival of Holi is also celebrated by Sikhs.)

Throughout the northern half of the world the spring months see many celebrations of the return of light and new life to the world after the gloom of winter. At this time of the year in India people celebrate the Hindu festival of Holi. This description is by the Indian actress and writer Madhur Jaffrey.

◆

HOLI IS THE Indian Spring Festival, a time when winter crops, such as wheat and mustard seeds, are harvested. I cannot tell you how much I looked forward to this festival. In fact, I longed for it a good 364 days of the year.

The reason was that our whole family did *such* unusual things to celebrate Holi.

First of all, on the day of the full moon around late February or early March, we built a huge bonfire. This was called 'burning Holi', because on this day, ages ago, a wicked princess, Holika, was consumed by flames that she had intended for her innocent nephew Prahlad.

Frankly, I cared less for Holika, who was burnt in ancient ☛

history, than I did for the stuff we actually threw into our own bonfire. We threw whole sheaves of green wheat, whole bundles of green chickpeas, still on their stalks, pinecones filled with strategically hidden pinenuts, and then watched them as their skins got charred.

Only the outside skins were allowed to burn. That was the trick. Each one of us then used a stick to pull out whatever we wanted to eat. My favourite was the chickpeas – tiny chickpeas still in their green skins. Of course, the skins would turn brownish-black but the peas themselves would be deliciously roasted. Everything would be hot – we would almost burn our fingers trying to peel the chickpeas and remove the shells from the pinenuts. Their taste would have to last us for the rest of the year as we licked our lips and remembered. By the end of it all, our faces were black and our clothes and hands were sooty, but no one seemed to mind, not even our parents.

The funny thing about Holi was that we could 'burn' it one night and 'play' it next morning. While the 'burning' had to do, naturally, with fire, the 'playing' had to do with water and colours.

It was said that Lord Krishna, the blue god, played Holi with the milkmaids, so who were we to do any less?

As the Spring Festival approached, an army of us young cousins would, in great secrecy and in competing groups, begin its preparation of colours.

At Holi, all Indians, of all ages, have the licence to rub or throw colours – waterbased, oil-based or in powder form – on the victims of their choice. No one is considered worthy of exemption, dignified grandmothers included.

Holi is a leveller, and there was no one we wanted to level more ☞

than those against whom we held grudges. A special ugly colour was prepared for them.

First, we would go to the garage and call on one of the chauffeurs. 'Masoom Ali? Masoom Ali?' we would call.

Masoom Ali would poke his head out from the pit under the gleaming Ford. 'I am busy. Why are you children always disturbing me? Always coming here to eat my head. Barrister Sa'ab, your grandfather, wants the car at noon and I still have much work to do.'

'Just give us some of the dirtiest grease from under the car.'

'So, Holi is upon us again? Why don't you children use the normal red, green and yellow colours?'

'If you give us the grease, we won't spray you with the awful magenta paint we have prepared in the garden watertank. It is a fast colour, too.'

'Threatening an old man, are you! All right, all right. Just don't eat my head.'

The grease would be combined with mud, slime and permanent purple dye. The concoction would be reserved for the lowliest enemies. Elderly relatives got a sampling of the more dignified, store-bought powders, yellow, red and green. For our best friends, we prepared a golden paint, carefully mixing real gilt and oil in a small jar. This expensive colour, would, as I grew older, be saved only for those members of the opposite sex on whom I had the severest crushes – transforming them, with one swift application, into golden gods. ◆

MADHUR JAFFREY

14

St Patrick's Day (17 March)

Much of what we 'know' about the patron saint of Ireland is legend. His birthplace may have been on the Clyde, on the Severn estuary – or in France. Besides the St Patrick credited with taking Christianity to Ireland, there was also a St Patrick of Nevers, France. It may be that details of the two lives have become entangled. This reading presents an 'accepted' life of Patrick.

NB: The Christian doctrine of the Trinity teaches that God is one being whom Christians know in three forms: Father, Son and Holy Spirit.

17 March is St Patrick's Day and St Patrick is the national saint of Ireland – even though he wasn't Irish. So how did this come about?

◆

ST PATRICK IS the patron saint of Ireland. Nobody knows now exactly when he was born and there are conflicting accounts of where. However, most people think that he was the son of a farmer living on the coast of France, in a place which is now Boulogne, and that he was probably born around the middle of the fourth century.

When he was about sixteen years old, Patrick was captured by pirates in a raid on the coast, and carried off to Ireland, where he was sold as a slave to a landowner and set to mind sheep and pigs among the bogs and hills of Antrim. Although he had been brought up as a Christian, he had not, hitherto, thought much about religion. But now, in his exile, he thought about it constantly, and in his misery his belief in God became a great comfort to him. He began to experience strange dreams which seemed to him to have some deep religious meaning, and one night, after he had been for about six years in captivity, he ☞

woke suddenly from sleep with a voice ringing in his ears telling him that he was to return to his own country, and that a ship was waiting for him. Believing that Christ, or some holy saint, had spoken to him, Patrick arose at once and set off towards the coast, where he did, in truth, find a ship which brought him back to his native land.

For a little while he lived with his family. Then again he experienced one of his vivid dreams. He thought a man brought him a letter headed 'The Voice of the Irish,' and at the same time he heard voices calling to him: 'Come again, holy boy, come and walk again in the midst of us.'

Patrick was greatly affected by this dream, and he made up his mind that he must return to Ireland and preach Christianity to the people. He trained as a priest, went to Rome to obtain the Pope's blessing on his project, and, after some delays, set sail for Ireland, where he remained for the rest of his life, teaching and converting the people.

Innumerable legends are told about St Patrick. He is supposed to have rid Ireland of snakes by charming them into the sea. When a robber stole one of his goats and ate it, the goat bleated from the criminal's stomach when the saint called it by name, and thanks to Patrick's holiness, he was able to extract the poor creature, safe and sound, without in any way injuring the man. His power of working miracles extended after his death, for when he died the sun did not set for the whole period of the prolonged funeral ceremonies, but continued to shine by day and night.

There is one famous story about St Patrick, which is almost certainly true, the story of the way in which the saint used the leaf of the shamrock to explain the mystery of the Trinity to his puzzled hearers – The Three in One and One in Three. It ☞

is because of this story that all patriotic Irish people wear a spray of shamrock leaves on St Patrick's Day.

The end came when St Patrick was over ninety. He had wished to die in Armagh, when in 444 the cathedral church had been founded, but it most probable that he died in the year 461 in Saul on Strangford Lough, where he had built his first church.

CHRISTINE CHAUNDLER

The work of evangelizing Ireland was full of peril. St Patrick writes, towards the end of his life: 'Daily I expect either a violent death or to be robbed and reduced to slavery or the occurrence of some such calamity … I have cast myself into the hands of Almighty God, for he rules everything; as the Prophet said, "Cast your care on the Lord, and he himself will sustain you" '. His writings reveal his intense love of humanity second only to his love of God and explain his enormous influence. ◆

BROTHER KENNETH, CGA

15

The Annunciation (25 March)

The Annunciation of Our Lord to the Blessed Virgin Mary (to give the day its full title) marks the time when Mary first heard from the Angel Gabriel that she was to be the mother of Jesus. It is of course nine months before Christmas Day. Sometimes known as Lady Day, it is one of the four quarter days (see Michaelmas). Until 1751 it was officially regarded as the start of the New Year.

    NB This passage may be used in March or as a Christmas reading. (See also passages 7 and 8.)

25 March is the day many Christians call the Annunciation, that is, the announcing by an angel to Mary that she was to be the mother of Jesus – even though she was still a young girl and a virgin. As you can work out, the reason for remembering the event at this time of year is that 25 March is exactly nine months before Christmas Day.

This reading suggests what it might have been like for Mary – and for the angel who had to tell her the news.

◆

THE ANGEL GABRIEL sat in the corner and watched.

The girl was only thirteen. Fourteen, at most. Barely a woman, by the shape of her. With long, dark hair and bright olive skin. Not beautiful, but far from plain. Pretty.

The last thing he wanted to do was scare her. Like he'd scared that old priest Zechariah.

You did everything possible to ease the shock, Gabriel assured himself. No blinding flashes of light. No angelic choirs. You just appeared to him there beside the altar. He was in the temple, for heaven's sake! What better place to meet an angel?

But the old man had still been spooked. He clutched at his heart. He wobbled and shook like the smoke curling up from the altar.

'Don't be afraid,' Gabriel had said. 'The news I have for you is good. Your wife will have a baby. You will call him John. He will prepare God's people to meet the Messiah.'

The announcement was nothing like he'd practised it, of course. He'd had to blurt it out all in one breath because the old man looked like he was about to keel over.

Gabriel hugged his knees and scrunched himself back into the corner. He hated these surprise visits, and that's all there was to it.

The girl was whistling now. Doing her ordinary, everyday chores – like this was some ordinary everyday, and not the most extraordinary day of her life.

The angel rested his chin on his knees. Think, Gabriel, think, he muttered to himself. She's young. But she's probably fragile like that old priest. So how do you do it? How do you tell her that God is about to change her whole life, without scaring her to death?

Mary began to sweep as she whistled. And as the dust motes danced in front of her broom, catching the sun and changing shape like dirty little clouds, Gabriel had an idea.

What about a vision? He asked himself. It always worked with the prophets. The dust rises and takes on the form of a man. 'Mary,' the dust-man says, 'your are going to be the mother of the Son of God!'

Gabriel shook his head, then buried it in his arms. No, no, no, he decided. Still too spooky. And besides, all it takes is a strong breeze and the poor girl has to dust her house all over again!

It was too late now, anyway. Mary had put her broom away and was across the room preparing dinner. Gabriel climbed up out of the corner and stretched. Then he followed her to the table.

Bread. She was making bread. And as she mixed the ingredients, another idea started to knead itself together and rise in Gabriel's head.

He could write the message in the flour on the table. Of course! An invisible hand, like the one that scratched those letters on the wall in Babylon. But it would have to be brief. It was a small table, after all. And there wasn't much time. Mary's parents were both gone, and there was no telling when they would by back. He wouldn't want to be surprised in the middle of his message. Gabriel hated surprises!

And then somebody knocked on the door. Gabriel jumped, startled by the sound. Mary quietly turned and walked to the door, wiping her hands as she went. It was a girl about Mary's age. Gabriel watched as they hugged and exchanged greetings. She had a brief message for Mary.

It wasn't long before Mary said goodbye and shut the door again.

I could do that, Gabriel thought. Knock at the door, like some unexpected visitor, and just give her the message … But what if she got scared and slammed the door in my face? Or what if someone passed by and saw us? She'll have enough explaining to do when the baby comes. She won't need to make excuses for some mysterious stranger.

And then Gabriel sighed. A long, frustrated angel sigh. Gabriel ☛

had run out of ideas. Gabriel was running out of time. So Gabriel sighed.

Perhaps it was the sigh. Perhaps it was something else that Mary heard. For whatever reason, she spun around and seemed to hang suspended in the air for a second – like one of those dust motes – her hair flung out behind her, her feet barely touching the floor. And her eyes. Her eyes looked right into Gabriel's.

He hadn't noticed her eyes before. Brown, shining eyes. Young and alive. They should have looked right through him, but they didn't. They stopped where he stood, and they touched him. Somehow she could see him. Somehow she knew he was there.

'Hello, Mary,' he said finally, because there was nothing else to say. 'God is with you, and wants to do something very special for you.'

Mary didn't say anything. But she didn't faint either. And that was a great relief to the angel. She just stood there, shaking ever so slightly, and stared at her guest. He could see those eyes swallow up his words, see the questions and concern in those eyes as the girl tried to puzzle out the meaning of his greeting.

'There's no need to be afraid,' Gabriel assured her, although it was hard to know exactly what she was feeling. Was she trembling with fear? Or was it more like excitement? Gabriel couldn't tell. And he didn't like that one bit. This girl was nothing like what he had expected. This girl was a bit of a surprise.

'Look,' he continued, ' God is very pleased with you. So pleased, in fact, that he wants you to be the mother of a very special child – Jesus, the Messiah. The Deliverer whom your people have been waiting for all these years.'

Surely this would shock her, Gabriel thought. And he was ready to catch her if she should fall. But all she did was sit herself down to think. She played with the hem of her dress, folding and unfolding it. She twisted her hair.

Say something, thought Gabriel. Say anything!

And finally she did. 'I don't understand,' she said. 'How can this happen? How can I become someone's mother when I'm not yet someone's wife?'

This was the last question the angel expected. This girl wasn't hysterical or alarmed. Her question was plain, straightforward and practical.

Gabriel cleared his throat and answered the question as best he could. 'The Holy Spirit will visit you. You will be wrapped in the power of the Almighty. And you will give birth to the Son of God.'

Mary had never heard of such a thing. And it showed. In her bright brown eyes it showed.

'Listen,' Gabriel explained, 'God can do anything. Think about your cousin Elizabeth. Well past child-bearing age. Barren, by all accounts. And yet she's expecting a son!'

Mary looked up at the angel and shook her head. She was still trying to take it in. But she wasn't afraid, he could tell that much. She was strong, this girl. A doer. A coper. A fighter. And when she finally weighed it all, Gabriel knew what her answer would be even before she gave it. Those eyes of hers were shining fierce and bold.

'I'll do it,' she said. 'I'll do it. I will be whatever God wants me to be.'

Gabriel nodded. Then he turned to leave. He reached out to ☛

open the curtain – the curtain between heaven and earth – and saw that his hand was trembling.

He turned back to look at Mary one last time. And in the mirror of her eyes, Gabriel saw a shocked angel face.

Mary smiled at him.

He smiled back. Perhaps surprises aren't so bad after all, he thought.

Then Gabriel pulled the curtain behind him and said goodbye to the girl. The girl who had surprised an angel. And who would one day surprise the world. ◆

BOB HARTMAN

16

Miss Mary Magdala

This passage is taken from a modern 'novelization' of the Easter story,
The Davidson Affair. *It may be used in two parts, if so required.*

Today's reading is a re-telling of the Easter story, supposing it happened in modern times. In it, Jesus becomes Jesus Davidson and his disciples or followers (whom the Bible describes as John, son of Zebedee and Simon bar-Jonah, also known as Simon Peter) become John Zebedee and Peter Johnson.

In this excerpt, a television reporter remembers interviewing another follower, Mary of Magdala (who was the first to see Jesus after he rose from the dead) about what happened that first Easter morning.

◆

I SAID, 'AND you saw him there, in the garden outside the tomb?'

'That's right. I saw him and talked to him.'

I heard the patience in her voice and smiled, watching the screen. She was right, of course. Once you had swallowed the incredible idea of God living in the world as a man, everything else was completely logical.

I said, 'How did you come to be in the garden so early in the morning? Was it pre-arranged before he died? A sort of rendezvous?'

She laughed. 'Nothing so dramatic. It was simply our first opportunity to visit his tomb. We have a strict rule about not

☞

working on the Sabbath, as I expect you know. We had to wait until first light yesterday before we could go.'

'Yes, but why did you go? Was it just a sentimental journey?'

'In a way, I suppose it was,' she said frankly. 'But practical too. We took spices and ointment and – oh, it sounds absurd now, a bunch of women in heavy mourning going to preserve a corpse. But it was all we could think of doing. We'd had to stand by and watch them take him away and kill him. And the burial on Friday was very rushed. We had to get finished before the Sabbath started at sunset. Yesterday morning we decided to do things properly. Give him a decent burial at least.' She smiled. 'I expect it all sounds very odd to you, Mr Tennel. But our Jewish funeral customs are important to us.'

'I understand,' I said.

'We were terribly worried about how we were were going to get into the tomb – what with that great stone slab sealing the entrance and the guard there and everything. But of course, when we got there, the guards had gone and the tomb was wide open. And when we looked inside, it was empty.'

I nodded. 'You've considered the possibility of grave-robbers?'

'It was our first thought. I remember Salome – she was one of the group – saying in that rather acid voice she puts on when she's upset, "Even when the poor soul's dead they can't leave him in peace." '

I looked at her quickly. 'They?'

'The supreme council, the Sanhedrin.'

'You thought the Sanhedrin had arranged to have the body removed?'

'Yes, of course. Who else would want to do such a thing?'

'Why the Sanhedrin?' I said.

'I don't know. Perhaps to prevent the tomb from becoming a shrine. If it hadn't been for Saul Joseph offering his own tomb they'd have buried him in quick-lime in the prison yard. That's what usually happens.'

'I wondered about that.'

She nodded. 'Mr Joseph went personally to the Governor-General and got his permission to bury the body. The Sanhedrin were very put out about it, I believe.'

I could understand their alarm. A dead hero in a magnificent tomb was a ready-made focal point for future trouble.

'But it wasn't that at all, of course,' she said. 'We rushed back to the house and told the men. And John Zebedee and Peter Johnson went back straightaway to see for themselves. I followed behind but I hadn't a hope of catching up with them.'

I said, 'I'd like to get this quite right. It's important, I think. Are you in fact saying that the men were surprised at your news of the empty tomb?'

'And angry. Peter especially. I've never seen him so wild.'

'It would be true to say, then, that these men who were his closest friends never expected him to come back from the dead?'

'None of us did, Mr, Tennel. None of us.'

'Although he had on several occasions promised to do just that?'

'In spite of that we didn't expect to see him alive again. I'm ashamed to have to say it, but it's true.'

'What happened when you got to the tomb the second time?'

'I saw Peter coming out. I hardly recognized him, he looked so old and beaten. John took his arm and they went off together, walking slowly. They passed right by me but I don't think either of them knew I was there. They were like men walking in their sleep.'

'And did you go after them?'

'No. I stayed on. I don't know why. I was weeping and terribly upset, and …'

'I quite understand, Miss Magdala. This has all been a tremendous strain on you.'

She looked at me steadily and said, 'You don't believe it, do you? You don't believe he's alive again?'

'I'm open to conviction,' I said.

She shook her head. 'You think I'm not quite myself. A little bit off-centre. You think it's all been too much of a shock for me. Well, it was a shock, finding that empty tomb. A terrible shock.'

'Yes,' I said. 'Of course.'

'The thought of them mauling him about. Dragging him out of his grave in the middle of the night and digging a hole somewhere and dropping his body in and stamping the ground down on top of him. Just for a moment or two, there by myself in the garden when the men had gone, I thought I was going out of my mind.' She smiled, a warm, sane smile. 'And then he came and spoke to me.'

'Jesus Davidson? You're sure?'

'Yes. He was suddenly there and he asked me why I was crying. ☞

He sounded so – so normal and relaxed I didn't think it was him at first. Funny isn't it, the way a familiar voice sounds strange when you don't expect to hear it? But then he spoke my name, "Mary" he said. And I knew who he was and turned round and saw him there.'

Again it was said with the devastating simplicity, as though she had wakened from a nightmare and recognized the familiar room and the figure of a parent bending over her.

'Did he say anything else?' I said.

'He gave me a message. For Peter and the men. He called them his brothers. I put my arms round him and hugged him. He was there and I was so glad to see him, and at the same time terrified in case he disappeared again. I held him tight to make sure of him. But he freed himself gently and told me to take this message back to the house.'

'What was the message? Can you tell us?'

'Oh yes. It's not a secret. We're finished with secrets now. It's all out in the open for everyone to hear. I mean, if killing him couldn't silence him, nothing can. He said "Go and tell my brothers I am ascending to my Father and yours, to my God and your God. Tell them I am going first to Galilee and they must come and meet me there." '

'And you took that message back to them?'

She nodded. 'I ran all the way. I was so excited I could hardly get the words out at first.'

'Did they understand what he meant, Miss Magdala?'

'Yes. It was exactly what he had promised. He told us all about it long before any of this happened; how he came from God and was going back to God. He told us plainly, not once but many times.'

'And yet at first, when you found the tomb empty, you didn't even consider the possibility of a resurrection.'

'I know,' she said. 'He told us exactly what would happen, and we wanted to believe him, but I don't think any of us really expected it to come true.' She shook her head. 'Looking back now over the last couple of years I think we must have broken his heart a hundred times simply by not being able to understand the truth about him and what he was trying to do for us.'

STUART JACKMAN

17

Wesak

Each Buddhist country has its own festivals. Events in the life of the Buddha are commemorated at different times of the year so, for example, Japanese Buddhists celebrate the Buddha's birthday on 8 April. Those who follow the Theravada school of Buddhism (which teaches we are each a responsible and separate individual as opposed to being inextricably interlinked one with another) celebrate the birth, enlightenment and death of the Buddha all on one day: the night of the Full Moon of the month of May. In India it is called Vaishaklia Puja; in Thailand and Sri Lanka it is called Vesak or Wesak.

Buddhists do not believe in God in the same way that followers of other religions do but they do follow the teachings of a man now known as the Buddha. He lived about 2500 years ago in India and many Buddhists remember three events in his life on the same day: the day (or night) when there is a Full Moon in the month of May.

He was not always known as the Buddha. Before that, he was a wealthy prince called Siddhartha Gotama. He led a very sheltered and comfortable life but when he was a young man he learned the truth about suffering, old age and death. He became unhappy with his life in the royal palace and set off to find a way of escaping the troubles of this world. Buddhists call this 'escape' *moksha.*

◆

SIDDHARTHA ADOPTED A life of extreme self-denial and penances, meditating constantly. He settled on the bank of the Nairanjana River, determined to force himself into the state of mind that would lead to *moksha.* For six years, through rain and wind, hot and cold weather, he stayed there, eating ☛

and drinking only enough to stay alive. His body became emaciated, and his former physical strength left him. His holiness
was so evident that five other holy men joined him, hoping to
learn from his example.

One day, the Buddhist tradition holds, Siddhartha realized
that his years of penance had only weakened his body. In such
a state of physical exhaustion, he could not meditate properly.
He stood up and stepped into the river to bathe. But he was so
weak that he could not raise himself out of the water. The
Buddhist scriptures say that the trees on the river bank bent
their branches down so that he could reach them.

At that moment, a milk-maid named Nandabala came into
sight. She offered Siddhartha a bowl of milk and rice, and he
accepted it gratefully. When the five holy men who had been
his pupils saw this, they left because they thought he had abandoned his quest to achieve true holiness or *moksha*.

Refreshed by the meal, Siddhartha sat down under a fig tree
(known to Buddhists as the *Bo tree*, the Tree of Enlightenment) and resolved that he would not arise until he had found
the answer he had sought for so long.

The Buddhist scriptures say that Mara, an evil god who constantly tempted people with desire, saw that Siddhartha was
near to his goal. Mara sent his three sons and three daughters
to tempt Siddhartha. They tormented him with thirst, lust, and
discontent, offering all sorts of pleasures to distract him.

But Siddhartha was not swayed by them. He entered a state of
deep meditation, in which he recalled all his previous rebirths.
He gained knowledge of the cycle of births and deaths, and the
certainty that he had cast off the ignorance and passion of the
'I' self that bound him to the world. At last, he had attained
enlightenment.

This experience was the beginning of the history of Buddhism as a religion. Siddhartha became the Buddha, the 'enlightened one.'

As tradition has it, the Buddha could then have cast off his body and his existence. Instead, however, he made a great act of self-sacrifice. Having discovered the way to end his own suffering, he turned back, determined to share his enlightenment with others so that all living souls could end the cycles of their own rebirth and suffering. He thus set an example of compassion and wisdom or self-knowledge for others that would be a hallmark of his followers. ◆

MADHU BEZAZ WANGU

18

Whitsun

Whitsun is the traditional name by which Pentecost has been known in Britain. It occurs seven weeks (or 50 days) after Easter. For Christians, it commemorates the coming of the Holy Spirit to the followers of Jesus (see Acts 2).

This time of the year is known as Pentecost or Whitsun. Pentecost is a special time of year for both Jews and Christians.

TO JEWS, PENTECOST is also known as the Feast of Weeks, or Shavuot. It is an early harvest festival which celebrates the wheat harvest. Two loaves of bread, made from newly-harvested wheat, used to be taken to the Temple in Jerusalem as a sign of gratitude for the harvest. Nowadays, it is more important to Jews as a time for remembering how God gave them the Ten Commandments when they were in the wilderness. The story of how Moses, the leader of the Jews at that time, went up Mount Sinai and was given the Commandments by God is read in synagogues at this time.

The word 'Pentecost' comes from a Greek word meaning fiftieth. The festival occurs 50 days after the Jewish Passover and also the Christian Easter.

Christians remember how, seven weeks (or 50 days) after the first Easter Day, the disciples of Jesus were together in Jerusalem to celebrate Shavuot, or Pentecost. That morning, they had a strange and wonderful experience, which they described as being 'filled with the Spirit of God'.

Christians believe that at that moment a special power came into the disciples: the power of the Holy Spirit. Christians say the Holy Spirit (sometimes called Holy Ghost) comes from God and is *part* of God, and gives strength to believers. Whatever did happen in that room that day, it gave the apostles courage. They went out into Jerusalem, and there Simon Peter spoke to the crowds.

Because it was an important Jewish festival, many Jews had come to Jerusalem, including those who did not speak the language spoken by the apostles – yet when Peter spoke (according to the Bible), everyone heard him speak in their own language.

The Bible goes on to say that, because of what Peter said, three thousand people believed that day that Jesus came from God, was crucified and then came back to life. So for Christians, Pentecost is the birthday of Christianity, the birthday of the Christian Church. Services are held as reminders of what happened to the first followers of Jesus at the first Pentecost after the resurrection.

In Britain, the day is sometimes called Whitsun (or White Sunday). This is because it used to be a popular day on which to hold baptism services and the people who were being baptized would wear white.

In parts of Lancashire and Yorkshire, it is a tradition for Christians to go on walks of witness at Whitsun, as a way of showing they are not ashamed to be Christians. These are known as Whit Walks. Usually, the members of each church or Sunday School meet at their own place of worship and have a short service, after which they walk in procession through the streets of their town or village. They stop at certain places and sing, sometimes meeting up with the members of other churches. ☞

Here is a description of the Whit Walks that used to be held in Manchester, written by Frances Lennon who lived in a suburb of Manchester called Trafford.

It is often said that it is always raining in Manchester. We never do 'chance it' without our umbrellas and there could always be a rainbow to look forward to afterwards. Whether there was rain, hail, shine or fog, Manchester and Salford Scholars turned out in splendour every day during the whole of Whit Week. With banners flying, dripping wet, they did not even notice that dye from the linen roses stained their pretty dresses, for this was Manchester and Salford's Profession of Faith.

Trafford's schools were considered to be too far out of town to join in this magnificent parade. We were great spectators at the city walks. All denominations were represented, together with refugees and immigrants. Each denomination was strong in its own belief, complimented each on their strength and admired each other for it. Starting out from St Ann's Square, led by the Bishop of Manchester, came the Cathedral choir, followed by school children from every parish in the city. Every poor child was 'rigged out' with new clothes given by various charitable organizations by voluntary workers.

On Whit Friday the Roman Catholic Schools were led by the Bishop of Salford. Brass bands and Irish pipers played as they had never played before. The sounds of rousing music echoed through the soot-grimed streets of our city, to the tunes of 'Land of Hope and Glory', 'God save the King', 'It's a long way to Tipperary' and 'Faith of our Fathers'. As the procession drew to its close, the Italian community appeared around the corner with a life-size statue of the Madonna carried by sturdy young men. It was laden with hundreds of fresh lilies. Like a thunderbolt came the clapping of thousands of people as they ☛

lined the streets. Children were lifted high on the shoulders of their Dads to witness the Profession of Faith and see the statue of the Madonna in the streets. ◆

FRANCES LENNON

19

Midsummer Fire (24 June)

In the Christian calendar, 24 June marks the birthday of John the Baptist. The date also marks a much older festival: the summer solstice, which was celebrated across Europe by fire festivals.

It is suggested that the second of the following short passages be used only where it will generate some revulsion and might be followed by a brief discussion about (for example) which present-day customs might horrify people in five hundred years' time. (Sir James Frazer was a folklorist and anthropologist.)

This time of the year sees the longest day of the year, a day known as the summer solstice. For Christians, it is also the birthday or feast day of John the Baptist – who was born six months before Jesus.

◆

JOHN THE BAPTIST was the prophet who proclaimed the coming of Jesus Christ, and prepared the way for him. During the Middle Ages he was looked upon as the patron saint of 'the common man', and his feast day, commemorating his birth, was a time of great celebration. On the Eve of the festival there were torchlight processions, and dancing round enormous bonfires.

Long before John the Baptist was born, fire festivals were held at Midsummer. It falls about three days after the Summer Solstice – the day when the sun reaches its highest point before starting to decline. 'Solstice' means to stand still.

Primitive people worshipped the sun as the giver of light and warmth. There are still plenty of 'sun-worshippers' who travel hundreds of miles to anoint themselves with oil, and then lie ☞

on their back for hours in silent communion with the sun! With only limited means of artificial lighting and heating, totally dependent on it for the growth of crops, it is not surprising that our pagan forebears looked on the sun as a god. As the seasons changed, they celebrated the sun-god's return or mourned his departure. The believed that the best way of pleasing him was to imitate him as closely as possible – 'Imitation is the highest form of flattery' – so they lit huge fires in his honour and danced round them sun-wise, or, as we would say, clock-wise. Turning 'widdershins' – against the sun – was unlucky and only done by witches making spells. We still deal playing cards and give the Christmas pudding a lucky stir, in a clock-wise direction.

Evil spirits were suspected of being on the prowl once the sun had begun to lose its power. Lighting fires helped to scare them away. Young men leaped through the flames to prove their manhood, and cattle were driven through the hot embers as protection against disease.

Yet again the Church took over primitive customs it could not quite suppress. People could still light their bonfires and have their fun, but now it was in honour of John the Baptist. Choosing Midsummer Day as his feast day was a stroke of genius. John the Baptist had said of Jesus, 'He must increase and I must decrease.' After Midsummer Day (John the Baptist's birthday), the days begin to shorten, while after Christmas (the birthday of Jesus), they start to lengthen again.

PETER WATKINS AND ERICA HUGHES

One of the largest fire festivals was the midsummer feast, tied, since Christianization, to St John's Day. For a long time, it was celebrated both in the country and in cities. Great piles of ☞

combustible material would be erected on village greens or town squares, and lit on the proper evening at sunset. Rubbish that had been collected over many months now went up in flames. To heighten the suspense people might throw puppets ('straw men') on the fire, or, as was customary in many places, living animals. Thus in early modern times St John's Day was celebrated in Paris with a bonfire in which cats were burned alive. Frazer summarized the proceedings as follows.

'In the midsummer fires formely kindled on the Place de Grève at Paris it was the custom to burn a basket, barrel or sack full of live cats, which was hung from a tall mast in the midst of the bonfire; sometimes a fox was burned. The people collected the embers and ashes of the fire and took them home, believing that they brought good luck. The French kings often witnessed these spectacles and even lit the bonfire with their own hands. In 1648 Louis XIV, crowned with a wreath of roses and carrying a bunch of roses in his hand, kindled the fire, danced at it and partook of the banquet afterwards in the town hall'.◆

JOHAN GOUDSBLOM

20

Ramadan and Id-ul-Fitr

Because the Muslim year is shorter than the Western year, the annual events in the Muslim calendar are not constant or 'fixed' in the Western calendar. So, for example, the month of Ramadan is 'earlier' each year. Ramadan is the month in which Muslims fast each day during daylight hours and marks the time when the Qur'an was revealed to the Prophet. It ends with the festival of Id-ul-Fitr.

What would you find hardest to give up? Watching television? Your best computer game? Or talking, or even eating? If you were to give up eating, for how long could you manage to do so? Members of the different religions sometimes try to go without food for a period; that is, they 'fast'.

◆

IMAGINE WHAT IT is like to go without anything to eat for twelve hours or more each day for a whole month. This is what members of the Muslim religion do each day during the month of Ramadan.

Ramadan is the ninth month of the Muslim year and is special because it was the month in which the Prophet Muhammad began to receive the teaching of Islam from God.

To remind themselves of this, Muslims fast each of the thirty days of Ramadan during daylight hours. That is, they don't eat or drink (or smoke) from dawn until it is completely dark again at night.

During this month, they are also meant to say extra prayers and to try to read the whole of their holy book, the Qur'an. All adult Muslims are expected to keep the fast but very old ☞

people, people who are ill and women who are pregnant or feeding a baby are excused.

Muslims fast not because they think that food is bad or eating is wicked. They fast for three reasons.

1 Going without food for a length of time makes you enjoy your next food very much more than you might have done. A meal at the end of a fast is certainly something to look forward to more than one that follows a meal you had only two or three hours before!

2 Fasting is a reminder that many people are too poor to eat whenever they feel like it – and it's a reminder that many people live in parts of the world where there is a shortage of food.

3 Fasting is a kind of discipline. Very often, we reach for something to nibble the moment we feel the slightest bit hungry. Fasting 'disciplines' people not to give in the moment they feel a pang of hunger: it makes the mind stronger than the body!

Fasting is one of five rules or 'pillars' which Muslims must obey. Another is *zakat* which is the duty or obligation to give money (or food) to the poor and others in need. Money may be given to help with the building of a hospital or mosque — or to help a poor student to study at a college or university. Helping in this way is obviously good for the person receiving the money but Islam teaches it is also good for the person giving help, as the following story or parable shows.

There was once a rich man and a poor man who owed him money. 'Sir, I can't pay you what I owe,' said the poor man, 'but, if you give me time, I'll pay you when I can.'

'Very well. Pay me when you can,' said the rich man.

Islam teaches that this rich man will be rewarded by God for ☞

being generous. But Islam also teaches how much better it might have been.

'Sir, I can't pay you what I owe,' said the poor man, 'but, if you give me time, I'll pay you when I can.'

'You keep what little money you have,' said the rich man. 'Forget what you owe me: it will be my *zakat*.'

Zakat is paid each year at the festival of Id-ul-Fitr.

'Id' means 'celebration' and is celebrated at the end of Ramadan, on the first day of the next month, Shawwal. It begins with an early meal. Then everyone puts on their best clothes and goes to the mosque and, later, they visit relatives and friends to swap presents and to give each other sweets. People wish each other 'Id Mubarak' ('Blessed be your celebration') and give each other Id cards. ◆

STORIES, PARABLES AND LEGENDS

'Learn to handle a writing brush and you'll never handle a begging bowl'
  CHINESE PROVERB
'Two watermelons cannot be held in one hand'
  PERSIAN PROVERB

21

The Gift of Fire

The Greek myth of Prometheus has some parallels with the story of Jesus: each suffered in order to benefit the human race. This passage may be read as a starter for discussion about the similarities and differences between it and the Christian message; simply as a story in its own right, an example of Greek mythology; or as a parable that warns of the benefits and dangers fire has brought us.

The Ancient Greeks believed there were many gods. Zeus was the chief who lived on Mount Olympus. After the creation of humans, Zeus determined they should be 'kept in their place' as underlings and so he denied them the gift of fire.

Prometheus (who was a kind of god called a Titan and who had created humankind) decided to help the human race by stealing fire from heaven (or Olympus) – even though he knew this would infuriate Zeus. As you hear the story, you might wonder what the world would be like without fire: no heat, no warmth, no hot food, no bombs ...

◆

SO MAN CAME to the Earth, and woman too; and with them came every kind of plague, mischief and disaster. Prometheus' people were hardly equipped to survive; their creator was forbidden to teach them necessary skills – and now Zeus, although he could not personally destroy what another god had made, arranged things so that the world's seasons would do his work for him.

Winter came ... and with it came humankind's first snow. It whispered across fields and forests, settling on the branches like a soft, white death. It slipped soundlessly into cracks between the rocks, and choked the gullies where sheep huddled and died. In lakes and the sea snowflakes disappeared and died. There was no sound.

In caves, under trees, men and women cowered for warmth. They were naked, their skin putty-coloured and pitted with cold. They looked at the falling snow with gentle eyes: without intelligence, they saw no link between the white drifts and the chill that dulled their bones. Like sheep they huddled and watched, and died.

From up above, where the gods feasted in the palace halls of Olympus, warmed by iron fire-baskets glowing on the polished floors, Prometheus looked down and pitied them. If once they understood, if once the spark of knowledge glowed, their minds would become fertile with the secrets of nature, the secrets of the gods. Wrapping his shadow-cloak about him, he stood up and slipped away. No one noticed: sweating, laughing, joking, the gods continued their feast.

Wrapped in his cloak, soaring like a night-bird, Prometheus passed from the home of the gods to the Earth below. He made his way deep inside, to the caverns of Sicily. Here, in the searing heat below the earth's crust, were the blacksmiths' forges where the Cyclopes sweated and toiled, shaping earth's iron bones into thunderbolts for Zeus. Fires flickered and roared; hammers thudded and anvils rang; waste rock, white-hot, flowed out through vent-holes on the surface, the volcanoes of Sicily.

Unseen, Prometheus knelt by a stream of glowing fire. From his belt he took a stalk of the green fennel-plant and split it open. The inside was hollow and damp: it would keep a glowing coal alive. Quickly he took a coal, slipped it inside the stalk and drew back into the shadows.

Fire! Prometheus' last gift to mortals. The fire of intelligence, to save them from death and teach them the secrets of the gods. When Zeus next looked out over the Earth (a morning later, to the gods; to mortals, a dozen generations), the world had changed. From every part of it pencils of smoke rose up from the wink and glint of cooking-fires. Men and women hurried about, eager and purposeful. They wore clothes of animal-skin and woven cloth; they had learned farming, sailing, a thousand crafts and skills; they were busy with markets, parliaments, fishing, hunting and harvesting. And above all, they had learned speech: a hum of voices, a bee-swarm of languages, rose up and drowned the wind's rustle, the murmur of the sea.

Zeus' anger was a lightning-storm, a blare of thunder. The sky darkened; the earth shook; the gods shrank back in fear. And for Prometheus, Fire-thief, there was no escape. There was the hiss of a thunderbolt, a flare of light, an eruption of pain. Black, greasy smoke; a stench of charred flesh; silence.

There was worse to come. Might and Force, the gods' slaves, gathered up the rags of Prometheus' body. They took Prometheus to Mount Caucasus, a jagged tooth of rock in thin, cold air. Might and Force stretched him on tiptoe and held his arms high while Hephaistos chained him to the rock.

Their job done, the gods went back to Olympus. Prometheus was left alone. He could see and hear nothing. His charred flesh stuck to the rock; his muscles locked with cramp; his wrists and ankles were ripped ragged by the chains. Then, in the echoing dark, he heard wings whirr. A black shape loomed over him. There was a searing pain as a curved beak tore into ☞

his ribs, stripping its way past bone and sinew till it found his liver.

The vulture of Zeus. All day it gorged on his flesh. At night it rested, and his wounds healed ready for the next day's pain. Prometheus, Fire-thief, was locked in an eternity of suffering. He knew before he stole that this would be his punishment. He knew it and chose it. To save his creation, he chose to destroy himself. ◆

KENNETH MCLEISH

22

The Happiest Man in the World

This is another story from Ancient Greece which asks whether money brings happiness.

What would you need to make you the happiest person in the world? Many people would answer money: unlimited money. This is a story from Ancient Greece about the wisest man in the world, the richest man – and the happiest one.

◆

WHEN SOLON, THE wisest man in the world, had written a complete set of laws for Athens, the world's first democracy, about 2500 years ago, he decided that he needed a holiday.

So, he thought that he would go away from Athens for exactly ten years so that he could have a look at the rest of the known world. While he was away, he said, no one would be allowed to alter in any way the laws that he had made. After a test lasting ten years, surely everyone would know whether his laws were workable or not?

On his travels, Solon decided to call on Croesus, the King of Lydia, who happened to be, at that time, the richest man in the whole of the known world.

Croesus, flattered by this, told his servants to entertain Solon in the most magnificent way. 'Show my guest through all my most important treasure houses,' he said. 'Hide nothing from him.'

So, Solon was conducted through all of Croesus's most glittering treasures – through cellars stacked with gold, through vaults glittering with heaped up diamonds, with rubies, emeralds, and all manner of precious stones.

When this conducted tour of Croesus's enormous wealth was over, Croesus asked Solon to tell him who, in his honest and considered opinion, was the happiest man in all the world?

Solon thought long and hard. 'I think that the happiest man in the world must have been a man called Tellus who lived, once, in the land I come from. He had enough money to live on comfortably, but not so much that he had to worry about it. He had sons who loved and honoured him and admirable grandchildren, too. He gave his life in the defence of his country, and in return he was given a State burial with full civil and military honours. Who could be happier than he?'

Solon meant Croesus to learn a lesson from this, but Croesus was merely offended. To think that anyone who had less money than he should be thought to be any happier! 'Well, who would you say is the second happiest man you have ever known?' he snapped. At least Solon would not dare to suggest that anyone other than himself could qualify for the second prize? But Croesus was wrong. Solon had not finished yet.

'The second happiest man I have ever known would have been one of two brothers who lived, like Tellus, in Athens,' he replied. 'Like Tellus, they had enough to live on, but not too much, and they were also immensely strong. One day, their mother wanted to attend an important religious festival, but the oxen which should have pulled her carriage to the temple were still out in the fields. So, the young men harnessed themselves to the carriage and they pulled her there as successfully as the oxen would have done. The Athenian people were very impressed by this, and they had important statues made of the young men who had been so good to their mother.'

When Croesus heard that Solon thought that two common young men, who had been ready to act as beasts of burden, were happier than he was, he was furious. 'What about *me?*' he thundered. 'Why do you think that these ordinary people are happier than I am? Haven't my servants shown you how rich I am?'

Solon was not put out at all by that question. 'But you are still alive!' he replied. 'No one who is still alive can be called the happiest man in the world, or even the second happiest. Consider this – a man can reasonably expect to live about 70 years, if he is lucky. That means that he has more than 25,000 days to enjoy, or to endure. Not one of those days will be exactly like the day that went before it, or the day that is destined to follow. So, how can I possibly tell what the future holds for you? I will call you happy, possibly, when I know that you have gone down to the grave in peace.'

Solon was, indeed, a wise man, for shortly after that Croesus's kingdom was invaded, his capital city was besieged and captured, and the King, stripped of his riches, was put on a big pile of wood ready to be burned. Croesus was saved from a horrible death on this occasion by a sudden downpour of rain, but he could hardly have been called 'happy' even then. ◆

HERODOTUS

23

Parables Jesus **Told**

One of Charles Dickens' least known books is his The Life of Our Lord. *Indeed, considering his frequent attacks on sham piety and religious humbug, it comes as something of a surprise to discover that he wrote his own version of the Gospel story. However, he did not write it for publication but for his own children and it was not published until 1934 when the last of his sons died. This passage may serve as an example of (or introduction to) the work of a pre-eminent novelist or as a simple retelling of two of the parables told by Jesus and of an incident from his life. Discussion might follow as to what might be modern equivalents of the parables.*

One of the greatest English writers was Charles Dickens. His stories (such as *David Copperfield* and *Oliver Twist*) appeared as serials in popular magazines over a hundred years ago. Some people say they were the 'soaps' of the nineteenth century.

For his own children, he wrote a biography, a life story of Jesus. And this is part of Dickens' story of *The Life of Our Lord*.

◆

THERE WERE, IN that country where Our Saviour performed his miracles, certain people who were called Pharisees. They were very proud, and believed that no people were good but themselves; and they were all afraid of Jesus Christ, because he taught the people better.

Now the Pharisees received these lessons from Our Saviour scornfully; for they were rich, and covetous, and thought themselves superior to all mankind. As a warning to them, Christ related this parable of Dives and Lazarus.

☞

'There was a certain rich man who was clothed in purple and fine linen, and fared sumptuously every day. And there was a certain beggar, named Lazarus, who was laid at his gate, full of sores, and desiring to be fed with the crumbs which fell from the rich man's table. Moreover, the dogs came and licked his sores.

And it came to pass that the beggar died, and was carried by the angels into Abraham's bosom – Abraham had been a very good man who lived many years before that time, and was then in Heaven. The rich man also died and was buried. And in Hell, he lifted up his eyes, being in torments, and saw Abraham afar off, and Lazarus. And he cried and said, "Father Abraham have mercy on me, and send Lazarus that he may dip the tip of his finger in water and cool my tongue, for I am tormented in this flame." But Abraham said, "Son, remember that in thy lifetime thou receivedst good things, and likewise Lazarus evil things. But now, he is comforted, and though art tormented!"'

And among other parables, Christ said to these same Pharisees, because of their pride, that two men once went up into the Temple, to pray; of whom, one was a Pharisee, and one a publican. The Pharisee said, 'God I thank thee, that I am not unjust as other men are, or bad as this publican is!' The publican, standing afar off, would not lift up his eyes to Heaven, but struck his breast, and only said, 'God be merciful to me, a sinner!' And God – Our Saviour told them – would be merciful to that man rather than the other, and would be better pleased with his prayer, because he made it with a humble and a lowly heart.

The Pharisees were so angry at being taught these things that they employed some spies to ask Our Saviour questions, and try to entrap him into saying something which was against the law. The emperor of that country, who was called Cæsar, having commanded tribute-money to be regularly paid to him by the people, and being cruel against any one who disputed his right to it, these spies thought they might, perhaps, induce Our Saviour to say it was an unjust payment, and so to bring himself under the emperor's displeasure. Therefore, pretending to be very humble, they came to him and said, 'Master you teach the word of God rightly, and do not respect persons on account of their wealth or high station. Tell us, is it lawful that we should pay tribute to Cæsar?' Christ, who knew their thoughts, replied, 'Why do you ask? Show me a penny.' They did so. 'Whose image, and whose name, is this upon it?' he asked them. They said, 'Cæsar's.' 'Then,' said he, 'render unto Cæsar the things that are Cæsar's.' ◆

CHARLES DICKENS

24

Take up Thy Bed

The Jewish actor-writer David Kossoff has written a series of portraits of characters who appear in the Bible, including this one of the lame man at the Pool of Bethesda. The story is told in John 5: 1–15. Each portrait is narrated by a different character. Here, David Kossoff describes the incident through the eyes of the lame man's nephew.

The Bible stories about Jesus make it clear that Jesus worked as a healer as well as a teacher. This work of healing did not please everybody. For example, when Jesus healed a man on the Sabbath (the day of the week on which no work was supposed to be done), the man he helped was criticized by the religious leaders of the day. This re-telling of that story has been written as if it is being told by the nephew of the man who was healed.

◆

MY MOTHER'S ELDER brother was born sickly, and, by the time he was a young man, had almost entirely lost the use of his legs. He had no belief in doctors at all, having been in their hands since birth. In the family he was known as Uncle Bethesda, which was not his name but where he spent most of his life. At the pools of Bethesda, here in Jerusalem. For years and years he lay on a low bed near to the Fifth Arch, by the smaller pool. He lay with other incurables, believing, as they did, that the first one into the pool 'after the Angel had moved the water' would be cured. An ancient legend. The trouble was that no one knew when the Angel would come – and there were many sufferers both nearer to the water and more active. So, for year after year, he lay there on his back, resigned, cheerful ☞

– he had my mother's humour – and pleasant. He was among friends; it was a community.

Now, the happening. I was in synagogue one Sabbath. Passover time. The Pharisee Mother-Synagogue. Every part of the service perfect, as written, as laid down. To every side, the serious, stern, righteous faces. The service ended and we were filing out. Suddenly there was an excitement. One of the helpers at the pool came running. He was breathless, hardly able to speak. 'Quick!' he shouted, 'your uncle!' My first thought was that he was dead. I set off at once – it wasn't far – and some of the synagogue elders and my colleagues came too. It was good of them, but I would have preferred to be alone. Grief is a private thing.

As we drew near to the Sheep Gate we saw an amazing sight. Not what it was, *who* it was. As a sight it was ordinary. A man carrying a narrow bed on his head. Not unusual. A porter; a market carrier. Walking slowly, carefully. A man of about fifty-five, sixty.

It was my uncle. I stopped, my mouth open. I'd never seen him vertical. He saw me, and proceeded at the same pace, watching his feet walking, with a sort of wonder, smiling. He came to a standstill in front of me.

'A man did it,' he said to me, 'a young man. No more than thirty-five. Dressed poorly, with a Galilee accent. He stopped by me and we talked. He was friendly and had not heard the Angel legend. I was telling him how, when the water moved, I always missed it. How, in any case, I could never be first. "Do you really want me to walk again?" he said to me. "Then get up! Walk! Get up, pick up your bed, and walk!" And I did. I had no doubts. I got up – I was very wobbly – and then I picked up my bed and I walked. And here I am.'

I felt strange. My uncle, always lying on his back, was part of the order of my life. I felt I was present at a great occasion; beyond my understanding; to do with God, and miracles. My uncle, with his bed on his head, stood smiling at me. Then the most venerable and respected of the elders stepped forward.

'Is it not written,' he said, 'that on the Sabbath it is wrong for a man to carry a burden? Do you not know it is wrong for you to be carrying that bed?'

The other elders lined themselves up by the one who'd just spoken. A jury; a line of silent reproach. My uncle carefully lowered his bed to the ground and looked along the line. Then he looked at me and started to laugh. He put his hands on my shoulders and laughed and laughed, like my mother, till the tears ran down. He hugged me to him, he hung on me, helpless, shaking, the laughter pouring from him like a great delirious wind of joy. Soon, for I put up no resistance, I was helpless as he, as wet with tears, as incapable of speech. The wind of his joy swept away for ever the dustiness of my life.

I picked up his bed and we walked away, not daring to look back at the line of motionless, affronted faces. Once round the corner, he stopped, drew himself up and straightened his features in a parody of the disapproval we had just left. He peered down at me, held it for a moment and then collapsed in hysterics. And so we made our way home, to my mother's, for Sabbath lunch. Two men, carrying an old bed, screaming with laughter, wet-eyed with joy and freedom. ◆

DAVID KOSSOFF

25

The Talkative Turtle

This parable comes from the Buddhist tradition and might be more suitable for younger age groups. It is a warning to all chatterboxes...

Today's story is not about anyone here of course... it's just a warning to anyone else who might talk too much, who might always be so busy talking they never listen... It's a very old story and it was first told by Buddhists.

◆

ONCE UPON A time (as all good stories begin) in a distant part of India there lived a rajah. That is to say, a ruler who (though not a king) was a prince of great power and wealth. And, besides that, he was a serious chatterbox. He could talk for hours and, since he was the rajah of that area there was no-one who dare tell him to shut up. So he never knew how boring he was.

Now this was in the time of the Buddha, the founder of Buddhism, a wise and clever man who travelled around India teaching what he knew to be the truth. But not even the Buddha dared tell the rajah that his talkativeness was making him not only unpopular but ridiculous in the eyes of his courtiers, servants and (worse) all the people of that region.

But he was to be given the opportunity in a very strange way. In front of the rajah's palace was an ornamental lake in which there lived a turtle. And during the cool season each year, a pair of wild geese came to live on the lake. Over the years, the turtle and the geese had become great friends and used to spend hours each day chatting to each other (I said this all happened once upon a time).

In fact, the *turtle* spent hours each day chattering away while the geese just had to listen to this talkative turtle who so loved the sound of his own voice that he shut up only to make the occasional dive to the bottom of the lake.

One day, when he had been talking without stopping for three hours, he suddenly exclaimed how much he would like to be able to fly – like the geese. Now, despite the fact that the turtle could bore the geese rigid, they were prepared to humour him.

'Why don't you?' one of them asked.

'But how can I?'

'Oh, it's not that difficult,' said the other goose. 'You see that stick the gardeners have left over the there? Well, we'll each take an end of it in our beaks and you use your teeth to grip the middle – then we can take off and give you a trip through the air.'

'And all you have to do is remember to keep your mouth shut,' added the first goose.

'Oh, I can do that,' said the turtle. 'Yes, I'd like to do that.'

So the geese got the stick, and carefully manoeuvred themselves until they had each got a firm grip of the two ends. Then they waddled over to where the turtle was so he could bite on the middle. When they were all ready, the geese took off and up they flew, high over the palace - with the turtle hanging from the middle of the stick.

As luck would have it, they flew over a place, just outside the palace gates, where some children were playing. One of the boys looked up and saw the flying turtle.

'Hey!' he said to the others. 'Look at that.'

They all looked up. After watching for a moment, one of the girls shouted out, 'That turtle looks really stupid.'

And of course the turtle couldn't resist answering back.

It landed on the palace courtyard with a horrible crash that shattered its shell to pieces. The rajah and the Buddha were among the first to reach the spot. It was, of course, quite dead.

'How tragic,' said the Buddha. 'If we only knew when to keep our mouths shut.'

The rajah looked at him. 'And what do you mean by that?'

'I was not referring to anyone in particular, your highness. I was speaking about anybody who is inclined to talk too much. Such people never listen to others and miss hearing all sorts of good things. And, like the turtle, they run the risk of landing themselves in trouble.'

The rajah was silent. But from that day onwards he was very less talkative — and he soon became very much more popular with his people. ◆

26

The Baal Shem-Tov

This eighteenth-century story is a translation from the Yiddish. The Baal Shem-Tov was the founder of the Jewish Hasidic movement which emphasized communal prayer, song and dance. It teaches the importance for our well-being of knowing that we have been forgiven for any wrong-doing.

This story is over 200 years old and comes from eastern Europe. It is about the Baal Shem-Tov who was the leader of a group of Russian Jews, and it's also about one of his followers, Reb Shmuel. The story is about a time when many Jews were being made to give up their religion and were forced to turn Christian against their will.

A pogrom is an organized and violent attack on a whole people, such as the Jews.

◆

FEELING HIMSELF ON the brink of death, the Baal Shem-Tov, the Master of the Good Name, decided to leave the few riches that he had to his disciples. To one he gave his prayer shawl; to another his silver snuff-box ...

His most faithful servant, Reb Shmuel, waited for his turn to come, but when the Master had given all his goods away, there was nothing left. Then the Baal Shem-Tov turned towards him with a smile: 'To you, I give my stories. You will travel the world over so that people may hear them.'

Surprised, Reb Shmuel thanked the Master, in whom he trusted completely, without fully understanding just what it was he had been left.

The Master died ...

Reb Shmuel found himself alone. He said to himself, 'What kind of inheritance have I received? Stories that nobody wants to hear?'

He remained alone, poorer than ever. One day a rumour began that there was a man, far away, who was prepared to pay large sums of money to hear stories about the Baal Shem-Tov. Reb Shmuel found out more about it and let it be known he was the man for the job. He was sent an invitation and, after a long journey, he arrived one Friday morning in a big city in Russia. He was welcomed by his host – no less than the president of the community.

That same evening, the president gathered all his friends together to join in a grand Sabbath meal prepared in honour of their special guest. As the meal was drawing to a close, the president stood up and said: 'We have the honour to have in our midst the secretary and disciple of the Baal Shem-Tov, who has come amongst us especially in order to tell us stories of his Master. Reb Shmuel, please tell us more.'

Reb Shmuel stood up, deeply moved to be able to speak about his beloved Master at last. He looked over his audience warmly and wanted to start telling them some of his stories. He opened his mouth to speak and, horrors! Nothing! His mind had gone blank! He could not remember a single story, not even the tiniest memory ...

The president, seeing him upset, said: 'Reb Shmuel must be worn out after his long journey. After a good night's sleep he will be himself again, and he will be able to remember some excellent stories to tell us.'

The next day, in the middle of the second meal of the Sabbath, Reb Shmuel stood up to speak, and, once again, nothing ... Embarrassed and upset, he sat down again. The president, once ☞

more, was kind and understanding, and promised the assembly that all would go well during the third meal.

But during the third meal the same thing happened, and the next morning Reb Shmuel, bitterly ashamed, found himself setting out on his journey home. His host was cold and distant towards him, and few were the people who came out to wish 'good journey' to the man whom the whole town had named 'the man with no stories' …

The horses had already set off at a brisk pace when Reb Shmuel stood up on the sledge and shouted: 'Stop, stop! I've got a story!'

The horses were reined in and, standing up where he was, Reb Shmuel said to the president, who was looking at him with a spark of hope and interest: 'It's just a small anecdote, I'm not sure if it would interest you … ' The president encouraged him with a slight nod of his head.

'It was a winter's night. The Baal Shem-Tov woke me: "Reb Shmuel, harness the horses, we're going out." We travelled through the icy snow, across deep forests until, after several hours, we arrived at a large, very beautiful house. The Master went in and, after only half an hour, he came out. "We're going home!" he said.'

As the story ended, the president started sobbing convulsively. Reb Shmuel looked at him in amazement.

Through his tears, the president could see the astonished faces of the men around him: 'Let me explain. The person that the Baal Shem-Tov was visiting that night was me! At that time, I had a very important position in the hierarchy of the Christian church. My job was to organize forced conversions, events which always occurred with violence and persecution of the ☞

Jews. When the Baal Shem-Tov burst into my home on that memorable night, I was preparing one of the cruellest decrees of my whole career ... He had hardly crossed the threshold when he began saying in a voice that grew louder and louder and more and more passionate: "How long will this go on? How long will you torture your own brothers? Didn't you know that you yourself were a Jewish child, rescued from a pogrom, taken in by a Polish family who kept your origins a secret? The time has come to return to your brothers and your tradition!" I was overwhelmed, and immediately decided to leave everything and start my life again from scratch. I asked the Master: "But will there come a day when I shall be forgiven for my crimes?"

The Baal Shem-Tov replied: "The day that somebody tells you this story, that is the day when you know you have been forgiven ... " ' ◆

MARC-ALAIN OUAKNIN AND DORY ROTNEMER

translated by Sarah Matthews

27

Bubblefoot

This is an abridgement of a short story by the children's author, Leon Garfield. It was originally published in a book issued to commemorate 25 years of the Samaritans – and especially their work with young people.

This story is set some time in the past. Or it may be the future – or it may be now. It's about young Bubblefoot who has a deformed foot and is on the edge of starving. He makes a living in the London streets guiding rich drunks back to their homes. Until one night he meets someone different and whose home is different.

◆

Shadows cluster, as if frightened of the dark; monsters lurk but dare not show themselves. It is a weird, hot-and-cold night, stinging with pins and needles and full of torn curtains that brush the eyes. Bubblefoot is weary unto death, and would like to go to sleep ... for a long, long time.

He sits himself down and considers the gruesome world that lies between sleeping and sleeping ... then he gets up again, with a sniff and a wipe of his snout.

'Bubblefoot 'ere, sir. 'Ere's Bubblefoot.'

Just his luck. A last gent has come floating out of somewhere on wings of wine. A very torn and bleeding gent, who looks like he's had more than words with some landlord before being booted out. A lean and whiskery gent, whose eyes keep rolling round and round, as if they're a bad fit.

'A fightin' gent,' thinks Bubblefoot gloomily. 'Them's worse'n the screamin' ones, worse'n the cryin' ones, worse'n ☞

96

the sick 'uns … because you never gets paid.' But duty must be done.

'Jes' tell us where yer lives, sir, an' Bubblefoot'll see yer 'ome.'

No good. Bubblefoot's never had such an awkward, boozy, battered gent in all his born nights. Look at him now! Lifting up a finger as if to see which way the wind's blowing! He's off.

'Follow me … '

First he goes along a thin old street, bending forward as if it's uphill when it's down; and then he starts staggering as if he's carrying something heavy enough to break his back. 'Watch out, mister!' calls Bubblefoot, hopping after. 'That's where them 'orrible creechers come crawlin' out o' the wall!'

'What creatures?' He leans against a doorway to rest.

Bubblefoot limps up to tell him (as if he didn't know!). He tells him of the snakes and spiders, the great pink rats and all the other terrible phantoms that inhabit the vineyards of the night. He tells him of households falling, falling in streamers of blood and tears; of bricks that weep and hearts built so strong and high that they shut out the light. Proudly he tells him everything he knows about; for it's not often that Bubblefoot has a chance to talk.

'And where are they now?' asks the gent abruptly, as if coming out of a deep reverie. He pushes himself upright and glares ferociously, with wine-bright eyes.

' 'E's goin' to fight,' thinks Bubblefoot wearily. ' 'E's goin' to bash in a winder or sumfink. Them fightin' gents is always the worst!'

'I'll smash them!' shouts the ragged one, making fists as wild as fireflies. 'I'll crash them! I'll blow them all to Kingdom come!'

Then, to Bubblefoot's further discomfiture, he launches himself into the middle of the street and begins a war-dance of fists, boots, elbows and knees.

'I'll smash them! I'll crash them! Like that! Like that! And another one! Begone! Begone, you foul things?'

Now down the street he capers, whirling round corners, swinging on posts. Sometimes, with arms outstretched, like a great tattered bird, he swoops, bending from side to side; hunting ... chasing ... pouncing! Then up the sides of the houses where the green spiders crawl ...

'Begone! Begone, I say!'

'Oh mister,' thinks Bubblefoot, hopping and limping in and out of the way. 'Yer've 'ad a skinful tonight, all right!'

Suddenly he stops his antics. He turns about and presents to Bubblefoot the most enormous smile.

('A joker!' thinks Bubblefoot. 'Worse, even, than them fightin' gents!')

'We've won!' says the joker. 'Now for a victory dance!'

'But us is poorly mister. Dreadful poorly ... '

'Dance! Dance!'

'But us 'as a disability, mister. Us 'as a rotten foot!'

'Dance! Dance!'

Then before Bubblefoot can hop away, he finds himself caught and whirled up and around. ('Them dancin' gents is worst of all!')

Round and round, down streets and alleys, through courts and across solemn squares; windows come out on stalks and the houses turn over and stand on their chimneys – which are toes. ☞

Stars and cobbles ... lamps and eyes ... and a roaring in Bubblefoot's ears as breath of wine beats round him like a billowing sea. No time to limp; nothing to limp on ... Bubblefoot prances on air.

'Oh mister!' he wails breathlessly. 'Tell us where's yer 'ome?'

'Oh I'll tell you – I'll tell you – ' cries out the dancing gent, into Bubblefoot's passing ear. 'I'll tell you – ' and he tells him jokes and stories ... sings him snatches of song ... and he's away laughing ... laughing fit to burst.

'Oh mister, mister!'

'It's something catching, Bubblefoot! Catch it – catch it while you can!'

It's the laughter that's catching and, try as he might to stop himself, Bubblefoot begins to laugh. He laughs and coughs and laughs and sneezes, and once he laughs bright blood. The dance stops. The houses put up their chimneys and smooth down their doors and bricks. The cobbles go back into the street and the stars return to the sky. Bubblefoot leans panting against a wall; and the dancer says:

'It's time to go home, now.'

'Where, mister? Where is it?'

There's a door, tall enough for a horse to go through without nodding. 'Here,' says the ragged one; and pushes it open. 'Will you come in?'

Bubblefoot ponders. Such a thing has never happened to him before. 'Nar,' he says at length. 'Yore pa would 'ave us out sooner'n spit!'

'We'll be quiet. Quiet as mice.'

'Nar!' says Bubblefoot. 'Yore ma'd smell us a mile off!' ☞

The ragged one chuckles and takes Bubblefoot by the hand. 'It's my house, you know.'

All is dim within. Huge pale walls vanish up, up into a gloom. Many carved seats, some with grinning faces. And far off, a great table, set with golden candlesticks and a white cloth. It is more splendid, even, than the Nag's Head.

'Sit here, Bubblefoot. Rest.'

'Where are yer goin', mister?'

'To look for my pa.'

'Let me come wiv' yer, mister?'

The ragged one pauses ... and shakes his head. 'Wait for me here.'

'Will yer be long gone?'

'I'll be back ... I'll be back ... '

He goes, soft as a dream, and Bubblefoot is left alone. Slowly his eyes close ... and he sleeps. ◆

LEON GARFIELD

28

Three Parables

These three short parables from the Sufi tradition may be used together or separately. Sufism is a sect of Islam. Sufis seek to come close to God through self-denial, prayer and other exercises including (occasionally) fire-walking and frenzied dancing (e.g. the 'whirling Dervishes'). Sufism has at times been at odds with orthodox Islam but many Sufis have been respected storytellers.

The first parable is as much about how we learn as being an attack on the absurdity of most horoscopes; the second may be seen as a reminder to delight in simple things and the third a cryptic reminder that many of us are only half awake to reality.

This very short story was (*or* these very short stories were) first told by a man called Idries Shah who was born in the year 1924 and who was a descendant of the Prophet Muhammad. He told these stories in order to teach certain things. As you listen, try to work out what is the lesson or moral of the story.

◆

Astrology

A certain respected thinker and teacher had written a book on astrology. Some people said that he must be a magician or insane; others believed that this action had shown that there was truth in astrology.

Ultimately a dervish who had travelled many miles to see the sage asked him about the problem, saying, 'Surely astrological work is inconsistent with the Path of the Wise, and the Work of the Elect?'

The sage answered: 'I make absolutely sure that all my pupils study my book on astrology. In this way they are able to un- ☞

derstand that astrology does not work. When they are completely skilled in the art, I make them interpret horoscopes. These we compare, and we always find such discrepancies in interpretation, when properly tested, that it becomes self-evident that the system is useful only for imaginings.'

The visitor said: 'Could you not simply tell them that astrology is not a true science, as others do?'

'Firstly,' said the sage, 'if the telling had been effective when done by others, who would still believe in astrology? When did telling equal understanding? Secondly, when you have thoroughly investigated one superstition, you are unlikely to be able to sustain, or adopt, another.'

'So it is not astrology in particular which you seek to dispose of?'

'No. Astrology is one of the easiest absurdities to study, because its practitioners have allowed themselves to be pinned down to rules.'

The Legend of the Three Men
Once upon a time there were three men, who went on a journey together.

They came upon a small coin by the roadside. As they had no other money, each started to argue with the others as to what they should buy with it.

The first man said, 'I want something sweet to eat!'

'No,' said the second, 'I want several sweet things to eat.'

'No!' said the third. 'I want something to quench my thirst.'

A wise man passing by stopped and they asked him to adjudicate between them. 'Choose,' they said, 'which of us should have his desire.'

'I will do better than that,' said the sage, 'for I can undertake ☞

to satisfy you all.' He went to a near-by shop and with the money bought a bunch of grapes, which he divided between them.

'But this is something sweet to eat,' said the first.

'But this is several sweet things to eat,' said the second man.

'But this is something with which to quench my thirst,' said the third man.

Feeling

Uwais was asked: 'How do you feel?'

He said: 'Like one who has risen in the morning and does not know whether he will be dead in the evening.'

The other man said: 'But this is the situation of all men.'

Uwais said: 'Yes. But how many of them *feel* it?' ◆

IDRIES SHAH

29

The Blessing of El-ahrairah

This passage is taken from the modern classic, Watership Down, *in which Richard Adams creates a saga about a band of rabbits escaping from disaster to seek a new life and a new world – a theme present in much Christian literature. This excerpt is a sort of parenthesis within the main narrative: one of the rabbits (called Dandelion) tells the others a creation story.*

This passage comes from a book some of you may know: *Watership Down*, which is about a journey made by a group of highly intelligent rabbits seeking a new home when their habitat is about to be destroyed. At one point in the story, one of the rabbits tells the others a story about Frith who is the god of the rabbits and El-ahrairah, a prince among rabbits. As you listen, you might try to decide whether it really is a story about rabbits – or one about people.

◆

'LONG AGO, FRITH made the world. He made all the stars too and the world is one of the stars. He made them by scattering his droppings over the sky and this is why the grass and the trees grow so thick on the world. Frith makes the brooks flow. They follow him as he goes through the sky and when he leaves the sky they look for him all night. Frith made all the animals and birds, but when he first made them they were all the same. The sparrow and the kestrel were friends and they both ate seeds and flies. And the fox and the rabbit were friends and they both ate grass. And there was plenty of grass and plenty of flies, because the world was new and Frith shone down bright and warm all day.

'Now El-ahrairah was among the animals in those days and he

had many wives. He had so many wives that there was no counting them and the wives had so many young that even Frith could not count them and they ate the grass and the dandelions and the lettuces and the clover and El-ahrairah was the father of them all.' (Bigwig growled appreciatively.) 'And after a time,' went on Dandelion, 'after a time the grass began to grow thin and the rabbits wandered everywhere, multiplying and eating as they went.

'Then Frith said to El-ahrairah, "Prince Rabbit, if you cannot control your people, I shall find ways to control them. So mark what I say." But El-ahrairah would not listen and he said to Frith, "My people are the strongest in the world, for they breed faster and eat more than any of the other people. And this shows how much they love Lord Frith, for of all the animals they are the most responsive to his warmth and brightness. You must realise, my lord, how important they are and not hinder them in their beautiful lives."

'Frith could have killed El-ahrairah at once, but he had a mind to keep him in the world, because he needed him to sport and jest and play tricks. So he determined to get the better of him not by means of his own great power but by means of a trick. He gave out that he would hold a great meeting and that at that meeting he would give a present to every animal and bird, to make each one different from the rest. And all the creatures set out to go to the meeting place. But they all arrived at different times, because Frith made sure that it would happen so. And when the blackbird came, he gave him his beautiful song, and when the cow came, he gave her sharp horns and the strength to be afraid of no other creature. And so in their turn came the fox and the stoat and the weasel. And to each of them Frith gave the cunning and the fierceness and the desire to hunt and slay and eat the children of El-ahrairah. And so they went away from Frith full of nothing but hunger to kill the rabbits.

'Now all this time, El-ahrairah was dancing and mating and boasting that he was going to Frith's meeting to receive a great gift. And at last he set out for the meeting-place. But as he was going there, he stopped to rest on a soft, sandy hillside. And while he was resting, over the hill came flying the dark Swift, screaming as he went, "News! News! News!" For you know, this is what he has said ever since that day. So El-ahrairah called up to him and said, "What news?" "Why," said the Swift, "I would not be you, El-ahrairah. For Frith has given the fox and the weasel cunning hearts and sharp teeth and to the cat he has given silent feet and eyes that can see in the dark and they are gone away from Frith's place to kill and devour all that belongs to El-ahrairah." And he dashed on over the hills. And at that moment El-ahrairah heard the voice of Frith calling, "Where is El-ahrairah? For all the others have taken their gifts and gone and I have come to look for him."

'Then El-ahrairah knew that Frith was too clever for him and he was frightened. He thought that the fox and the weasel were coming with Frith and he turned to the face of the hill and began to dig. He dug a hole, but he had dug only a little of it when Frith came over the hill alone. And he saw El-ahrairah's bottom sticking out of the hole and the sand flying out in showers as the digging went on. When he saw that, he called out, "My friend, have you seen El-ahrairah, for I am looking for him to give him my gift?" "No," answered El-ahrairah, without coming out, "I have not seen him. He is far away. He could not come." So Frith said, "Then come out of that hole and I will bless you instead of him." "No, I cannot," said El-ahrairah, "I am busy. The fox and the weasel are coming. If you want to bless me you can bless my bottom, for it is sticking out of the hole." '

All the rabbits had heard the story before: on winter nights, ☛

106

when the cold draught moved down the warren passages and the icy wet lay in the pits of the runs below their burrows; and on summer evenings, in the grass under the red may and the sweet, carrion-scented elder bloom. Dandelion was telling it well and even Pipkin forgot his weariness and danger, and remembered instead the great indestructibility of the Rabbits. Each one of them saw himself as El-ahrairah, who could be impudent to Frith and get away with it.

'Then,' said Dandelion, 'Frith felt himself in friendship with El-ahrairah, because of his resourcefulness, and because he would not give up even when he thought the fox and the weasel were coming. And he said, "Very well, I will bless your bottom as it sticks out of the hole. Bottom, be strength and warning and speed for ever and save the life of your master. Be it so!" And as he spoke, El-ahrairah's tail grew shining white and flashed like a star: and his back legs grew long and powerful and he thumped the hillside until the very beetles fell off the grass-stems. He came out of the hole and tore across the hill faster than any creature in the world. And Frith called after him, "El-ahrairah, your people cannot rule the world, for I will not have it so. All the world will be your enemy, Prince with a Thousand Enemies, and whenever they catch you, they will kill you. But first they must catch you, digger, listener, runner, prince with the swift warning. Be cunning and full of tricks and your people shall never be destroyed." And El-ahrairah knew then that although he would not be mocked, yet Frith was his friend. And every evening, when Frith has done his day's work and lies calm and easy in the red sky, El-ahrairah and his children and his children's children come out of their holes and feed and play in his sight, for they are his friends and he has promised them that they can never be destroyed.' ◆

RICHARD ADAMS

30

The Peaceable Mongoose

This fable illustrates the problems society throws at those who are different or who want to be different.

This is a story with a moral. It's about a mongoose – and mongooses are small furry animals, common in India, which are very good at killing snakes such as cobras. When you've heard the story, you must decide whether the moral is true – and whether that always has to be the case.

◆

IN COBRA COUNTRY a mongoose was born one day who didn't want to fight cobras or anything else. The word spread from mongoose to mongoose that there was a mongoose who didn't want to fight cobras. If he didn't want to fight anything else, it was his own business, but it was the duty of every mongoose to kill cobras or be killed by cobras.

'Why?' asked the peacelike mongoose, and the word went around that the strange new mongoose was not only pro-cobra and anti-mongoose but intellectually curious and against the ideals and traditions of mongoosism.

'He is crazy,' cried the young mongoose's father.

'He is sick,' said his mother.

'He is a coward,' shouted his brothers.

'He is a mongoosexual,' whispered his sisters.

Strangers who had never laid eyes on the peacelike mongoose remembered that they had seen him crawling on his stomach, ☛

or trying on cobra hoods, or plotting the violent overthrow of Mongoosia.

'I am trying to use reason and intelligence,' said the strange new mongoose.

'Reason is six-sevenths of treason,' said one of his neighbours.

'Intelligence is what the enemy uses,' said another.

Finally, the rumour spread that the mongoose had venom in his sting, like a cobra, and he was tried, convicted by a show of paws, and condemned to banishment.

MORAL: *Ashes to ashes, and clay to clay, if the enemy doesn't get you your own folks may.* ◆

JAMES THURBER

31

The Man Who Planted Trees

This is an abridgement of a modern environmental classic first published in (somewhat surprisingly) Vogue magazine. It is a story which reminds us of the need to care for and to restore our environment, God's creation.

This story is told by a Frenchman who, when he was a young man, used to go on walking holidays in the mountains of Provence in southern France. At that time, almost no one lived there – and nothing grew there: just grass and a few wild flowers.

◆

AFTER THREE DAYS' walking I camped near a ruined and deserted village. I'd run out of water the day before, and had to find some. These clustered houses, although in ruins, suggested that there must once have been a fresh water spring or well here. There had indeed been a spring, but it had dried up long ago.

After five hours' walking I'd still not found water and there was nothing to give me any hope of finding any. All about me was the same dryness, the same coarse grasses. Then I thought I glimpsed in the distance a small black silhouette, and I took it to be the trunk of a solitary tree. I started toward it. It was a shepherd.

He gave me a drink (from his water-gourd) and, a little later, took me to his cottage. He drew his water – excellent water – from a very deep natural well above which he had constructed a primitive winch with a bucket and chain.

It was understood from the first that I should spend the night ☞

there; the nearest village was still more than a day and a half's walk away.

That evening, he went to fetch a small sack and poured out a heap of acorns on the table. He began to inspect them, one by one, with great concentration, separating the good from the bad. I offered to help. He told me that it was his job. When he'd set aside a large enough pile of good acorns he counted them out by tens. When he had thus selected 100 perfect acorns he stopped and we went to bed.

The next day I asked if I might rest here for a day. He nodded but said nothing. Taking a long iron rod with him, he went outside, opened the pen and led his sheep up onto the mountainside.

As I wanted to know more about him, I decided to follow. When he reached some grass where the sheep could graze, he left the dog in charge of the little flock and invited me to go along with him. He climbed to the top of the ridge, about 100 metres away.

There he began thrusting his iron rod into the earth making a hole in which he planted an acorn; then he refilled the hole. He was planting oak trees. I asked him if the land belonged to him. He answered no. Did he know whose it was? He didn't.

After the midday meal he resumed his planting. I suppose I must have been fairly insistent in my questioning, for he answered me. For three years he had been planting trees in this wilderness. He'd planted 100,000. Of these, 20,000 had sprouted. Of the 20,000 he still expected to lose about half. There remained 10,000 oak trees to grow where nothing had grown before. That was when I began to wonder about the age of this man. He was obviously over fifty. Fifty-five, he told me. His name was Elzéard Bouffier. ☛

I told him that in 30 years his 10,000 oaks would be magnificent. He answered quite simply that if God granted him life, in 30 years he would have planted so many more that these 10,000 would be no more than a drop of water in the ocean.

Besides all this, he was now studying the reproduction of beech trees and had a nursery of seedlings grown from beechnuts near his cottage. He was also considering birches for the valleys where, he told me, there was a certain amount of moisture a few yards below the surface of the soil.

It was not until five years later that I was able to visit that part of the country again. As I approached the deserted village I glimpsed in the distance a sort of greyish mist that covered the mountain-tops like a carpet. Since the day before, I'd begun to think again of the shepherd tree-planter. 'Ten thousand oaks.' I reflected, 'really take up quite a bit of space.'

Elzéard Bouffier was still there – but he'd changed jobs. Now he had only four sheep but, instead, 100 beehives. He'd got rid of the sheep because they threatened to nibble his young trees.

The oaks were now ten years old and taller than either of us. I was literally speechless and, as he did not talk, we spent the whole day walking in silence through his forest. It measured eleven kilometres in length and three kilometres at its greatest width. When you remembered that all this had sprung from the hands and the soul of this one man, without any technical help, you understood that men could be as effectual as God in the business of creation.

He'd got on with his second plan, and young beech trees as high as my shoulder were spreading out as far as the eye could reach. He also showed me handsome clumps of birch planted five years before. He'd set these out in all the valleys where he'd guessed, rightly, that there was moisture just below the ☛

surface of the ground. What's more, the young trees had caused a chain reaction in nature. Now water was flowing in brooks that had been dry since the memory of man.

Some years later, when I again revisited the area, he told me how he'd received a visit from a forest ranger who notified him of an order against lighting fires out of doors for fear of endangering the growth of this *natural* forest. It was the first time, the man told Bouffier, that he'd ever heard of a forest growing all of its own accord!

Two years after that, a whole group of people from the Government came to examine the 'natural forest'. There was a high official from the Forestry Department, a deputy and other officials.

One of these officials was a friend of mine, and later I explained the mystery to him. One day the following week we went together to see Elzéard Bouffier. We found him hard at work, some ten kilometres from the spot where the inspection had taken place.

This forester was not my friend for nothing. He knew how to keep silent. Before leaving, my friend simply made a brief suggestion about certain species of trees that the soil here seemed particularly suited for. He didn't force the point. 'For the very good reason,' he told me later, 'that Bouffier knows more about it than I do.' At the end of an hour's walking – having turned it over in his mind – he added, 'He knows a lot more about it than anybody. He's discovered a wonderful way to be happy!'

It was thanks to this officer that not only the forest but also the happiness of the man was protected. My friend appointed three rangers to the task of protecting the forest against people who might chop down the trees to sell as firewood.

I saw Elzéard Bouffier for the last time when he was 87. Now, there was a bus running along the valley. I no longer recognized the route of my earlier journeys and it seemed to me, too, that the bus took me through new countryside. It took the name of a village to convince me that I was actually in that region that had been all ruins and desolation.

What was once a deserted village was now alive! The ruins had been cleared away, broken walls torn down and five houses rebuilt. The village had 28 inhabitants, four of them young married couples. The new houses were surrounded by gardens where vegetables and flowers grew in orderly confusion. It was now a village where you'd like to live.

From that point on, I went on foot. On the lower slopes of the mountain I saw fields of barley and corn; deep in the valleys the meadows were turning green. Little by little the other villages were being rebuilt. People from the plains, where land is costly, had settled here, and brought the farms back to life.

When I reflect that just one man was able to cause this land to spring from the wasteland, I am convinced that in spite of wars and everything, human beings *are* admirable. But especially I am taken with an immense respect for that old and unlearned peasant who was able to complete a work worthy of God: Elzéard Bouffier, the man who planted trees. ◆

JEAN GIONO

32

The Mystery *of the* Marie-Celeste

This is the perfectly true story of a sailing ship found abandoned but with sails perfectly set between the Azores and Portugal. The ship's one boat, sextant, chronometer and crew were missing. No trace of them was ever found: there was no sign of turmoil on board. This reading is provided as a challenge the pupils' imagination and as a reminder that there are mysteries without solution in this world.

Here's a perfectly true story. What do you think was the explanation? Or do we simply have to say it is a mystery for which there is no answer?

◆

ABOUT 3.00 PM on 5 December 1872, the captain and crew of the *Dei Gratia* were over half way across the Atlantic Ocean on a journey from New York to Gibraltar when they sighted a smaller ship ahead of them. She also appeared to be heading east, and as they gradually overhauled her they realized that something was seriously wrong. The strange vessel was changing direction with the wind and seemed to be out of control. The crew of the *Dei Gratia* hoisted a signal but there was no reply. Coming closer to the mystery ship, Captain D R Moorhouse hailed her through a megaphone but there was no answer from the silent, deserted decks.

A boat was lowered and the captain, the second mate and two seamen pulled across to the smaller vessel. Now they could read on her stern – *Marie-Celeste* New York. Tying their boat alongside, the captain and the mate clambered aboard, determined to solve the mystery. Perhaps there had been a mutiny. Perhaps the crew had caught some terrible disease and were all

☛

115

dead or dying. They wondered what dreadful scene would greet their eyes as they made their way below.

To their amazement they found nothing. No sign of disorder, no damage, no blood, no bodies, nothing which would indicate what disaster had befallen the crew. The ship was deserted yet it was in perfect condition! In the seamen's quarters washing was hanging on a line to dry. Some razors were found, clean and free from rust. In the galleys were the cold ashes of a fire, and some cooking pots in which breakfast had obviously been prepared.

The two men made their way to the captain's cabin. There were later tales that there the table was laid for breakfast which was half eaten. There was one plate half full of porridge, and an egg had its top sliced off ready to eat. A bottle of cough medicine stood on the table with its cork beside it. In the mate's cabin there was a piece of paper with an unfinished sum on it.

Search as they would, the captain and mate of the *Dei Gratia* could find no trace of the crew. The ship's log contained no hint of tragedy. The last entry was for 24 November, eleven days earlier. The ship was recorded as being some 650 kilometres to the west of her present position. During this time the wind had been blowing constantly from the north, yet the *Marie-Celeste* had travelled almost due east.

Today, 100 years later, the mystery of the *Marie-Celeste* is still unsolved. ◆

SCHOOLS COUNCIL

33

Learn the Lesson

These two disconnected anecdotes may be used, separately, to start short discussions: 'What lesson, or moral, can we learn from this story?' It may be necessary to explain 'posthumous' and 'lethal' before using the second anecdote.

First story
This is a very short story with a simple message or moral. As you listen, decide what that moral is.

Second story
This is another story with a moral. There are two words in it you may not know. 'Posthumous' means 'happening after someone's death' – so a posthumous report about someone is written after they are dead. And the other word is 'lethal' which means deadly. So what's the moral of this story?

◆

THE CAPTAIN ON the bridge of a large naval ship saw a light ahead, set for collision with his vessel. He signalled to it: 'Alter your course ten degrees south.' The reply came back: 'Alter *your* course ten degrees north.'

The Captain then signalled: 'Alter your course ten degrees south. I am a Captain.' The reply came back: 'Alter your course ten degrees north. I am a Seaman third-class.'

The Captain, furious by now, signalled back: 'Alter your course ten degrees south. I am a battleship!' The reply: 'Alter your course ten degrees north. I am a lighthouse.'

☞

There were three zoology students, and each was sent to a different part of the world to find out about spiders.

The first was sent to Africa. After a few weeks a report arrived for his professors, saying that he'd discovered some spiders that climbed trees.

The second student was sent to South America. After a few months a posthumous report arrived saying that he'd discovered a lethal species of spider.

The third was sent to Australia. They heard not a word from him for a whole year, but then he came back in person, bringing with him a carton full of the particular species of spider that he'd been studying.

Very excitedly, he rang up his professors and got them all to meet him one morning. When they were all sitting round the table, the student put one of the spiders in the middle of it.

He looked hard at it and said, 'Walk!', and it obediently walked around the table and came back to the middle. The student said to it again, 'Walk!' and again the spider walked round the table and came back to the middle.

Then the student caught up the spider, and his professors watched aghast as he picked off its eight legs, one by one. Then he put it down again in the middle of the table.

He looked at it hard. 'Walk!' he said. Nothing happened.

'Walk!' he said again, more loudly. Still nothing happened.

'There!' he exclaimed. 'That proves my theory! Spiders without legs are deaf!' ◆

STEPHEN GAUKROGER AND NICK MERCER

34

The **Bricklayer**

This story is best known from the humorist Gerard Hoffnung's recording of it. It is offered here first for its sheer entertainment value and secondly as a parable teaching the need to plan ahead.

It is a passage well worth rehearsing. As Hoffnung proved, timing is everything.

How many times have you been told to plan before you start some project or other piece of work? Because, whatever the job, if you don't think ahead, you'll get into trouble. As this building worker did.

◆

Dear Sir,

By the time I arrived at the house where you sent me to make repairs, the storm had torn a good fifty bricks from the roof. So I set up on the roof of the building a beam and a pulley and I hoisted up a couple of baskets of bricks. When I had finished repairing the building there were a lot of bricks left over since I had brought up more than I needed and also because there were some bad, reject bricks that I still had left to bring down. I hoisted the basket back up again and hitched up the line at the bottom. Then I climbed back up again and filled up the basket with the extra bricks. Then I went down to the bottom and untied the line. Unfortunately, the basket of bricks was much heavier than I was and before I knew what was happening, the basket started to plunge down, lifting me suddenly off the ground. I decided to keep my grip and hang on, realizing that to let go would end in disaster – but halfway up I ran into the basket coming down and received a severe blow on the

☞

shoulder. I then continued to the top, banging my head against the beam and getting my fingers jammed in the pulley. When the basket hit the ground it burst its bottom, allowing all the bricks to spill out. Since I was now heavier than the basket I started back down again at high speed. Halfway down, I met the basket coming up, and received several severe injuries on my shins. When I hit the ground, I landed on the bricks, getting several more painful cuts and bruises from the sharp edges.

At this moment I must have lost my presence of mind, because I let go of the line. The basket came down again, giving me another heavy blow on the head, and putting me in the hospital. I respectfully request sick leave. ◆

JEAN L'ANSELME

translated by Michael Benedikt

35

Nothing to be **Done?**

*This is a story which celebrates creative thought: if only we learn to think
constructively and imaginatively we can achieve more than we imagine.
It is also a reminder that youthful inventiveness deserves respect as much
as experience.*

Being young doesn't mean you're not intelligent. If you only
use your mind and your brain, you can often think of ways out
of problems that older people don't see. This is a true story
from Denmark.

◆

Copenhagen, 13 November 1953.

IN THE FIRE brigade's call centre the telephone rings. It is 3
a.m. Erik, the young fireman on night duty, takes up the receiver. He is 22. 'Fire brigade here ...'

No reply. But he hears heavy breathing. And then an agitated
woman's voice: 'Help, help! I can't get up. I'm in a pool of
blood.'

'Keep calm, we're coming straight away. Where are you?'

'I don't know.'

'Are you at home?'

'Yes. I think so at least.'

'Where is it, what street?'

'I don't know. I'm dizzy. I'm losing blood.'

'Well tell me your name.'

'I can't remember anything. I must have banged my head.'

☞

'Stay by the phone please.' Erik goes to a second phone and dials the exchange. A man's voice replies.

'Can you, please,' says Erik, 'give me the number of the person calling the fire brigade just now?'

'No I can't. I'm the night watchman and don't know anything about technical things. And today being Saturday the right people are not around.'

Erik hangs up. Then an idea strikes him. He asks the woman: 'How did you manage to find the fire brigade number?'

'It's written on the phone. I must have taken it with me as I fell.'

'Have a look to see whether your number isn't on it.'

'No there's nothing else on it. But please come quickly.' The voice is getting weaker.

'Tell me, what can you see from where you are?'

'I can see … I can see windows and the street lamps outside.'

Aha, thinks Erik, she lives on the street side and can't be higher up than the 3rd floor if she can see the lamps.

'What sort of window is it?' he inquires again. 'Is it square?'

'No it's a long one.'

So, thinks Erik, she must be living in a downtown area.

'Is there a light in your room?'

'Yes, the light's on.'

Erik wants to ask more but there is no reply. Time is passing. What can he do?

From the nearby fire station Erik rings up the fire brigade chief. He puts the problem to him. The chief's opinion is: ☞

'Nothing to be done there. We can't possibly find the woman. And besides,' he complains, 'the fire brigade main line is being occupied meanwhile by this woman. Supposing there's a fire somewhere.'

Erik refuses to give up. During his training he was taught that a fireman's first duty is to save lives. Suddenly he has a wild idea and tells his chief. But the captain is taken aback.

'That's mad! People will think there's been an atom bomb. In the middle of the night in a town with a million inhabitants!'

'Please,' begs Erik, 'we must act quickly before it is too late.'

Silence at the other end of the line. Then Erik hears: 'All right we'll do it. I'll be right over.'

A quarter of an hour later 20 small fire brigade vehicles are out in the old part of the town with sirens wailing. Each one has a certain district to quarter.

The woman gives no further sign but Erik can hear her breathing. After ten minutes Erik calls: 'Now I can hear a siren through the receiver!'

Straight away the captain speaks on his intercom: 'Car no. 1. Shut off your siren.' He refers to Erik.

'I can still hear the siren,' says the young man.

'Car no. 2. Shut off your siren.'

At the twelfth car Erik says in triumph: 'The siren has stopped now.'

The captain gives the order on the radio: 'Car no. 12 put your siren on again.'

Erik informs him: 'I can hear it again but now it's fainter.'

'Car no. 12. Turn round,' says the captain.

Shortly afterwards from Erik: 'It's getting louder, it's quite loud, it must be in the street.'

'Car no. 12. Look to see which window has a light showing.'

A growl comes back: 'Hundreds of lights on. They're all at their windows!'

'Use your loudhailer,' orders the captain.

Erik hears the loudspeaker through the telephone: 'Ladies and gentlemen, we are looking for a woman in danger of her life. Her light is on. Please put your lights out.'

The lights go out, only one window remains alight. Shortly after, Erik can hear the door being broken open; then a man's voice comes over the phone: 'She's unconscious but her pulse is still beating. We're taking her straight to the hospital. I think she'll manage.'

Ellen Thorndall – that was her name – did in fact manage. She recovered consciousness. Even her memory returned after a few weeks. ◆

PIERRE LEFÈVRE

36

Blackout

This is part of a story by the late Jamaican novelist Roger Mais. It is a reminder that we can all, unthinkingly, be racist – and show it in unexpected ways.

This story is by a writer who lived in the West Indies. It was written at a time when they were fewer black people in countries such as America and Britain than there are now. As you listen, ask yourself whether the woman in the story knows she is causing offence and also ask yourself which of her actions cause offence to the man in the story.

◆

THE CITY WAS in partial blackout; the street lights had not been turned on, because of the wartime policy of conserving electricity; and the houses behind their discreet *aurelia* hedges were wrapped in an atmosphere of exclusive respectability.

The young woman waiting at the bus stop was not in the least nervous, in spite of the wave of panic that had been sweeping the city about bands of hooligans roaming the streets after dark and assaulting unprotected women. She was a sensible young woman to begin with, who realized that one good scream would be sufficient to bring a score of respectable suburban householders running to her assistance. On the other hand she was an American, and fully conscious of the tradition of American young women that they don't scare easily.

Even that slinking black shadow that seemed to be materializing out of the darkness at the other side of the street did not disconcert her. She was only slightly curious now that she observed that the shadow was approaching her, slowly.

125

It was a young man dressed in conventional shirt and pants, and wearing a pair of canvas shoes. That was what lent the suggestion of slinking to his movements, because he went along noiselessly – that, and the mere suggestion of a stoop. He was very tall. There was a curious look of hunger and unrest about his eyes. But the thing that struck her immediately was the fact that he was black; the other particulars scarcely made any impression at all in comparison. In her country not every night a white woman could be nonchalantly approached by a black man. There was enough novelty in all this to intrigue her. She seemed to remember that any sort of adventure might be experienced in one of these tropical islands of the West Indies.

'Could you give me a light, lady?' the man said.

It is true she was smoking, but she had only just lit this one from the stub of the cigarette she had thrown away. The fact was she had no matches. Would he believe her, she wondered? 'I am sorry. I haven't got a match.'

The young man looked into her face, seemed to hesitate an instant and said, his brow slightly wrinkled in perplexity: 'But you are smoking.'

There was no argument against that. Still, she was not particular about giving him a light from the cigarette she was smoking. It may be stupid, but there was a suggestion of intimacy about such an act, simple as it was, that, call it what you may, she could not accept just like that.

There was a moment's hesitation on her part now, during which time the man's steady gaze never left her face. There was pride and challenge in his look, curiously mingled with quiet amusement.

She held out her cigarette towards him between two fingers. 'Here,' she said, 'you can light from that.'

In the act of bending his head to accept the proffered light, he came quite close to her. He did not seem to understand that she meant him to take the lighted cigarette from her hand. He just bent over her hand to light his.

Presently he straightened up, inhaled a deep lungful of soothing smoke and exhaled again with satisfaction. She saw then that he was smoking the half of a cigarette, which had been clinched and saved for future consumption.

'Thank you,' said the man, politely; and was in the act of moving off when he noticed that instead of returning her cigarette to her lips she had casually, unthinkingly flicked it away. He observed this in the split part of a second that it took him to say those two words. It was almost a whole cigarette she had thrown away. She had been smoking it with evident enjoyment a moment before.

He stood there looking at her, with cold speculation. ◆

ROGER MAIS

127

37

Being Accepted

This firsthand account of racism, written by a teenage Sikh girl, may be used when it seems necessary to raise and discuss this issue.

This true story was written by a teenage girl and it's about her experiences when her family moved home and she started at a new school. Do you think the same thing would happen to someone like her who came to this school? And what, if anything, can be done about it?

◆

MY NAME IS Sanjit and I live in Telford with my mum and dad and three brothers. We own two shops, but only one is running and we also own a house. We used to live in Wolverhampton but moved to Telford in 1981.

When my dad told us that we were moving, I thought great, what a nice break it will be from Wolverhampton. But when we moved to Telford I found it was different from what I thought it would be.

We first bought a corner shop in Madeley and the house was in Woodside. I thought the house was very nice but no other Asian family lived around us. I was eleven and didn't know much about racism but I did know a bit about the National Front. The first day when we were about to move in, we had a note through the door saying something like 'We don't need you here black bastards'. The letters NF were written on the front of our door. Even though I didn't know much about them, I did know that we were going to get some trouble around here. My mum was a little worried but my dad said it would soon pass.

When we settled down, me and my brother decided to play outside. While we were playing on our bikes a boy about ten came over and started to make trouble by calling me names such as Paki, saying niggers aren't welcome here. We started making friends around the neighbourhood after two or three months, but there was still this little prat and his mates who kept going on and on. We tried hard to ignore them but it was hard, so we'd get into fights and we would get the blame.

I think the worst experience came at school, because I was on my own, without my brothers to stick up for me. I was taken to my tutor group by the headmaster. I walked into the class behind him and I could feel pairs of eyes looking at me as though a leper had walked in. The headmaster introduced me to the tutor who seemed like a nice man. As soon as the headmaster left I could hear whispering behind me. I heard lots of things I had heard in my neighbourhood, but something really hit me. 'They should go back to their own country.' I was in my own country, I was born here. This is what they didn't know and I knew I was not welcome. A girl took me around the school.

My first lesson was music. I really like music except I knew I wasn't going to like this lesson. Two boys sitting opposite me kept laughing. I couldn't figure out what was so funny until a girl told them to stop taking the piss. They were making fun of me.

In maths we had a test and I finished first and got the top mark. 'Blackie is brainy,' I heard.

It took me a couple of months to make friends with some of the girls. I hadn't made friends with any of the boys because I found they were the more racist, though there was the odd girl too.

One day in home economics lesson, a boy was making so many racist remarks that he really got on my nerves. I told him to shut up or else. He didn't shut up because he was in front of all his friends, so I went over to him and pushed him. He thumped me so I got hold of him and swung him around. He landed on a table with his arm twisted. He shut up after that.

I don't know what it was, but from that day on I started making more friends with the boys and started getting less racial abuse. I guess I had to show them that they couldn't push me around any more.

In the fourth and fifth year I got to know more people. In the fifth year I found that I got on with the boys a bit more than the girls because I am into doing boys' stuff such as wearing ties, shirts and other boys' things. At the end of the fifth year I even played cricket with the boys, so you can see how it changed gradually over the years.

The latest remark I got at the end of the fifth year was: 'We got used to her'. I don't think this boy meant it in a racist way because we are really good friends.

But this made me think. Why did they have to get used to me? I was like everyone else. Why was it me they had to get used to? I don't think anyone should go through this kind of experience because it is very upsetting at times.

After this experience, I was afraid of going to college this year in case I had to go through the same experience again. But I found it was very different. I made friends quite quickly.

Even though I get odd remarks from my friends I don't take them so seriously because I know that they are only joking. But if I get a remark from someone I don't know, well, I just ignore them or tell them to grow up. But most of the time my ☞

friends stick up for me so I don't have to say anything for myself. ◆

SANJIT KAUR BAGRY

(NB: When one of her new classmates said, 'We got used to her,' he may have meant that in a friendly way. But why should they have had to 'get used to her'? Would something similar have happened to a new pupil who was of the same ethnic group as the rest of the class?)

38

A *Walk in the* Woods

This passage is an excerpt from the novel A Proper Little Nooryef *by Jean Ure. Jamie, an ordinary boy at an ordinary school, is persuaded to try ballet dancing to help his sister's dancing teacher. He proves to be exceptionally talented but has problems in accepting his gift. Here he is clumsily trying to prove his masculinity. It is a reading which may help to nurture respect for other people, especially of the opposite sex; and to encourage listeners to see things from other people's points of view.*

This is a story about a girl and a boy. One evening he persuades her to go for a walk in the woods. So who's to blame for what happens? And should they have been able to go for the walk without anything happening?

◆

'SHALL WE GO into the woods?' he said.

'What for?'

'Be nice in there. Nice and quiet.'

It'd be dark,' said Sharon. 'You couldn't see where you were going.'

'So who wants to?'

Sharon, apparently. She refused point blank to go into the woods. She said she'd rather walk up to the look-out and see all the lights marking the roads that led to London.

'Sometimes you can see St Paul's, Mr Hubbard says. If the conditions are right.'

He didn't believe that; St Paul's must be all of 40 miles away. Most likely what the Hubbard had said was that you could see as *far* as St Paul's. Still, he wasn't going to argue with her; it wasn't worth it.

Duly they trudged as far as the look-out: duly they gazed upon the lights. At least they were alone up there. Perhaps it was quite a good place to have come. The hillside sloped away before them, invitingly covered in ferns and long grass. He wondered how one began.

'Want to come and sit down?' he said.

'Not particularly.' She was still searching in vain for St Paul's. 'He said the sky had to be clear. I expect there's too much cloud.'

'Yeah, I expect so.' Anything to keep her happy. He caught her about the waist. 'Come and sit down.'

She wrinkled her nose. 'On the ground?'

'Why not?' What did she expect? A room at the Ritz? 'It's perfectly OK. It hasn't rained for decades.'

'It rained last Sunday,' said Sharon.

'Yeah, well, that was days ago. It's had a chance to dry out since then. See?' He bent down and rubbed his hand over the grass to show her. 'Dry as a bone.'

'Yes,' she said, 'but it might be dirty.'

Some people! He peeled off his sweater. 'There! How about that?'

Yes; she liked that. Had a touch of the old Walter Raleigh about it. Graciously, she sat herself upon it. He sat down beside her.

'Of course, there isn't any moon,' said Sharon. 'That would probably make a difference.'

Oh, bound to, bound to. (How was one supposed to stop them *talking*, for goodness' sake?)

He slipped his arm back round her waist, and obligingly she wriggled closer. This was better, thought Jamie. He was obviously getting the hang of it. It was simply a question of being masterful.

He tried kissing her, and instead of presenting herself with lips all puckered and pursed like a prune she actually parted them slightly, as if to indicate willingness. He began to feel that Doug had, quite definitely, been right: this was what she had wanted all along. All it had needed was a bit of positivity.

Encouraged, he slid his hand inside her bright pink top with the sparkly things round the neck. Instantly, she pulled away.

'Ja-*mie*!'

'What's the matter?'

'*Don't.*'

She only said it because she thought she had to; because it would have looked bad if she'd just let him go ahead without making any form of protest. She was just playing hard to get, that was all. 'Push 'em about a bit – show 'em you mean business.' What she needed was someone to be masterful. Very well, then.

'*Do you mind?*' Something went stinging like a whiplash across his face: it took him a second to realise that it was Sharon, belting him one, 'You just keep your hands to yourself! I didn't come up here to be mauled about.'

He might have retorted, then what did you come for? (bearing in mind that the Common was notorious) but he was still reeling from the blow she had dealt him. He wouldn't be at all ☛

surprised if she'd broken his nose. For such a puny creature, she packed one hell of a powerful punch.

'You must be bonkers!' Already she was up on her feet, trampling with cold disregard all over his sweater. 'You must be out of your tiny mind!'

Jamie thrust a lock of hair out of his eyes. 'There's no need to get all uptight.'

'You've got a nerve!' shrieked Sharon. 'You bring me up here and maul me about and then tell me that *there's no need to get all uptight*?'

'Well – be reasonable.' He wondered if he had red marks across his face, and if so whether they'd be gone by Monday. 'There are some girls that actually like it.'

'If you think,' said Sharon, 'that I'm one of *that* sort, then you obviously don't know very much about girls, that's all I can say.'

They walked back home with half a yard of daylight between them. ◆

JEAN URE

39

Four Eyes

Many people hate the idea of having to wear glasses – or anything else which makes them 'different'. This passage might be used as assurance that 'you are not alone' and also as a reminder of the way many of us take the gift of sight for granted.

Many people think that wearing dark glasses is 'cool' (or whatever) but wearing ordinary glasses is naff. But some people do have to wear glasses and this passage is a reminder of just what glasses can do to help those people. The narrator is remembering when he was a small boy early in this century.

◆

A MEDICAL EXAMINATION at school had revealed the fact that I was short-sighted. The doctor took me solemnly between his knees, looked into my face, and said, 'If you don't get some glasses, you'll be blind by the time you are fifteen, and I shall tell your parents so.'

I was rather proud of this distinction. Fifteen. That was so far ahead that it meant nothing to me, except a sort of twilight at the end of my life. My parents thought otherwise, and one Saturday afternoon I was taken to a chemist's shop. Behind the shop was a room where my eyes were tested in the rough and ready way customary in those days. The chemist hung an open framework that felt like the Forth Bridge around my ears and on my nose. Lenses were slotted into this, and twisted about, while I was instructed to read the card of letters beginning with a large E.

I remember still the astonishment with which I saw the smaller ☞

letters change from a dark blur into separate items of the alphabet. I thought about it all the following week, and found that by screwing up my eyes when I was out of doors I could get to some faint approximation of that clarity, for a few seconds at a time. This made me surmise that the universe which hitherto I had seen as a vague mass of colour and blurred shapes might in actuality be much more concise and defined. I was therefore half prepared for the surprise which shook me a week later when, on the Saturday evening, we went again to the shop, and the chemist produced the pair of steel-rimmed spectacles through which I was invited to read the card. I read it, from top to bottom! I turned and looked in triumph at Mother, but what I saw was Mother intensified. I saw the pupils of her eyes, the tiny feathers in her boa necklet; I saw the hairs in Father's moustache, and on the back of his hand. Jack's cap might have been made of metal, so hard and clear did it shine on his close-cropped head, above his bony face and huge nose. I saw *his* eyes too, round, enquiring, fierce with a hunger of observation. He was studying me with a gimlet sharpness such as I had never before been able to perceive.

Then we walked out of the shop, and I stepped on to the pavement, which came up and hit me, so that I had to grasp the nearest support – Father's coat. 'Take care, now, take care!' he said indulgently (though he disapproved of all these concessions to physical weakness). 'And mind you don't break them!'

I walked still with some uncertainty, carefully placing my feet and feeling their impact on the pavement whose surface I could see sparkling like quartz in the lamplight.

The lamplight! I looked in wonder at the diminishing crystals of gasflame strung down the hill. Clapham was hung with necklaces of light, and the horses pulling the glittering omni-☛

buses struck the granite road with hooves of iron and ebony. I could see the skeletons inside the flesh and blood of the Saturday-night shoppers. The garments they wore were made of separate threads. In this new world, sound as well as sight was changed. It took on hardness and definition, forcing itself upon my hearing, so that I was besieged simultaneously through the eye and through the ear. ◆

RICHARD CHURCH

40

Red the Bully

*This passage may help to raise the subject of bullying and ways to
overcome it. Discussion might centre on whether the way the narrator
defeats his bully is realistic or desirable and what other courses of action
are possible.*

This is a story about a bully and his victim. The victim (who
is the storyteller) tries two ways of overcoming his fear and
the bully. One doesn't work; the other does – but is it a way
open to everyone? He ends up by saying there is a way to
defeat every strong man, every bully. 'There is a special
ju-jitsu.' A special magic. Is there?

◆

I REALIZED THAT what mattered in the struggle for life was
to overcome my fear of those who were stronger.

The ruler of our street was a boy of about sixteen who was
nicknamed Red. Red was big and broad-shouldered beyond his
years. Red walked masterfully up and down our street, legs
wide and with a slightly rolling gait, like a seaman on his deck.

From under his cap, its peak always at the back of his head, his
forelock tumbled down in a fiery cascade, and out of his round
pock-marked face, green eyes, like a cat's, sparkled with scorn
for everything and everyone. Two or three lieutenants, in
peaked caps back to front like Red's, tripped at his heels.

Red could stop any boy and say impressively the one word
'money'. His lieutenants would turn out the boy's pockets,
and if he resisted they beat him up hard.

Everyone was afraid of Red. So was I. I knew he carried a heavy ☛

139

metal knuckle-duster in his pocket. I wanted to conquer my fear of Red. So I wrote a poem about him. This was my first piece of journalism in verse.

By the next day the whole street knew it by heart and exulted with triumphant hatred.

One morning on my way to school I suddenly came upon Red and his lieutenants. His eyes seemed to bore through me. 'Ah, the poet,' he drawled, smiling crookedly. 'So you write verses. Do they rhyme?'

Red's hand darted into his pocket and came out armed with its knuckle-duster; it flashed like lightning and struck my head. I fell down streaming with blood and lost consciousness. This was my first remuneration as a poet. I spent several days in bed.

When I went out, with my head still bandaged, I again saw Red. I struggled with myself but lost and took to my heels. At home I rolled on my bed, biting my pillow and pounding it in shame and impotent fury at my cowardice. I made up my mind to vanquish it at whatever cost.

I went into training with parallel bars and weights. After every session I would feel my muscles; they were getting bigger, but slowly. Then I remembered something I had read in a book about a miraculous Japanese method of wrestling which gave an advantage to the weak over the strong. I exchanged a week's ration card for a textbook on ju-jitsu.

For three weeks I stayed at home, practising with two other boys. Then I went out.

Red was sitting on the lawn in our yard, playing *vingt-et-un* with his lieutenants. He was absorbed in the game. Fear was still deep in me, urging me to go back. But I went up to the players and kicked and scattered the cards.

Red looked up, surprised at my impudence after my recent flight. He got up slowly. 'You looking for more?' he asked menacingly. As before, his hand dived into his pocket for the knuckle-duster. But I made a quick jabbing movement and Red, howling with pain, rolled on the ground. Bewildered he got up and came at me, swinging his head furiously from side to side like a maddened bull.

I caught his wrist and squeezed slowly, as I had read in the book, until the knuckle-duster dropped from his limp fingers. Nursing his hand, Red fell down again. He was sobbing and smearing the tears over his pock-marked face with his grubby fist.

That day Red ceased to be the monarch of our street. And from that day on I knew for certain that one need not fear the strong. All one needs is to know the way to beat them. For every strong man there is a special ju-jitsu.

What I also learned on this occasion was that to be a poet, I had not only to write poems, but know how to stand up for them. ◆

YEVGENY YEVTUSHENKO

SAINTS ARE SINNERS WHO KEEP ON TRYING

'A questioning man is halfway to being wise'
  IRISH PROVERB
'Compete, don't envy'
  ARAB PROVERB

41

Legion and Jairus

This reading is an introduction to three characters from the New Testament. Mark 5 tells of the deranged man who called himself Legion, the woman 'with an issue of blood' and the 'ruler of the synagogue' named Jairus.

The passage may be divided and used on separate occasions and either or both halves may be used in conjunction with a Bible reading or as a way of pointing out a central Christian belief: Jesus had very special gifts as a healer.

Christians believe that the four books in their Bible called Gospels describe the life of Jesus. In one of them, Mark's Gospel, we hear about three of the stranger things Jesus did. One was curing a man who was mentally ill. In those days, people often believed someone who seemed 'mad' was 'possessed by a devil'. The second involved curing a woman who had great faith in him as a healer; and for the third 'miracle' he apparently brought a young girl back to life. So what do you think really happened in each case?

◆

FIRST THERE IS the wild lunatic who lives among the mountain tombs in the country of the Gadarenes on the eastern shore of the Sea of Galilee. He is an alarming figure. People had tried to bind him with chains, but such was the strength of his frenzy that he always broke loose. He wandered about in this rough mountain-place, shrieking and cutting himself with stones. Jesus met this man, and the 'devils' inside the lunatic shouted out that Jesus was tormenting them. Jesus asked the man's name. 'My name is legion,' he replied, 'for we are many.'

It is an exchange which has all the ring of truth, and which ☞

could have taken place at any time, and in any place between a mad divided self, and a sane man. Jesus the exorcist and healer commanded the devils to come out of the man; and he 'sent' them into a neighbouring herd of pigs. Presumably, the wretched man's shrieks were enough to frighten the pigs, who ran violently down the slopes, and fell to their destruction in the Lake. The local farmers, understandably enough, came to ask Jesus if he would move on. It was one thing for visiting Jews [like Jesus] to abstain from eating pigs; but another thing altogether when they invaded the farms of Gentiles and destroyed their livelihood.

Like all the stories in Mark, it has been adapted so that a preacher can use it to tell the early Church some truth, as they understood it, about Jesus. In his lifetime on earth, Jesus had a great power of healing. Jesus will, Mark teaches us, be able to heal our inward conflicts and divisions if we come to him. That is the sermonizing point of the story. But the wild man in the cave seems very real. More real, strangely enough, than Jesus.

Then we met Jairus: a very different man. He was the ruler of the synagogue in Capernaum [and] is a man in despair about his daughter, who is lying at the point of death. Jesus made his way to the house and on his way, he met another unhappy person: a woman who for twelve years had been suffering from haemorrhages – 'an issue of blood'. She believed that if she could only touch the hem of Jesus's clothing, she will be healed. She came up behind him in the crowd, and Jesus rounded on her. 'Who touched me?' The disciples were astonished, since he had been touched and jostled by so many people. Yet at that moment, we are told, he was aware of the healing power within him being used up. Goodness went out of him. Full of anxiety and fear, the woman came forward and ☞

145

admitted that she had touched him. And she is healed. After this healing, Jesus made his way to the house of Jairus, and found the full paraphernalia of a funeral in progress, with hired mourners wailing and the family in a state of shock. When Jesus said that the girl was not dead, he was laughed to scorn. Undeterred, he cleared the house of people and went to the young girl's bedside. '*Talitha cumi!* Damsel arise!' When the little girl opened her eyes, Jesus realized that she would be hungry. He told the family that they should keep the healing a secret and that they should give the girl something to eat.

The words of Jesus to the daughter of Jairus were taken up as a rallying-cry among nineteenth-century feminists. 'Damsel arise!' were words which emblazoned colleges and schools which, for the first time in history, had been founded with the specific purpose of educating women. This was not completely fanciful. By contrast with St Paul and the early Christians, Jesus neither feared women, nor treated them as a sub-species. It would appear that he was prepared to defy convention in this regard and to befriend women in a time and place when the sexes were not supposed to mix on socially equal terms. ◆

A N WILSON

42

Pontius Pilate

This is another reading which provides background to a character in the Gospels. Obviously this one may conveniently be used as Good Friday approaches.

At the time of the crucifixion of Jesus, Judaea was under Roman rule and almost certainly only the Roman Governor could pronounce the death penalty.

Crucifixion was the Roman method of execution. Jewish death sentences were traditionally carried out by stoning or burning.

When Jesus became unpopular with the Jewish leaders in Jerusalem, they could not put him to death themselves because the country, Judaea, was under Roman occupation. The Roman Governor, who had the real power, was a man called Pontius Pilate.

◆

PONTIUS PILATE WAS a Roman official, possibly a Spaniard by birth. In his early manhood he became a member of the Ordo Equester, the Knights of the Cavalry, a company of gentlemen who could afford the minimum property qualification of 400,000 sesterces*. He had served for a time under Germanicus in Germany, and had married Claudia Procula, a lady having connections with the imperial family. Tradition reveals that she was the illegitimate daughter of the third wife of the future emperor Claudius. In 26 CE Pilate was made the sixth procurator, or governor, of Judaea.

ROSALYN A KENDRICK

So why was this powerful Roman so reluctant to put to death the man called Jesus? Especially as Pilate could be quite a brute.

When we read the trial before Pilate, one thing is crystal clear; Pilate was quite certain that Jesus was not guilty. Pilate wanted to let Jesus go and yet Pilate could not let him go – why? Quite simply, because Pilate was in a spot. His past rose up against him and made it impossible to do what he knew he ought to do. Pilate must have been a good governor and a wise administrator, because Judaea was one of the most difficult provinces in the Roman Empire and only a very efficient official would have been put in charge of it. But when he came to Judaea, Pilate got off on the wrong foot straight away.

What happened was this. The Roman troops were stationed, not in Jerusalem, but in the Roman government headquarters at Caesarea, between 20 and 30 miles away; when troops were needed, when Jerusalem was crowded and there was a chance of trouble, detachments of them were brought from Caesarea and stationed temporarily in Jerusalem. Now a Roman soldier's standards were not flags like the standards of British regiments; they were poles with little metal busts of the Emperor on the top. The Emperor in those days was held to be divine, and so to the Jew the little metal bust on the top of the pole was a graven image, an idol, an image of a strange god. All Roman governors and commanders, up to the time of Pilate, had removed these little images before they marched their troops in, in deference to the religious feelings of the Jews. But Pilate said, 'Not on your life. I'm not taking away the figure of the Emperor for these Jews or anyone else.' And he marched in with the figure of the Emperor on the standards. There was no riot; the Jews simply besought Pilate with all their hearts to take away the image and not to desecrate the city. They followed him down to Caesarea and for five days they tagged on behind him in their hundreds, with their prayers and their requests. On the sixth day he said he would meet them in the amphitheatre and give them his answer. Some thousands of them were there, and his answer was that unless they stopped their requests on the spot, the soldiers who surrounded them would kill them in cold blood. The Jews simply bared their necks and said, 'Kill us, but don't desecrate our city.' Now even Pilate could not kill thousands in cold blood: he had to climb down.

But Pilate was curiously unteachable. He wanted to bring a water supply into Jerusalem and to build an aqueduct – an entirely laudable and praiseworthy undertaking. But aqueducts cost money. He had no money, and so raided the Temple treasury (which counted its money in nothing less than millions). Of course the Jews wanted water all right, but they did not want the Temple treasury raided – they went up in a blue light straight away and rioted. Pilate then dressed his troops in plain clothes, gave them cudgels beneath their cloaks, and sent them in among the crowds. Unless the riot stopped, at a given signal the soldiers were to do a bit of beating up. But something went badly wrong. Instead of just beating up, the soldiers got quite out of control and two thousand Jews lay dead in the streets of Jerusalem that night.

Pilate's whole trouble was this: that a Roman governor could be reported to the Emperor for mismanagement. In this the Jews had the whip hand of Pilate. They were saying, 'If you don't condemn this man [Jesus] you're not Caesar's friend.' In effect, they were saying, 'If you let this man go we are going to report you to Caesar, and you've had it.' And Pilate simply could not make the stand. But he still tried to shuffle out of the responsibility, even to the very last minute. He suddenly dis- ☛

covered that Jesus was a Galilean by original residence, and at that time there was present in Jerusalem, as Luke tells, the Herod who was King of Galilee, an area not under Pilate's jurisdiction. So Pilate took the chance and decided that he would send Jesus to Herod to see if Herod would take the responsibility of condemning him. But Herod would not. He simply examined him and sent him back to Pilate. ◆

WILLIAM BARCLAY

(* Cicero said an annual income of 600,000 sesterces was needed to lead the life of a gentleman in Rome in 50BCE. 400,000 sesterces = 100,000 denarii – perhaps 1000 times the income of a Palestinian peasant farmer of the time.)

43

The Young Prophet

This passage, perhaps more suitable for the younger age groups, is a Muslim account of the early years of the Prophet of Islam, Muhammad, who was born about the year 570 CE. It might be used to mark a Muslim festival or to show that all religions have a belief in one Creator God.

Muslims, when pronouncing the name Muhammad, follow it with the blessing 'Peace and blessings of Allah be upon him'. Non-Muslim readers must decide if or when it is appropriate to follow this practice.

Muslims, people who follow the faith of Islam, recognize many of the great teachers and leaders of the Jewish faith: Abraham and Moses, for example. They also believe Jesus was a great prophet. But for Muslims the greatest prophet was Muhammad. And this is the story of his childhood. He was born in a city called Makkah (or Mecca); both his parents had died by the time he was six and he was then brought up by his grandfather.

◆

WHEN MUHAMMAD WAS only eight years old his grandfather, Abdul Muttalib, died. Muhammad went to live with his uncle, Abu Talib. Abu Talib was a kind and intelligent man. He loved Muhammad very much.

Muhammad was only a child, but he wanted to work and help his uncle. He asked if he could look after the goats of people in Makkah. He already had plenty of experience in looking after his grandfather's goats.

At first, Abu Talib did not want to let Muhammad work. But the boy was determined, so Abu Talib agreed. Looking after goats was not easy work, but Muhammad enjoyed it. He was a ☞

good goatherd. He knew where the best grass was and he always brought his goats home well-fed. Sometimes, with a few of his friends, he would drive his goats over the desert sands in search of green valleys and oases.

Muhammad did not mind the burning heat of the Sun or the harsh winds of the desert. He loved the beauty of the world he saw, lit by the Sun during the day and the Moon by night. Muhammad looked carefully at the beauty around him and thought a lot about what he saw. He did not think that the idols could have made a world as splendid as this. His grandfather had often taken him to see the idols, but he had never worshipped them. He felt sorry for the Arabic people who worshipped the idols. He felt in his heart that men were blind not to see the greatness of Allah, the one Almighty God.

Muhammad's friends thought he was funny when he spoke of Allah. They were afraid for him, too.

'Muhammad, do be quiet', they said. 'Don't anger the idols or there will be terrible trouble. They alone are powerful.' Muhammad told his uncle he could not believe the idols had made the Sun and Moon, the heat and the cold, the stars and the clouds, all the wonderful things in the world. Abu Talib was astonished at Muhammad's words. He tried to answer, but nothing would convince Muhammad. He knew that Allah had created the world.

When Muhammad was twelve, he was travelling in a trading caravan through the desert. Abu Talib was leading the caravan from Makkah to Syria. Abu Talib had not wanted Muhammad to come on the journey. He thought it would be too long and too difficult for a child. During the day, the Sun burned the skin of the travellers, and at night the cold bit into their bones. ☞

But Muhammad had been determined, and he had proved himself able to put up with the discomforts of the journey.

After many days the caravan came to Busra, a fertile oasis in the desert. The travellers stopped to rest in the shade of the trees. The traders did not know that their arrival had been watched by a wise old man. He had noticed some white clouds travelling above the caravan as they came near to Busra. When they stopped, the clouds had stopped above them. If the old man's learning did not deceive him, there was something very special about these Arabian traders. He was very eager to meet them. He decided to give them a party, so he prepared some food. Then he sent a messenger to invite the traders to his house.

Now Abu Talib did not want to go to the man's house. He knew the old man was a Christian and his teaching was different from the beliefs of Abu Talib and his people. In the end, though, Abu Talib was persuaded to go. One of the traders knew the old man and told Abu Talib he was a good man.

'He won't talk about his religion', said the trader. 'He is very wise and understands the stars. What could be wrong with going to see him?'

The old man met Abu Talib at the door of his house, and welcomed him. 'I pass through here often, sir', said Abu Talib. 'Why have you invited me to your house this time?'

'I wished to pay my respects, sir', said the old man. He did not say anything about the strange clouds.

'Just to me?' asked Abu Talib.

'No, to all of you. I open my home to you all. The meal is already prepared', replied the old man.

Abu Talib and all the traders who were travelling in the caravan ☞

went into the house and the old man invited them to sit down. But he felt someone was missing, so he asked, 'Is there no one left outside?' Jabir, the servant who looked after Muhammad, replied, 'No, sir. All the men are here. There's only a boy who's stayed outside. He's resting under the trees.' The old man insisted that the boy was invited too, and Jabir went to fetch Muhammad.

During the meal the old man watched Muhammad. He felt that this boy was special. When he spoke to him and discovered that his name was Muhammad, that he looked after goats to earn his living (as the prophets Musa and Isa – or Moses and Jesus – had done) and hated the idols that some Arabs then worshipped, the old man was sure that this child was the one he had learned about. The clouds had been a sign to him. This boy was to be the last prophet and messenger of Allah.

The old man spoke to Muhammad's uncle. 'Your child will face many difficulties and dangers. Guard him well and look after him. The Jews are looking for him, and if they find him, they will kill him. This boy is to become the last prophet and messenger of Allah.'

Abu Talib was amazed at the old man's words. And he was afraid. They had to continue to Syria to sell their goods, and there were Jews in Syria. But the old man said, 'Do not be afraid, Allah will protect His prophet.'

The caravan of traders went on to Syria but they did not stay there long. All the time the old man's words rang in Abu Talib's ears. As soon as they could, they returned safely to Makkah. ◆

ABDUL RAHMAN RUKAINI

154

44

The Prophet's Escape

This further Muslim reading describes another incident in the life of the Prophet.

A passage describing the key episode, the Call of the Prophet, may be found in the companion anthology to this, 100 Readings for Assembly, in passage 50, The Prophet Muhammad.

This is another story about Muhammad, the Prophet of Islam. When he grew up, he received a call from God and also the teaching which was to be written down as the Muslim holy book, the Qur'an. Muhammad then set about preaching God's word in his home city of Makkah (Mecca) but that did not make him popular with the leaders of the people there (the Quraysh). One night, Muhammad and his close friend and follower Abu Bakar were able to escape from the city. Even so, they were followed ...

◆

ABU BAKAR'S HEART was beating so fast. He found it difficult to breathe. He knew that he and the Prophet were in great danger. Silently he prayed to Allah for protection.

The Prophet Muhammad sat silently by Abu Bakar's side. They were hiding in a cave in the mountains of Thur and their enemies were searching for them. But still the Prophet was calm and unafraid.

When the leaders of the Quraysh found they had been tricked and Muhammad had managed to escape from Makkah without being seen, they set out to look for him. Groups of men went off in different directions.

One group, led by a man who was clever at following tracks, ☞

arrived at the bottom of the mountain of Thur. Their eyes searched the mountainside, looking for signs of Abu Bakar and the Prophet. Abu Bakar could see them from his hiding place in the mouth of the cave. The hunters were talking to a goatherd and looking up towards the cave. Abu Bakar was so afraid they would climb the mountain and find the cave where he and the Prophet were hidden.

'It doesn't look easy to climb', said one of the hunters. 'It's so steep and there are no foot-holds.' The man was tired. He wanted to give up the search. He and his friends had been promised a hundred camels by the leaders of the Quraysh if they found Muhammad. He didn't think it was worth risking his life on the steep mountainside for a hundred camels. But his friends did, and they carried on. They didn't know whether Muhammad was right or not, and they did not care. They knew the leaders of the Quraysh were always attacking Muhammad, and they were being paid good money to find him.

One of them was a good climber. Soon he was near the top of the mountain. Muhammad and Abu Bakar knew the man was near. Abu Bakar held his breath but the Prophet calmly recited the words of the Qur'an:

'Remember when the unbelievers plotted against you to kill you or send you into exile. They tried to trick Allah but Allah will repay them, as He does all who lie and cheat.'

The words calmed Abu Bakar for a moment, but then he saw the climber right at the mouth of the cave! The man's hands were scratched and bleeding from his climb. He was looking at his hands, then something caught his attention. It was a spider in the centre of its web. The web hung right across the entrance to the cave. And on a hollow in the rock, a dove had made her nest. The man looked closer. The bird was sitting on her eggs. ☞

The man was sure no one had gone into the cave through this entrance. The dove and the spider had clearly been there a long time. He began to walk round to look for another way into the cave.

Abu Bakar's heart leapt. Only Allah could save them. Allah had made the spider and the dove appear. But now the man was standing right by another entrance to the cave. Abu Bakar moved closer to the Prophet.

'If he bends down, he'll see us', he whispered. Muhammad knew his friend was afraid and recited these words from the Qur'an:

'If you do not help him, Allah will help him, as He helped him when he and another were driven out by the non-believers. Then in the cave when he said to his friend, "Do not be afraid. Allah is with us," Allah strengthened his spirit and sent to his aid unseen helpers. Allah is mighty and wise.'

Abu Bakar stopped feeling afraid. The man outside the cave did not bend down. He shouted down to his friends below to continue their search for the Prophet elsewhere. ◆

ABDUL RAHMAN RUKAINI

45

Guru Nanak and the Banquet

The first teacher of Sikhism was Guru Nanak ('Guru' means teacher).
He was born in 1469CE in a village called Talwandi in what is now
Pakistan. The people in that area were either Hindus or Muslims.
Nanak's faith embraced what he saw as good in both these religions.

He rejected the Hindu caste system (though it may not be appropriate
to stress this point in every assembly) and taught the equality of all men
and women.

NB The sound '-ji' [pronounced 'gee'] after a name or title is a mark
of respect.

Does being rich make you important? Or in some way
better than other people? The man who was the first teacher
of the Sikh religion about five hundred years ago, Guru
Nanak, thought not. He travelled around India and what is
now Pakistan teaching (among other things) that all men
and women are equally important and that it is what you do
that makes you good or bad.

◆

ONE OF THE cities Guru Nanak visited was Eminabad, not
far from the Sikh holy city of Amritsar. One evening when he
had finished teaching there, a carpenter called Lalo went shyly
up to him. 'Guru-ji,' he said. 'I'm only a poor man and you're
a great and wise man, but you're a traveller and a visitor to our
city and so I should like to offer you a meal tonight.'

'Lalo, *you* are a kind and generous man,' replied Guru Nanak,
'and I'll be delighted to accept.'

'But you must know that I can't offer much. Some water to
drink and vegetables and rice, that is all. And a little bread
perhaps.'

☞

158

'That is all I need and all I want. I am delighted to accept your invitation.' And so they walked back together, through the crowded streets, to the tiny house where Lalo lived.

In another part of the city, there lived a rich businessman called Malik Bhago. He hadn't bothered to go and listen to Guru Nanak; he'd been too busy carrying out his business deals but he'd heard talk of how Guru Nanak was a respected person.

'I shall invite him to dinner,' said Malik Bhago to himself, 'and when he comes, that'll prove to everyone in the city that I'm a good and popular person – just like Nanak.'

Which of course he wasn't.

He was cruel to his workers, he was unfair and he was mean. But he *was* rich and powerful, so people did what he said. And when he ordered his servants to find Guru Nanak and invite him to dinner that evening, that is what they set out to do. They looked everywhere, except they never thought of looking in the house of someone like Lalo. But at last they found someone who'd seen Guru Nanak going home with Lalo, so the servants raced to Lalo's house. They raced there because they knew that Malik Bhago's temper wouldn't be getting any better with waiting.

'Guru Nanak,' they said breathlessly as soon they'd found him, 'you must come to Malik Bhago's house at once. You're invited to dinner.'

'Must?' asked Guru Nanak.

'Everyone does what Malik Bhago says,' said Lalo very quietly. 'And you'll get a very much better meal.'

'No,' said Guru Nanak. 'I'll stay here. I was glad to accept Lalo's kind invitation.'

159

'But our master will be very angry if you refuse him,' said one of the servants.

'I really think you should go,' added Lalo.

Guru Nanak was silent for a few moments. 'Very well,' he said at last. 'I'll go. But I'll take a piece of that bread you have baked, Bhai Lalo.'

Everyone looked amazed. Not because of what he'd said about the bread. What surprised them was that Guru Nanak called him 'Bhai Lalo'. The word or title 'bhai' (which means 'brother') is used only when you wish to pay someone a very great honour.

The servants led Guru Nanak through the streets to Malik Bhago's house and, when they got there, Malik Bhago invited Guru Nanak to sit down. But just as they were about to eat, Guru Nanak took two pieces of bread, one in each hand. One was the piece that Bhai Lalo had baked; the other was from Malik Bhago's house. And then Guru Nanak squeezed both pieces of bread. Out of the bread that Bhai Lalo had baked dripped pure, fresh milk – and out of the bread from Malik Bhago's house there came drops of blood.

'What does this mean?' asked Malik Bhago.

'It means,' said Guru Nanak, 'that I would prefer to eat Bhai Lalo's plain food, which has been earned by his hard work and prepared with care by himself, rather than eat this banquet which has been made possible only because you've become rich by cheating the poor and by tricking those with whom you do business.'

And as Malik Bhago watched the last drops of blood trickle from his piece of bread, he was silent.

'I think,' he said after a while, 'I think that tomorrow I shall ☛

come to hear you teach. I think I have made ... mistakes in the past. I think I must–'

'Be more generous to other people?' suggested Guru Nanak.

'Exactly what I was going to say.'

'And what you will do, I hope,' said Guru Nanak.

'I'll try.'

'And you'll invite Bhai Lalo to supper?'

'Lalo? To supper? But he's just –'

'To God, a poor person is as important as a rich person.'

Malik Bhago was silent. ◆

161

46

John Wesley

John Wesley (1703–1791) was the founder of the Methodist Church. He was the fifteenth child of an Anglican clergyman, the Rev. Samuel Wesley – and also, briefly, his curate. He later devoted his life to evangelical preaching, touring Britain and abroad. Wesley wanted his 'methodist system' to remain within the Church of England but it became increasingly independent. His achievement was to revive the faith in a period of some indifference.

The lives of John (and Charles) Wesley are commemorated in some churches on 24 May.

You have probably seen a church building labelled 'Methodist Church'. But how did the organization called the Methodist Church begin, back around the year 1760? It was all because of the enthusiasm of one man who felt that the people of his day did not believe and live their religion firmly and keenly enough. He was called John Wesley and, at that time, most people in England were supposed to be members of the Church of England.

◆

HE MADE HUNDREDS of thousands of men better, in an age which was apparently dead to religion, dead to seriousness, dead to everything that was not frivolous, empty and vain.

How did John Wesley do this great work? How was it that he saved the soul of England in the eighteenth century? He mounted a horse and rode to all the parts of England where the working classes lived; and preached to them the religion of Jesus. He avoided the rich; he made his appeal to the magnificent forces of England's working classes.

John Wesley was a clergyman's son. His father had nineteen ☞

children. John had no luxuries. His mother whipped her children in order to teach them to cry softly. He was strictly trained, but the harshness of his childhood could not destroy in him the glowing light which illumined his noble spirit – the light of God's love. He believed implicitly that God *loves* every man, woman, and child; loves them, and desires them to be good that they may be capable of appreciating the joys which await those who love what is right and hate everything that is evil.

When he went to Oxford, Wesley had £30 a year, lived on £28, and gave £2 away. Next year he had £60, lived on £28, and gave £32 away. Next year he had £90, and the year after £120, but he still lived on £28 a year, and gave the rest away. It is said that during his life he gave away £30,000.

There were some very foolish men in the Church of England at that period, who so ill-treated Wesley that, though he was a churchman, he worked on his own lines. He built chapels wherever he went, organized a great society of worshippers, and preached in the fields and in the streets to anybody who would listen. Sometimes he was roughly used by the mob, but he never lost heart. He used to travel some 5000 miles every year, generally on horseback. He lived to be 88, and almost his last word was the joyful exclamation: 'The best of all is, God is with us!' That was the secret of his life. He felt that God was with man, helping, in His own wise way, the work of improving the human race. ◆

CHILDREN'S ENCYCLOPEDIA

47

No Schooling

The author of this passage was born in 1837 in Clerkenwell, London, the son of a furniture maker. He worked at this trade for some years, while educating himself. Eventually he gave up the cabinet-making trade to become a professional organist and music teacher. He told his story of self-advancement through hard work and thrift in a short unpublished biography (from which this excerpt is taken), written in 1923 when he was 86. As we now expect state provision, it is an 'unfashionable' tale in some ways but it remains an example of how a person can beat the system – and also one of remarkable contentment.

Not having to go to school may seem a very pleasant idea. But what was it like in the past when there were no schools – except for those who could afford to pay? This is the story of a person whose family couldn't pay. He was born in 1837 in London where his father earned a little money making furniture, in what was known as the cabinet trade. Later in life, John Shinn (that was his name) taught himself enough to become a professional musician – and he wrote about his life when he was an old man, aged 86. As you listen, you might think whether you really would like not having to go to school, and whether you will be as happy when you are 86.

◆

THE GREATEST AND most serious misfortune of my life has been the loss of schooling or education. At the time of my school age my parents were very poor and in great distress. There was no free education and private schools were few and very expensive, therefore my education was entirely lost, which has been to me the greatest trouble, but that was no fault of mine. The want of education has been a most serious draw- ☞

164

back all through my life. As a child I was passionately fond of drawing and painting and spent much of my time in that way, when I could get paper and paints to work with, but our distress at that time made this a great difficulty. The few halfpence I did get were all for that purpose, which afforded me very great pleasure and satisfaction and occupied my time and mind. Sundays were long and weary days when we were kept in for want of decent clothes. My mother who was a good pious woman did her best to keep us occupied during the long dull winter Sundays. During the evening she would read to us from the Bible and other suitable books and when we were tired would lead us in singing some favourite hymns for a change and thus we got through the time. Sometimes, (after dark) when our clothing was shabby, she would take us to some chapel a distance from home, where we were not known, which made a little change for us children.

As my parents were unable to send me to school, I was sent into the workshop to occupy my time and give me something to do. In a little time I became useful in assisting my father in many ways, and gradually drifted into the cabinet trade (which I never liked) but there was nothing else to be done but to remain and do my best, and wait and see what the future brought forth. The life in a workshop in those days was very rough. The working hours were very long, from 7 a.m. to 8 p.m. Saturday was the same, no half holidays at that time. The only holidays allowed during the year were Christmas and Boxing Days, Easter and Whit Monday (not Good Friday), which left very little time for study or self-improvement. About this period we were in very straightened circumstances, and my brother Edwin and I were sent one day to try and sell two ottoman footstools to raise a little money. We could only sell them at furniture dealers. We carried them from Clerken- ☞

165

well to Walworth then on to Camberwell Green, then across to Kennington Green, from there to Westminster through St Giles's to Tottenham Court Road, and Euston Road and back to Clerkenwell, a distance of about twelve or thirteen miles, and brought them back unsold ...

In taking a survey of my life, I don't think I ought to be dissatisfied with the social position I have attained and the progress I have made considering the many hardships and difficulties I had to contend with through my whole life. What I have done has been done only by hard work and persistent perseverance. Considering the circumstances of my early life it is surprising that I have been able to do so much. My earnings have always been very modest, I may say small, but I could see from the first that unless I could put by something, however little, no progress could be made and no provision made for sickness, misfortune or old age, therefore from my early life I resolved to save something out of my small income for future help, which I have done the whole of my life. I have had many difficulties and trials to bear, the greatest trial has been the want of education, but this was no fault of mine. All the education I got I had to get for myself. It is a most unfortunate thing to lose all the advantage of schooling which is so essential in the present age. Seventy years back there were no Board Schools and private schools were very expensive, quite out of the reach of the poor working classes in those days. The want of a better education has always been a great drawback all through my life, it has always made me feel nervous and timid and gave me a great lack of confidence in myself, but I have done the best I could under the circumstances and must rest contented with what I have attained. Had I had the opportunities which I have seen many have, I could have done much more. One thing I shall always regret, that when my parents ☞

were getting old and were in need that my own circumstances prevented me from giving them more assistance. But I did what I could. ◆

JOHN SHINN

48

Florence Nightingale

Born in 1820, the 'Lady with the Lamp' is, superficially, one of the better known characters in our history: she is one of those people of whom we have an immediate mental image. But precisely what was her achievement?

The daughter of a wealthy landowner, she gradually wore down parental opposition to her taking a job and trained as a nurse in Paris. By 1853 she was superintendent of the London Hospital for Invalid Gentlewomen. In 1854, at the outbreak of the Crimean War, she agreed to take 38 nurses to run the military hospital at Scutari. She was involved in a continuous battle against officialdom but survived triumphantly and returned to reform the nursing profession, giving it a new status. Hers is a tale of achievement in the face of (largely) male prejudice.

A name you've probably heard is that of Florence Nightingale. She was a nurse during the Crimean War – and it was her habit of visiting the wounded and dying soldiers each evening, carrying a lamp, that got her the nickname, 'Lady of the Lamp'. That makes her sound rather wet. Far from it. She was a most determined woman who did much to establish nursing as a proper profession – and to win many battles against male prejudice.

◆

FLORENCE NIGHTINGALE WAS born in 1820 at the city [in Italy] from which she got her Christian name. She was an heiress. Her family owned three large houses; they travelled a great deal, and moved in a world of fashionable ladies and Cabinet Ministers.

But Florence was soon as weary of parties as a grown-up would be of baby food. She wrote that since she was six she had craved ☞

to have something to do. 'A profession, a trade, something to fill and employ all my faculties. The first thought I can remember, and the last, was nursing work.' She was born with a vocation, and could not rest.

Unhappily for her, people of that age considered it unwomanly for a girl to think of anything but marriage. Florence Nightingale had many suitors, and seems to have cared for one of them; but she wrote in her journal that if she married him she would have had to continue her Society life, and that she could not endure.

When she was 25 she dared to make an extraordinary proposal to her scandalized parents: might she go to Salisbury Hospital as a nurse? 'It was as if I had wanted to be a kitchen maid,' she wrote; and they refused flatly. In those days, remember, nurses were ignorant of their work, notorious for drunkenness, and often thoroughly bad characters.

However, she took up her Society life anew, like a heavy burden. Her family did not know that she was always reading medical books and paying secret visits to hospitals and workhouses. Once, when they were all abroad, she 'succeeded in slipping off to a nursing institution at Kaiserswerth,' where she worked for three months. By hook or crook she gathered knowledge.

At last, when she was 33, her parents despaired of stamping out her strange craving for work, and she was allowed to become superintendent of a charitable nursing home in Harley Street. She had been there for a year when the Crimean War broke out. It soon became known that the nursing base at Scutari was inadequately served, and a letter from Florence Nightingale offering her services crossed one from her friend, Sidney Herbert, a Cabinet Minister, asking for them. In a week's time she ☛

sailed for Constantinople at the head of a band of 38 nurses, taking with her large supplies of medical stores, though the War Office had assured her that 'nothing was wanted at Scutari.'

She arrived the day before the battle of Inkerman, ten days after [the battle of] Balaclava. She found a hospital built over cesspools. There was no ventilation. The floor-boards were rotten. The walls were covered with vermin. There were four miles of beds, packed together, with hardly room to pass down the lines. There was no materials for cleaning, no knives, no forks, no clothing, and no medical stores of any kind. Before she arrived at Scutari the total number of shirts washed at the hospital during the campaign had been seven.

Red tape bound everyone hand and foot. Once, when the men were bitterly cold and 27,000 shirts had arrived for them, it was three weeks before the necessary formalities were got through and they could be unpacked. But worst of all was the prejudice and jealousy with which the chief doctors regarded this woman's appointment.

Because she had a will of steel, a genius for organization, and a commanding personality, because she brushed aside red tape like a spider's web, Florence Nightingale was able to bring order, comfort, cleanliness, and health out of the chaos. The death-rate fell from 42 per cent to 2 per cent. The soldiers worshipped her. But it is terrible to think that Florence Nightingale was fighting for them against those who should have been working with her. Once a doctor who resented her authority ordered that no rations should be supplied to her, but her foresight outwitted this petty attempt to starve her out.

In 1856, when the wretched war was over, Florence Nightingale returned to England, a popular idol. But her heart was strained, and she suffered from prolonged fainting fits. The doctors ordered her complete rest, and thought her on the brink of death. That, she told them, was all the more reason why she should make haste with her work. The suffering of Scutari must never be repeated; the Army medical system must be reformed, and she must devote her life, short or long, to that work.

But the whole War Office was against reform, against anything *new*, good or bad, and it was only after herculean labours that Florence Nightingale forced the authorities to appoint a Royal Commission to report on the health of the Army. As she was a woman, she could not take open part; but she coached the members all through, and their report was founded entirely on matter supplied by her.

Reform was now inevitable. The Army medical authorities were made responsible for keeping the soldiers well, besides curing them when they were sick. Florence Nightingale had pointed out that the mortality in the old barracks was almost twice the mortality in ordinary life, and said: 'You might as well take 1100 men every year out on Salisbury Plain and shoot them.' But now dirt and muddle, like two great spiders swept from a dark corner, fled from the barracks. Reading and recreation rooms were provided, although the officers had laughed at Florence Nightingale at Scutari for 'spoiling the brutes' by providing them with books. The private soldier never had a better friend. ◆

CHILDREN'S ENCYCLOPEDIA

49

Don Bosco

John Bosco was born near Turin in 1815. In adult life, he became a priest (Don Bosco) and was influential in nineteenth-century Italian politics. He founded the Salesian Order of the Catholic Church but is chiefly remembered for his practical work in helping the young homeless in his native city. He died in 1888 and his Church declared him a saint in 1934.

Some Christians fail to do what their church teaches them to do. Many other Christians do a lot of good in the world: they *do* improve things for people less fortunate than themselves. One such person was an Italian priest called Don Bosco who lived and worked in Turin in the nineteenth century.

◆

HE BECAME INCREASINGLY concerned with young men who were totally abandoned to themselves, without a home, often unable to get jobs for lack of any skill. He had occasionally seen them in the streets in swearing, fighting groups. He had visited some of the hovels in which they lived and shared their wretched sleeping quarters with depraved men and criminals. And he had seen some of them in the city prisons. For these boys he dreamed of clean, airy buildings with spacious courtyards, dormitories, classrooms, workshops particularly, where a boy could learn to be a printer, a bookbinder, a cobbler, a machinist, a carpenter, a stone mason without leaving the grounds. He dreamed, hoped, prayed, and waited.

Late one cold, rainy night, a sixteen-year old boy, in tatters and soaked to the skin, knocked at his door.

'Come in lad. It's no night to be out in weather like this. Where are you coming from?'

'From Valsesia, Father.'

'That's a good many miles away. What are you doing in Turin?'

'I am a mason-apprentice, looking for a job. I've spent the three liras I had, and ... ' He was on the verge of tears.

'You mean you don't know where to go?'

'I have no one, Father.'

From then on, he set about establishing hostels for homeless young people and providing them with food, training and, eventually, jobs. He did much other good work.

But it was his consuming interest in the young, the poorest and most neglected among them, that won for him the admiration of the world. From his compassionate love for them came countless homelike establishments and a uniquely successful system of education based on reason, religion and kindness.

PETER RINALDI

Indeed, he became very well known throughout Italy – but in those days long before television, he wasn't a 'famous face'. People didn't always recognize him. This next story teaches a number of lessons, and not just about Don Bosco.

Once Don Bosco was visiting in the neighbourhood of Alba. In the evening he wanted to return to Turin but he missed the last train. In pouring rain he knocked at the nearest presbytery. The priest opened the door and asked who he was.

'I'm a poor priest from Turin. I've just missed the last train.'

'What is your position in Turin?'

'I have a small suburban parish.'

'Yes. Have you had supper?'

'If you would be kind enough to give me something I would be most grateful.'

'I'm sorry but I've nothing by me. The most I can offer you is bread and cheese.'

'That will suit me very well. Thank you.'

'Do you intend staying the night?'

'You see how it is ... this pouring rain ... and the train has gone!'

'Quite, but I've no spare bed.'

'Oh, that's no problem, a couple of chairs will do.'

'If that's the case then please come in. I'm really sorry I've nothing better to offer.'

While the housekeeper was bringing the bread and cheese the priest continued: 'So you're from Turin?'

'That's right.'

'D'you perhaps know a certain Don Bosco?'

'Yes, a little.'

'I've never met him,' said the priest. 'But I've something I'd like to ask him. D'you think he would help?'

'He's always ready to help others when he can.'

'I was thinking of writing tomorrow to ask whether he could take a child into his orphanage.'

'He certainly will, I can assure you.'

'Really? Are you a friend of Don Bosco's?'

'Yes, indeed, since childhood.'

'Well, can you arrange the matter for me perhaps?'

'Consider it settled in return for your present kindness.'

'But ... you ... who are you then?'

'I'm Don Bosco.'

'Don Bosco? You're Don Bosco! Now why didn't you say so at first? But forgive me for not receiving you properly ... Now who would have thought it! Do leave that cheese, I've just remembered there's something left over from lunch.'

Thoroughly embarrassed and perspiring the priest called his housekeeper, had a clean cloth put on the table and ordered fish, soup and ham omelette. He ran to the cupboard and fetched half a roast chicken and a bottle of good red wine. He could hardly do enough and Don Bosco smiled to himself meanwhile.

After the meal the guest was taken up to a handsome bedroom. The next morning the priest accompanied him to the station uttering ceaseless apologies.

When saying goodbye Don Bosco took his arm: 'Look, Father, let's learn a lesson from what has happened. When we have nothing we can give nothing. When we have a little we can give a little. And when we have much we can give what seems to be the right thing. But let it always be for love of neighbour and not out of self-interest.' ◆

PIERRE LEFÈVRE

175

50

William **Booth**

The distinctive uniform of the Salvation Army will probably be familiar to most pupils but many may know little about its work or its founder, William Booth, who was a notable Christian activist and social reformer.

   Booth (1829–1912) was a Methodist preacher but left that organization to act independently. In 1865 he founded a mission in Whitechapel, London which proved to be the forerunner of the Salvation Army (officially founded in 1878). The 'Army' is still known, not only for its music, but for its readiness to help those in the roughest circumstances.

You've probably seen them in their uniforms, perhaps with their collecting tins: members of the Salvation Army.

   Christians believe they should help one another – and especially that they should help the poor and homeless. Few people have done this more usefully than William Booth, the man who started the Salvation Army over 100 years ago. He was a preacher in the poorest parts of London when he realized it was no good preaching about Jesus to people who were starving. They needed food and real help – not just alcohol to help them forget their misery.

◆

ON CHRISTMAS MORNING 1868, after preaching in Whitechapel, William Booth returned home feeling dejected; he had seen the poor celebrating the festival by getting drunk and was determined that it should not happen again. The following year he organized 300 Christmas dinners for the poor, most of them cooked by Catherine [his wife] and an Army helper in their home kitchen. This marked the beginning of the Mission's social work.

☞

Realizing that people don't respond to the Gospel on an empty stomach, he opened a 'soup kitchen' selling hot drinks at all hours of the day. He also set up five 'Food-for-the-Million Shops' where cheap three course meals were available.

The Christian Mission, as it was now called, produced militant-type Christians who almost from the beginning began to use military-style terms. They were 'fighting for God' in the 'Hallelujah army', and Booth was their 'General'. In 1878 Booth described the Mission as a 'Volunteer Army', but his lieutenant, George Railton, protested. Booth replaced the term 'Volunteer' with 'Salvation' and the title stuck.

By early 1879 converts could be counted by the thousands, and the Army had 81 stations manned by 127 full-time evangelists and holding 75,000 services a year. Yet Booth still felt that there was an unexplained element missing. The solution came at an Army meeting in Salisbury. Faced with the possibility of trouble at an open-air meeting, Salvationist William Fry and his three sons offered to act as bodyguards. They brought their musical instruments with them to accompany the singing, and the first Army band was formed. For a while the General was not attracted by the idea of a band but was eventually forced to declare, 'Why should the Devil have all the best tunes?' Soon the band was to accompany Booth on his tours and was often a means of attracting people to his meetings.

Before long, the Army added other features which promoted the military image. Instead of a conference, the Army was now governed by a 'Council of War'; ranks and titles came later. In 1878 Catherine Booth designed a flag for the station at Coventry which became the Army standard; it had a crimson background with a sun in the centre, later replaced by a star with the words 'Blood and Fire'. And in 1880 a standard uniform was introduced to take the place of the imaginative outfits ☛

worn by the first converts; this included the distinctive bonnet for the women, still worn today.

As the Army success gathered momentum, so did the opposition – the decade beginning in 1880 witnessed a period of assaults more violent than anything experienced in the early days. In one year alone (1882), 669 Army soldiers were attacked and 60 buildings wrecked. All over the country Army processions were broken up, meetings disrupted, while at Hastings one woman was kicked to death.

The most prolonged battle was fought at Worthing, on the south coast. There in 1884 a 'Skeleton Army' some 4000 strong launched a series of attacks that went on over a period of three months. In the end, order was only restored when troops were called in from Brighton. By about 1890 the troubles began to die down as magistrates took a firmer line with offenders, and the Army won the right to parade the streets of England without being molested.

Now with a wider vision of his work, Booth declared that his intention was 'to get his arms right around the world', but the initial step came about as if by accident. It happened in 1878 when Amos Shirley from Coventry emigrated to America in order to find a job. With his wife and daughter, he rented a disused factory in Philadelphia and started Army-type preaching services to packed meetings. Two years later, George Railton sailed to New York and opened up a centre for the Army, followed by ten others in different parts of the country.

At home, Booth never missed an opportunity for dealing with a problem whenever he saw the need. Crossing London Bridge late one night he discovered men lying at the side of the road, covered with newspapers and trying to sleep. Next day he called his son [Bramwell] and told him to do something about ☛

it. Bramwell rented a warehouse by the West India Docks which became the Army's first hostel for the homeless, complete with a food shop serving cheap meals. In England at that time there were an estimated three million poor people – people who were starving and homeless.

He called his plan the 'Cab-Horse Charter', pointing out that just as every cab-horse was given food, shelter and work, so people should enjoy the same rights. In order to achieve this aim he called for a public subscription of at least £100,000, and another £30,000 every year to maintain the scheme.

The scheme, which foreshadowed the Welfare State by some 20 years, provided for a job centre, a bank which advanced small loans, a farm for training workers and a missing persons bureau. Within nine years, the Army had found jobs for 9,000 workers and every night gave lodging to over 3000 men and women.

When Booth died his funeral service was held at Olympia, West London. Unknown to anyone, Queen Mary slipped in quietly and sat at the back beside a shabby but neatly-dressed woman who afterwards confessed to the Queen that the Army had saved her from prostitution. As the coffin passed down the aisle, the woman slipped three faded carnations on to the lid. Curious, the Queen asked the woman, 'What brought you here to the service?'

'Well,' the woman replied, 'he cared for the likes of us.' ◆

GEOFFREY HANKS

51

Lilian Westall: Housemaid

This passage from the unpublished autobiography of a housemaid gives a clear picture of what life was like for many working women and girls at the turn of this century. Lilian Westall was born in 1893, left school (aged fourteen) in 1907 and worked in domestic service till 1914. She worked in a munitions factory during both world wars and as a hotel maid between the wars. She retired in 1964, aged 71. Her story is a useful reminder that we have made some progress and, for today's fourteen-year olds, a warning of what life could have been like.

Suppose you are aged fourteen. Not all that long ago, you'd be leaving school at that age. Ready for a job. And if you were a girl, the chances were you'd start work 'in service'. That is, as a full-time maid living in your employer's house. That's what happened to Lilian Westall at the start of the twentieth century. Her weekly pay was five shillings which would have been worth about £25 in today's money. And even for that, she had to work very long hours. This is her description of two of her first jobs.

◆

I WENT TO Chiswick to work for a dentist and his wife. They were very respectable people and much better off than my last employers. I was to live in, and the wages were five shillings a week; it sounded good when the mistress told me.

I was the only servant. I had to be up at six in the morning, and there were so many jobs lined up for me that I worked till eleven o'clock at night. The mistress explained that she was very particular; the house had to be spotless always. After all, they were professional people and used to very high standards. I had to clean all the house, starting at the top and working ☞

down, sweeping and scrubbing right through. Hearthstoning the steps from the front door to the pavement took me an hour alone. I was most conscientious.

The meals I remember well. For breakfast I had bread and dripping. There were often mice dirts on the dripping to be scraped off first. Dinner was herring, every day; tea was bread and marge. I didn't have a bath during the month I was there, I wasn't given the opportunity; in fact there was no time to comb my hair properly, which was long – down to my waist; it grew so matted my mother had to cut a lot of it off when I finally came home again.

My room was in the attic. There was a little iron bed in the corner, a wooden chair and a washstand. It was a cold, bare, utterly cheerless room. At night I used to climb the dark stairs to the gloomy top of the house, go over to my bed, put the candle on the chair, fall on my knees, say my prayers, and crawl into bed too tired to wash. Once, quite exhausted, I fell asleep whilst praying and woke in the early hours of the morning, stiff and cold, still kneeling, with the candle burnt right down, and the wax running over the chair.

I gave in my notice in the first week, but a servant was obliged to stay at least one month in those days, and wasn't paid, of course, until the end of that time. I found out that a succession of girls before me had stayed only one month, but there were enough youngsters looking for work to ensure that a regular supply was maintained.

My employers must have accepted religious need, for they let me have Sunday off, and I was able to go to church. I had no shoes good enough to wear, however, and I remember having to make the hard decision of spending one shilling and eleven ☞

pence on a pair of shoes, only to find that they pinched my feet terribly, and I hobbled painfully to and from church.

I applied for a post in a block of flats in the Baker Street area. At that time I had a bad cold; I was sniffing and snuffling as I waited in the hall. The mistress came out to interview me; she was aghast.

'Good heavens!' she said. 'You could be *most* infectious.'

She went hurriedly back into the room, closed the door, and addressed me in a muffled voice from the other side.

'Have you ever had measles?'

'No, mum,' I said, thickly.

'Have you ever had chicken-pox or mumps?'

'No, mum. Not as far as I know.'

There was a pause. 'Well,' said the voice, 'perhaps you'll be all right. Now this is what you must do. Go to bed and I'll tell cook to take you up a glass of lemon water.' I did as I was told. Cook came up as instructed, I sipped my drink and settled down comfortably, thinking that this was a very pleasant start to a new job. Ten minutes later cook was up again. She wanted help with the dinner, she told me to jump out of bed at once and start giving a hand. Anyway, I'd enjoyed the lemon water.

The mistress was a difficult person to work for. She was for-ever feeling the chair legs or under the table for signs of dust. Now and again she would find some, and I would be scolded harshly for neglect. At the end of the month, after I'd had my wages of £1, I put my few things in the little basket I took everywhere, leaned out of the window and dropped it down into the courtyard below. I'd had enough; working hard was one thing, continual scolding was another. I made my way ☛

down the stairs. At the bottom I ran into the yard, picked up my basket and was away. ◆

LILIAN WESTALL

52

The Small Woman

Christian missionaries have on occasion, it must be admitted, behaved crassly and in a patronizing manner – if not worse. However, they have also done much good work and their courage and selflessness is worthy of admiration.

Gladys Aylward was made famous by the film The Inn of the Sixth Happiness *which was based on her work in China during the invasion of that country by Japan in the thirties. Notably, she led 100 refugee children to safety across a mountain range and across other hostile territory. This incident shows her determination to do what she believed was right.*

For centuries, it was the custom in China to bind up the feet and especially the toes of young girls – because it was fashionable to have small feet. Parents would happily inflict quite cruel torture on their children, for the sake of custom and fashion (and the hope that they would be more likely to find a husband).

One person who did a lot to break the habit was a Christian woman called Gladys Aylward who had gone to China to teach people about Christianity. Although she was small (her nickname was 'the Small Woman'), she herself had largish feet.

When the Chinese Government tried to break the foot-binding custom, a local official (called a Mandarin) gave her an unpopular job.

◆

WITH A CONTEMPTUOUS flick of his fan the Mandarin said: 'It must be *you* who become foot inspector.'

'Me!' repeated Gladys in a strangulated voice. At moments like these her conversation seemed to fail her.

'You are the only woman in the province with big feet. You must take the job! It is very simple. You will travel from village to village and tell the people of the Government's decree. You will assemble the women in the centre of the village or in their houses and inspect their feet. If the feet of the infants are bound, you will unbind them. You will be armed with my authority and report to me personally. Do you agree?'

As he talked, Gladys's thoughts fell into place. She wondered why she hadn't thought of it before. A mule out to the most distant villages? A guard to protect her? It was an opportunity without parallel for her to visit every part of the province, preaching wherever she went. But would he accept this?

'You must realize, Excellency,' she said, 'that if I accept this position I shall try and convert the people of this province to Christianity wherever I go!'

There was a short silence. The retainers in the background appeared frozen in horror. She wondered if she had committed an unpardonable error. Then he said quietly: 'I care nothing for your religion or to whom you preach. This is a matter for the conscience of each individual. But it is important that you should do this work. The Central Government is impatient.'

Gladys was knowledgeable enough about local conditions by that time to realize that the Central Government was probably demanding facts and figures about the incidence of foot-binding from this mountain province. She smiled inwardly. This was certainly something to write home about; a foot in-spector on the payroll of the Mandarin.

She bowed low. 'I am anxious to be of assistance,' she said. 'I will gladly accept your position.'

Gladys Aylward never forgot the first village at which she ar-rived as official foot inspector. A small dark-eyed girl, aged about three, clung to her mother's trousers and looked nervously up at Gladys. A single glance was sufficient to tell that her feet were bound.

'That one,' said Gladys, trying to insert a note of authority into her voice. 'Unbind her feet!'

Two women neighbours and a grandmother had now appeared in the room. The mother took the child on her lap and all four women began to undo the bandages. To cover her own nervousness, Gladys maintained a running commentary, which she improvised as each fold of cloth fell away.

'That's it. Come on now. Hurry up! If God intended little girls to have horrible stubby little feet, He'd have made them like that in the first place, wouldn't He? Feet are to walk with, not to shuffle up and down with, aren't they? I don't care if the husbands say you should do it or not. They should try it sometime, and see if they like hobbling about on little club feet. Any other man who tells you to do it goes to prison at once; that's the law now.'

The last bandage dropped, revealing tiny white feet with toes bent downwards and up into the soles.

'Look at those feet!' exclaimed Gladys. 'Disgraceful, absolutely disgraceful! How d'you expect the poor child to walk properly with those feet?'

She almost pushed the women away, and, kneeling down, gently prised the toes up and away from the sole. The child regarded her with wide, timid eyes.

'There,' said Gladys softly.

She massaged the foot tenderly. Suddenly there was a quick liquid giggle of sound from the child, who wriggled with delight.

The spell was broken. ◆

ALAN BURGESS

53

'Jumbo' Wilson and Changi Jail

Bishop Leonard Wilson was Bishop of Singapore when the city was captured by the Japanese during World War Two. He was not immediately arrested but spent several months smuggling items to those whom the Japanese had interned in various camps. Then, in 1943, he himself was suddenly imprisoned in the notorious Changi jail where his Christian witness inspired his fellow prisoners. After the war, he baptised and confirmed a group of his Japanese guards.

How would you cope if you were suddenly arrested and put in prison? Especially if you had committed no crime? Now imagine what it must be like to be kept in the worst imaginable conditions and to be tortured. That happened during World War Two to a Church of England bishop.

Bishop Wilson's nickname was 'Jumbo'. He was a large, cheerful man who was Bishop of Singapore when the Japanese invaded that city during that war. For several months, the Japanese seemed to take no notice of him: then they suddenly arrested him and put him in Changi prison camp. Conditions were not good.

◆

THE INTERNEES WERE crowded, irrespective of race, sex, or state of health, in small cells or cages. They were so crowded that they could not lie down in comfort. No bedding or covering of any kind were provided, and bright lights were kept burning overhead all night. From 8 a.m. to 10 p.m. inmates had to sit up straight on the bare floor with their knees up, and were not allowed to relax or put their hands on the floor, or talk, or move, except to go to the lavatory. Any infractions of the rigid discipline involved a beating by the sentries. There ☞

was one pedestal water-closet in each cell or cage, and the water flushing into the pan provided the only water supply for all purposes, including drinking. It should be recorded here that nearly all of the inmates suffered from enteritis or dysentery. No soap, towel, toilet articles or handkerchiefs were permitted, and inmates had no clothing other than that they were wearing. The food supplied, normally rice, occasional vegetables, and weak tea with no milk or sugar, was less than half of that supplied by our own prisons' department as punishment diet ... The three women taken from Changi prison were detained in exactly the same conditions as the men, and shared cells with male prisoners of all races. They were afforded no privacy, even for their most intimate requirements, and any attempt on the part of European men to screen them was broken down by the guards... The buildings resounded all day and night with blows, the bellowing of the inquisitors, and the shrieks of the tortured... In these conditions, and this atmosphere of terror, these men and women waited, sometimes for months, their summons to interrogation, which might come at any hour of the day or night.

What happened when Bishop Leonard Wilson was arrested was described by another clergyman who was with him in Singapore.

In the evening of his arrival Leonard was questioned, the interrogation being punctuated with beatings, for between three and four hours. On the following morning, he was again taken to the torture room, where he was made to kneel down. A three-angled bar was placed behind his knees. He was made to kneel on his haunches. His hands were tied behind his back and pulled up to a position between his shoulder blades. His head ☞

188

was forced down and he remained in this position for seven and a half hours. Any attempt to ease the strain from the cramp in his thighs was frustrated by the guards, who brought the flat of their hobnailed boots down hard on to his thighs. At intervals the bar between his knees would be twisted, or the guards would jump on to one or both projecting ends. Beatings and kicks were frequent. Throughout the whole of this time he was being questioned and told that he was a spy. This was one of the times when he lost his nerve and pleaded for death.

Again, the next morning, he was brought up from the cells, and this time tied face upwards to a table with his head hanging over the end of it. For several hours he remained in that position while relays of soldiers beat him systematically from the ankles to the thighs with three-fold knotted ropes.

JOHN HAYTER

In 1946, when the war was over, Bishop Wilson spoke in a church service about what had happened to him:

After my first beating I was almost afraid to pray for courage lest I should have another opportunity for exercising it, but my unspoken prayer was there, and without God's help I doubt whether I could have come through. Long hours of ignoble pain were a severe test. In the middle of that torture they asked me if I still believed in God. When, by God's help, I said, 'I do,' they asked me why God did not save me, and by the help of his Holy Spirit, I said, 'God does save me. He does not save me by freeing me from pain or punishment, but he saves me by giving me the spirit to bear it.' And when they asked me why I did not curse them, I told them that it was because I was a follower of Jesus Christ, who taught us that we were all brethren. I did not ☞

like to use the words, 'Father, forgive them'. It seemed too blasphemous to use Our Lord's words, but I felt them. ◆

LEONARD WILSON

54

Auschwitz, 1944

This is another reminder of the atrocities of German Nazism during World War II. Like the previous passage, it is offered as a reading that will nurture a horror at our potential to be inhuman and as one to be read 'lest we forget'.

Many people suffered at the hands of the German Nazis during World War II – especially those who were sent to concentration camps such as one at a place called Auschwitz.

One family called Offer was sent there. They had twin boys, Moshe and Tibi, who were twelve at the time. This is Moshe's story. One of the so-called camp doctors was a Dr Mengele who carried out terrible experiments on the prisoners – especially on twins.

◆

WE WERE TAKEN out of the ghetto and placed in cattle cars. The journey took eight days – eight days without water, without food. It is painful for me to remember what went on there. It is too horrible to describe.

We arrived at Auschwitz in May 1944. I can even tell you the exact time: ten o'clock in the morning.

When they opened the doors to our cattle cars, there were a lot of dead children. During the trip, some mothers couldn't bear to hear the cries of their hungry babies – and so they killed them. I remember two blond, very beautiful children in my car whose mother had choked them to death because she could not stand to watch them suffer.

When we stepped off the trains, we could hear soldiers yelling,

☞

191

'Men on one side, women on the other side.' Some German SS guards were also shouting, 'We want twins – bring us the twins!'

Dr Mengele was making the selections. He stood there, tall, nice-looking, and he was dressed very well, as if he wanted to make a good impression. He had very soft hands, and he made fast decisions. I heard my father cry out to them he had twins. He went over personally to Dr Mengele, and told him, 'I have a pair of twin boys.' Mengele sent some SS guards over to us. My twin, Tibi, and I were ordered to leave our parents and brothers and follow them.

But we didn't want to be separated from our mother, and so the Nazis separated us by force. My father begged Mengele to give us some food and water. But Mengele motioned to an SS guard, who beat him up on the spot. As we were led away, I saw my father fall to the ground.

One morning, at roll call, my number and that of Tibi were announced as part of the group that was going for experiments. We were taken with some other children by ambulance to a laboratory. The doctors took many X rays of us.

Then, Dr Mengele walked in. He was wearing a white gown, but underneath his gown I could see his SS uniform and boots. He gave me some candy, and then he gave me an injection that was extremely painful.

'Nicht angst,' Mengele told me in German. 'Don't be afraid.'

One day, my twin brother, Tibi, was taken away for some special experiments. Dr Mengele had always been more interested in Tibi. I am not sure why – perhaps because he was the older twin.

Mengele made several operations on Tibi. One surgery on his ☛

spine left my brother paralyzed. He could not walk anymore. Then they took out his sexual organs. After the fourth operation, I did not see Tibi anymore.

I cannot tell you how I felt. It is impossible to put into words how I felt. They had taken away my father, my mother, my two older brothers – and now, my twin.

I was put along with other camp survivors on a train bound for I don't know where. It was very crowded. I felt a push, and I fell off the train. To this day, I don't know if it was because I was so skinny, or because someone was trying to save me. In any case, I landed in a field. My hand was broken from the fall from the train. I crawled through the field, and I looked up to see a big German in uniform. I started crying and asked him to kill me. I told the Nazi I was a Jew. 'I fell off the train, and I cannot take it anymore, so go ahead and kill me.'

But the old German soldier said to me, 'I won't kill you – I am going to hide you.' And so he took me to an attic where they were storing corn and other grain.

This old German soldier was very nice. Every day, he brought me some dry biscuits and water. From the window of the attic, I saw the war coming to an end. I saw trains go by, carrying munitions. I watched German airplanes being shot down and parachutists jumping out – and being shot themselves.

One day, in the middle of the night, I heard artillery fire. After that night, the German didn't come anymore. I no longer got food or water. And so I began eating the corn and grain.

For four days, I was without any food or water. I was very hungry, very thirsty. But I stayed in the attic because I was also very frightened.

Then one day I looked out from the window and saw a jeep. It ☞

193

was carrying American soldiers. I was so weak, I couldn't walk, and so I crawled on my hands and knees from the attic to the jeep. The American GIs spotted me and rescued me. They carried me in their arms to their jeep, and they gave me candy and chocolates. ◆

LUCETTE MATALON LAGNADO AND SHEILA COHN DEKEL

55

'Chesh' and the Cheshire Homes

Leonard Cheshire was born in 1917 and died in 1992. As a bomber pilot in World War II, he flew over 100 missions and was awarded the VC. In 1945, he was Britain's official observer at the dropping of the atom bomb on Nagasaki (see passage 96). After the war, he devoted himself to social work and found his faith by helping the sick.

This is the story of a bomber pilot who was awarded the Victoria Cross for his bravery in the war – and whom many people think should now be called a saint.

◆

TWELVE BOMBER AIRCRAFT flew steadily through the moonlit sky, their engines droning. They were British bombers, flying over France, making for a town called Limoges. This was over 50 years ago, during World War II – when Britain was at war with Germany, and the German army had occupied France. That meant that German soldiers were everywhere in France – forcing many French people to work for them.

And that had happened at Limoges. There, the Germans had set up a factory to build aircraft engines to use in planes that would attack Britain. Consequently the British planned to bomb it before any of these engines could be finished – but the Germans had 300 French women working there throughout each night so the British would have to kill them if the factory was to be destroyed.

The man selected to lead the bombing raid was known to all his friends as 'Chesh'; his proper name was Group Captain Leonard Cheshire and he decided on this tactic. When the twelve aircraft reached Limoges, instead of bombing the ☞

factory straight away, Chesh flew his own plane in low – hurtling noisily over the factory roof. He turned his aircraft, saw all the factory lights go off – and zoomed in again. This time, in the moonlight, he saw the women running as fast as they could, away from the building. Despite the risk of being fired at by the Germans, Chesh dived a third and fourth time to give the French time to escape. Only then did the twelve Lancaster aircraft drop their heavy bombs – and fly safely back to Britain.

Next morning, a light aircraft flew high over Limoges and reported back that the German factory had been totally destroyed. A few weeks later, a secret message reached England from the French workers thanking the bomber pilots for the warning Chesh had given them.

After Britain had defeated Germany, he was given one more important job. Britain and America were still at war with Japan and it had been decided to use a new and terrible weapon against Japan: the atom bomb, which was very much more powerful than any bomb that had been used before. Group Captain Leonard Cheshire was told to fly near to the atom bomb when it was dropped, to see what happened.

It brought the war to an end. Japan gave in and stopped fighting – but that one bomb killed 40,000 people. Chesh felt it was a terrible weapon, but he also thought it was right to use it then because, otherwise, the war would have gone on longer and just as many people would have been killed.

During the war, he had been on 100 bombing missions – far more than most pilots – and he was awarded a very special medal for his bravery, the Victoria Cross. But once the war was over, in 1946, what was he to do? He tried various jobs until at last he made up his mind. He bought a house called Le Court at Liss in Hampshire and made it into a home for people who ☞

had been soldiers, sailors or airmen during the war and who now had no family and nowhere to live. All went well at first but, after a year, the home was so in debt that the project was ended.

At this time, Chesh found he kept remembering one evening during the war. He had been drinking in a night club in London where some people were talking about God. He joined in their conversation: 'God is just another word for our conscience. It's only a voice that tells us what's right and wrong,' said someone. 'Nonsense,' replied a woman. 'God is real.' And that was what Chesh kept thinking about – especially during a time he had flu.

When he was better (and living on his own at Le Court), he heard that Arthur Dykes, one of the men who used to share the house with him, was now very ill and in hospital. Chesh went to see him. He found that Arthur was so ill that there was no hope of recovery and, because of this, the people at the hospital wanted Arthur to leave so that the bed could be used for someone they *could* cure.

But Arthur had no family. Chesh decided he would look after Arthur himself – even though he didn't like the idea of coping with a very ill person and being with him when he died. Despite this, he brought Arthur back to Le Court to look after him; to wash him and feed him; and when Arthur became very weak, Chesh had to lift him in and out of bed.

Then, one day, the telephone rang, and it was someone in London who had heard that Chesh was looking after Arthur and wondered if he could also look after another old person. Next day, an ambulance brought an old lady called 'Granny' Haynes to Le Court. She was 94 and so weak she too needed ☞

197

everything doing for her. She was Leonard Cheshire's second patient.

By now, Arthur knew he was dying but, because he was religious, he was not afraid of death. He was certain he would go to heaven when he died – and Chesh became very interested in Arthur's strong faith.

Then came the day when Arthur died. While Chesh was waiting for the doctor, he picked up a book that Arthur had been reading, about a man had become a Roman Catholic Christian (like Arthur). Chesh was impressed and talked to the local priest about the Church and what it meant to be a Christian. Shortly afterwards, Chesh became a member of the Catholic Church.

By now, many more old and sick people had been brought to stay at Le Court. Leonard Cheshire needed help in looking after them and so a group of people formed a committee to help run what was becoming known as 'the Cheshire Home'. Chesh was horrified at this name. He didn't want to become famous for 'good work' — but he *was* famous (because of what he had done in the war) and since people knew about him, they were prepared to give money to help run 'the Cheshire Home'. Soon, a second home was opened in Cornwall and it was shortly after this that he decided he would devote the rest of his life to helping the old, the seriously ill and the handicapped. He decided this because of his Christian faith – but he never forced his beliefs on those he helped.

More and more new homes were started and there are now 270 Cheshire Homes all around the world. ◆

56

Sherpa Tenzing

The first people to climb Everest were Sir Edmund Hillary and Sherpa Tenzing, members of an expedition led by Colonel John Hunt. They reached the summit on 29 May, 1953. The news reached Britain on Coronation Day, 2 June. Tenzing found a message of religious toleration and also of the love of God in the achievement. This passage may also help to strengthen and encourage a sense of ambition in those who hear it.

Imagine what it must be like to do something no one else has ever done before. The first person to set foot on the Moon … the first person to sail round the world … the first person to reach the South Pole …

Not only have you managed to do something that has never been done before: you have completed your ambition. Back in 1953, a group of climbers made the attempt to be the first to reach the top of Mount Everest, the highest mountain in the world which stands between India and Nepal. That expedition was led by a man called John Hunt but the two who actually made it to the summit were a New Zealander, called Sir Edmund Hillary, and the expedition guide, Sherpa Tenzing. Sherpas are mountain people who live on the lower slopes of the Himalayas.

What would you have done on reaching the summit? This is Tenzing's story of what he did.

◆

WE STEPPED UP. We were there. The dream had come true …

What we did first was what all climbers do when they reach the top of their mountain. We shook hands. But this was not enough for Everest. I waved my arms in the air, and then threw ☞

them round Hillary, and we thumped each other on the back until, even with the oxygen, we were almost breathless. Then we looked round. It was 11.30 in the morning, the sun was shining, and the sky was the deepest blue I have ever seen. Only a gentle breeze was blowing, coming from the direction of Tibet, and the plume of snow that always blows from Everest's summit was very small.

We turned off our oxygen. Even there on top of the world it was possible to live without it, so long as we were not exerting ourselves. We cleared away the ice that had formed on our masks, and I popped a bit of sweet into my mouth. Then we replaced the masks. But we did not turn on the oxygen again until we were ready to leave the top. Hillary took out his camera, which he had been carrying under his clothing to keep it from freezing, and I unwound the four flags from around my axe. They were tied together on a string, which was fastened to the blade of the axe, and now I held the axe up, and Hillary took my picture. Actually he took three, and I think it was lucky, in those difficult conditions, that one came out so well. The order of the flags from top to bottom was United Nations, British, Nepalese, Indian; and the same sort of people who have made trouble in other ways have tried to find political meaning in this too. All I can say is that on Everest I was not thinking about politics. If I had been I suppose I would have put the Indian or Nepalese flag highest, though that in itself would have been a bad problem for me. As it is, I am glad that the UN flag was on top. For I like to think that our victory was not only for ourselves – not only for our own nations – but for all men [and women] everywhere.

I motioned to Hillary that I would now take his picture. But for some reason he shook his head; he did not want it. Instead he began taking more pictures himself, around and down on all ☞

sides of the peak, and meanwhile I did another thing that had to be done on the top of our mountain. From my pocket I took the package of sweets I had been carrying. I took the little red-and-blue pencil that my daughter, Nima, had given me. And, scraping a hollow in the snow, I laid them there. Seeing what I was doing, Hillary handed me a small cloth cat, black and with white eyes, that Hunt had given him as a mascot, and I put this beside them. In his story of our climb Hillary says it was a crucifix that Hunt gave him, and that he left on top; but if this was so I did not see it. He gave me only the cloth cat. All I laid in the snow was the cat, the pencil, and the sweets. 'At home,' I thought, 'we offer sweets to those who are near and dear to us. Everest has always been dear to me, and now it is near too.' As I covered up the offerings I said a silent prayer. And I gave my thanks. Seven times I had come to the mountain of my dream, and on this, the seventh, with God's help, the dream had come true.

I am a religious man. I believe in God and in the Way of Buddha, and in my home I have always had a prayer-corner or prayer-room, which is the Buddhist custom. But I am not an orthodox man. I do not believe greatly in ritual, and not at all in superstition. In my life I have been on too many mountains to think that they are the home of demons. Also, and more seriously, I have known too many men of other faiths to believe that they are all wrong and Buddhists alone are all right. I am not an educated man – not a lama or scholar who can speak of matters of theology. But I feel that there is room on earth for many faiths, as for many races and nations. It is with God Himself as it is with a great mountain. The important thing is to come to Him not with fear, but with love. ◆

SHERPA TENZING

with James Ramsay Ullman

201

57

Another Country: Nelson Mandela and Willem de Klerk

One of the greatest leaders of the twentieth century must be a man who spent a large part of it in prison, Nelson Mandela. Without undervaluing his part in the dismantling of apartheid in South Africa, the role of the white leader, Willem de Klerk is also noteworthy. The writer is an award-winning South African journalist.

For much of the twentieth century, South Africa was ruled by white Afrikaners who believed in white supremacy and apartheid: savage and often cruel separation of the races. Black people were moved off their good land, and did not have the vote (even though they formed the vast majority of the population). They had to live in separate areas, go to separate schools, and were barred from so-called 'white' areas and amenities.

South Africa's move from apartheid to a non-racial, democratic state (in which everyone has an equal vote) was one of the miracles of the century. It came about thanks to the black leader Nelson Mandela (whom the Afrikaners had kept in jail from 1962–1990) and also to the white Afrikaner who decided it was time for change.

◆

WHEN FREDERICK WILLEM de Klerk strode to the podium in South Africa's wood-panelled Chamber of Parliament at 11.15 on the morning of 2 February, 1990, to open his first parliamentary session as president, everyone expected him to make a reformist statement of some kind. Talk of reforming the apartheid system had been in the air for months. After ☞

seven years of racial unrest, there was a clamour for political change: international pressures were on the increase, the country was under economic and diplomatic siege, the black townships were on the boil, living standards for the white minority were declining, and there was a general state of emergency. But expectations were tinged with scepticism. There had been too many letdowns in the past.

But this time it was to be different. This time the surprise was an announcement that went far beyond anyone's expectations. Not even de Klerk's opening line – 'The general election of 6 September, 1989, placed our country irrevocably on the road of drastic change' – prepared his audience for what was to come. These masters of double-talk had used such language before. But 35 minutes later everything had indeed drastically changed. In that time the new president, short, rotund, balding, polished but without much charisma, head cocked to one side like a sparrow and bobbing on his right foot as he spoke, turned three centuries of his country's history on its head.

He didn't just change the country, he transmuted it. In those 35 minutes de Klerk unleashed forces that within four years would sweep away the old South Africa and establish an altogether new and different country in its place. Another country with another constitution and another flag and another national anthem. And above all, another ethos.

He demolished the old Afrikaner vision of a white South Africa, of a *volkstaat* that was theirs by divine right and without which they could not survive as a national entity, and ensured that in its stead a new black-led South Africa would arise, as alien to traditional Afrikaner thinking as Palestinian majority rule is to Israelis.

Nine days after de Klerk's speech, on 11 February, 1990, ☞

Nelson Mandela was released. As billions around the world watched on television, he walked with the stiff gait of an elderly man through the gates of Victor Verster Prison to freedom, with his wife, Winnie, beside him. 'Gee, you know, I never expected there would be so many people there,' he told me later, as though still astonished that he should have become such a celebrity.

Late that afternoon Mandela addressed a feverishly excited crowd of thousands on Cape Town's Grand Parade, peering uncertainly in fading light at the script of a speech through spectacles that kept slipping from his nose.

Thus the new South Africa as it emerges at the dawn of a new millennium. A new country with new horizons – and new divisions. There will be enormous new challenges, too, but the democratic structures are there to resolve them and grow through them. For as the graffito says, building a new nation, a great nation which this may yet become, is a continuous process. The construction never ends.

'Viva Verwoerd!' Of all the ironies one encounters in the changing value system of the new South Africa, none is more startling than that chant of praise at an African National Congress rally for a name which more than any other is identified with apartheid. Hendrik Verwoerd, prime minister from 1958 until he was struck down by an assassin's hand in 1966, was both chief architect and the most ruthless implementer of the doctrine that turned South Africa into the world symbol of racial oppression. He was apartheid's Karl Marx and Stalin rolled into one.

Yet in mid-1993 his grandson, Wilhelm, joined the ANC together with his wife, Melanie, and at a rally in Cape Town soon ☛

afterwards that astonishing chant was raised in praise of them. Long live Verwoerd!

But for Wilhelm Verwoerd there was another and more personal motive – the expiation of guilt. 'There is this personal cross I bear,' he says, referring to his surname. 'It is something I cannot escape. I have to confront the ghosts.' F W de Klerk's insistence that South Africans should simply forget the past angers him. 'There is no way we can do that,' Verwoerd says. 'Unless we confront the past and look at what happened, these ghosts will continue to haunt us. It must all come out so that the sunlight can heal the wounds.' ◆

ALLISTER SPARKS

58

Rock On, Bobby

Religious conversion and 'born again' Christianity are topics often ignored within the curriculum – perhaps because they can seem embarrassing. Nevertheless, evangelical churches are growing in number and thriving. This passage is included to show that (a) conversion is a very real experience for many believers and (b) there are believers in unlikely walks of life.

You may have seen the comedians Cannon and Ball on television. What you probably didn't know at the time is that Bobby Ball was a committed or 'born again' Christian. (Some Christians say they have been 'born again' when they make a firm decision to start following the teaching of Jesus.) This is how Bobby Ball became a Christian when he was at his most popular and successful.

◆

SLOWLY I BEGAN to hate the life I was living. I began to hate the drinking every night, and the things that it led to, but I couldn't stop, I was too far down the road. I tried reading the Bible. Why? I don't know, perhaps I was trying to find God then, but it was no use, even that didn't bring me any solace. I began to get feelings of guilt, but as usual I managed to shove them to the back of my mind. Yet somewhere deep inside me I knew that I had to face God. But then again, I reasoned to myself, I was no different from any other man, apart from those 'born-again Christians'. I hadn't really done anything wrong, and I was quite sure that God would forgive me when I was dead. How foolish!

During the Christmas of 1986 we returned once again to Bradford and as usual my old friend Max Wigley came in to see me. It was great to see him, now we could have more discussions and arguments about the Christian message. I asked him many questions and he answered them very simply. In fact what he told me made me realize that God could be very real. What you must realize was that to me God was only a force, something found in the Bible and at church or Sunday school. God was for people who didn't have anything else in their life. I told Max that now my daughter was growing up I was becoming very embarrassed about watching a video with her even though it was PG rated, because of the bad language. And I also told him about my concern for the state of the world and how I thought that if Jesus was real he was the only one who could sort it out. Max told me later that he could see Jesus already working in my life, but at that time becoming a born-again Christian was the furthest thing from my mind. Max and I had quite a few talks, and the more we talked the more my guilt came to the surface. A few days later Max came to see me again and said that he felt we should have a talk. It was about an hour before the curtain went up, so we sat down to talk. What he told me changed my life for ever. He told me about the love and justice of God, using this illustration.

One day a judge came into court wearing his fine robes and wig and sat in his elevated chair behind his big bench. He looked into the dock, and there in the dock was his son, whom he loved very much and wanted to forgive for all the sins he had committed. However, as a judge he had to be just and needed to hear the case against his son. He listened as his son's sins were read out. Then after the hearing he pronounced his son guilty, and fined him £500. He then took his wig off and his fine robes and came down from his big chair and bench and ☛

walked across the floor of the court. He took his cheque book out, signed a cheque for £500 and paid the fine for his son.

Max pointed out that the judge had been both loving and just and that is what God has done for us through Jesus Christ. I realized that Max was telling me that God knows we have broken his laws and that we deserved to be punished, but he also loves us enough to come himself and take the punishment that we deserve.

This illustration had a great effect on me; I had never looked at God in this way. It made him seem more real. I knew that I needed to be forgiven for what I had done and coming before God, as the judge's son had in the illustration, seemed the only way. I told Max that I would like to become a Christian that night and asked him if he would wait until the end of the show. He said he would and then went around the other dressing-rooms to see the other artistes. The curtain went up and everyone got on with the show. But as I was going through the show I couldn't get Max out of my mind. Had I said the right thing? Did I want to become a Christian? Was I ready to become one? I felt that I had done the wrong thing by saying I wanted to become a Christian, because I felt I wasn't good enough, I felt I had sinned too much. I also felt that if I committed myself to the Lord and He was real I was sure that I would let Him down. It's not that I didn't want to get to know the Lord, it's just that my way of life had become like a drug to me. I felt very frightened and threatened. ◆

BOBBY BALL

59

The Princess

Sikhism (like Judaism) is not a proselytizing religion: it does not seek converts – and most Sikhs are of Indian or Punjabi origin. Some westerners have, however, converted to the faith. (See also passages 45 and 71.)

You may know that most Sikh men wear a turban (because they never cut their hair and the turban is to keep it tidy) and you may think that all Sikhs are Indian in appearance. Not so. Some Europeans convert to Sikhism because they approve of its teaching. One such person is Satya Kaur who was born in Portugal. When she became a Sikh she took the name Kaur, which all Sikh women have, and which means 'princess'.

◆

SATYA KAUR, FORMERLY Isabel Cepĕda, is a Portuguese Sikh – the only one she knows of. Converts to Sikhism are unusual, for it is in principle a tolerant religion which recognizes other faiths and does not proselytize. Its homeland is the Punjab, the land of five rivers now divided between India and Pakistan, and most of the Sikhs around the world have Punjabi roots.

The Punjabi Sikhs in London regard Satya and her Scottish husband, Shiv Charan Singh, with amazement, which takes one of two forms. Some think they are 'weirdoes' and wonder what their families must be like; others think they are wonderful and holy and want to fall at their feet. The response of non-Sikhs varies too. Satya used to be mocked and abused as she walked down the street – it happens less now, perhaps because she has relaxed into her Sikh identity and her elegant ☞

turban is taken for fashion. Her husband, however, stands out: 'with a big orange beard down to here', she indicates her midriff, laughing, 'and a big turban and blue eyes and a pale face, and he often looks scruffy anyway. He arouses a lot of antagonism,' she adds mildly.

In 1987 she took *Amrit*, Sikh initiation, and later that year she married her present husband, who had converted while working in Holland as a chef in a Sikh restaurant – called the Golden Temple.

The word *sikh* means 'disciple' – a follower of the teachings of the Ten Gurus. The last Guru died in 1708, having ordained that from then on the ultimate spiritual authority for the Sikhs would rest in the *Guru Granth Sahib*. This, their holy book, contains the writings of the Gurus, as well as poetry by Sufi saints and others. It is built around the 974 hymns of Guru Nanak, the First Guru, who was born into a Hindu family in 1469. 'India at the time was under the Moghuls and in a rocky state. There were forced conversions to Islam, and the Hindus were caught up in rituals,' Satya says. 'It needed a kind of cleansing, so that people could come back to the realities of spiritual life.'

Guru Nanak worked as an accountant as a young man, but was preoccupied with God. 'There is no Hindu or Muslim, so whose path shall I follow?' he declared after an experience which he described as being taken to the court of God and into his presence. 'I shall follow God's path.' From then on he lived as an itinerant preacher, seeking to remind people of the underlying truth of religion and warning them away from the increasing emphasis on ritual. Ironically, he became the founder of a new religion.

'Sikhs believe in one God,' says Satya. 'He's the Creator of ☞

everything and he pervades everybody. He's inside us, outside us, he's before us and he's after us; he's got no name, no form ... it's there and it's everything, it's just an almighty force.' The *Guru Granth Sahib*, she says, was written by men in a state of bliss and inspiration, with the light of God inside them. 'By chanting it, reading it, absorbing it, you get into the same state.' She brings down one of the eight volumes from the top room of the house, where it must always be kept, and opens the white cloth it is wrapped in as a sign of respect. The pages are printed in the original Gurmukhi, with translations in English and in the thick black characters of modern Punjabi. 'Whenever I am stuck or confused I say a prayer and open it and read whatever is there, and it usually uplifts me.'

For those who take *Amrit* (and this is a sign of commitment not made by all) there is a strict code of conduct. Every day they must get up early, have a bath, and meditate on God's name. Five prayers a day are required – three in the morning and two at night. Satya usually says hers on the train, on the way to the hospital where she is training as a midwife.

They must never cut their hair or shave or change their form in any way – 'Well, my ears were already pierced and I sometimes wear earrings, but I shouldn't,' Satya says. They should be householders, not celibates; they should earn their own living and give a tenth of it away. They are vegetarian (although some Sikhs simply avoid meat that is *halal*, slaughtered according to Muslim ritual), and do not drink or smoke or take any other intoxicants that alter the state of the mind. There is a lightness with constraints, which pervades her style and her philosophy. She rarely talks of darkness. 'It's normal to keep breaking your vows, nobody's perfect, God is forgiving. You've just got to keep doing your best.' ◆

JUDITH RICE

211

60

Parents

This 'prose poem' was written as a celebration of his late father (and of his mother) by the poet Adrian Mitchell: it stands as a tribute to all parents and might be used at the time of Mothering Sunday or Father's Day. (See also passage 90.)

Young people are often expected to dislike or even hate their parents – or at least not to get on with them. Of course that's not true but often it's not easy to admit your parents can also be friends. When the poet Adrian Mitchell's father died, he realized he had never written about his father; had never paid tribute to him. So he wrote this.

◆

MY FATHER DIED the other day and I would like to write about him. Because I think of them together, this means also writing about my mother, who died several years ago.

About a thousand people called her Kay, most of them people she helped at some time, for she was what chintzy villains call a 'do-gooder'. Nobody ever called her that to her face or in my family's hearing; if they had, she'd have felt sorry for them. Both her brothers were killed in World War I. She wore two poppies on Remembrance Day. She divided her life between loving her family, bullying or laughing innumerable committees into action rather than talk, giving, plotting happiness for other people, and keeping up an exuberant correspondence with several hundred friends.

She was not afraid of anyone. She was right. A Fabian near-pacifist, she encouraged me to argue, assuming right-wing ☞

positions sometimes so that I was forced to fight and win the discussion.

She tried to hoist the whole world on her shoulders. After each of her first two cancer operations, on her breasts, she seemed to clench her fists and double the energy with which she gave. She wasn't interested in unshared pleasure.

After the second operation she answered the door one day to a poor woman whom she didn't know. The woman asked where 'the wise woman' lived. My mother knew who she meant – a rich clairvoyant who lived down the road. Not trusting that particular witch, my mother asked what was wrong. The poor woman's doctor had told her she must have a breast removed, and she was very scared. My mother said, but there's nothing to that, look – and she took out the two rolled socks which she kept in her empty brassière and threw them up into the sunlight and then caught them again. So the poor woman came in, drank tea, forgot many fears, and went away knowing that she had seen the wise woman.

People called my father Jock. Face tanned from working in his garden, he survived four years in the trenches of World War I. He spoke very little. When he talked it was either very funny or very important. He only spoke to me about his war twice, and then briefly. In my teens I wrote a short, Owen-influenced poem about the war. My father read it, then told me of a friend who, during the lull between bombardments, fell to all fours, howled like an animal and was never cured.

Usually he avoided company. There was something in other people which frightened him. He was right. At the seaside he would sit on the farthest-out rock and fish peacefully. When visitors called at our house he would generally disappear into his jungle of raspberry canes and lurk.

Maybe there were 20 or 30 people in the world whose company he really enjoyed. They were lucky; he was a lovely man. Like Edward Lear, he was most at ease with children, who instantly read, in the lines radiating from corners of his eyes, that this was a man who understood their games and jokes.

He was short and lean and had fantastic sprouting Scottish eyebrows. He was a research chemist, but that didn't mean he only took an interest and pride in my elder brother's scientific work. He let me see how glad he was that I wrote and I still remember the stories he used to write for me and my brother.

A year or so before he died he was in London for the day. My father sometimes voted Tory, sometimes Liberal, but when he began to talk about Vietnam that day, his face became first red and then white with anger about the cruelty and stupidity of the war. I seldom saw him angry and never so angry as at that moment, a man of 70, not much interested in politics, all the grief of 1914-18 marching back into his mind.

People sometimes talk as if the ideological conflicts between generations have to be fought out bloodily, as if it is inevitable that children should grow to hate their parents. I don't believe this. Our family was lucky: my brother and I were always free to choose for ourselves – knowing that, however odd our decisions, we were trusted and loved. We all loved one another and this love was never shadowed. ◆

ADRIAN MITCHELL

THOUGHTS FOR A DAY

'Do not expect waterlilies in every pond'
INDIAN PROVERB
'Not to know is bad, but not to wish to know is worse'
WEST AFRICAN PROVERB

61

When the Curtain Goes Up ...

This very short passage may seem to be about death but it is actually about life and the way we live it. Its moral could said to be 'Don't waste your life' or 'How you live each day really matters'. The last sentence, referring to us at the time of our death, may benefit from repetition.

This very short reading may seem to be a warning about death. It's not. So just what is its message or moral?

◆

HAVE YOU EVER had to act in a play or perform in a concert? If so, you must have spent many hours rehearsing or practising beforehand. If you stumbled or forgot your lines you had another chance – dozens more chances. That is what rehearsals are for.

However, when the curtain goes up and those rows of empty chairs are now full of people, you have no more chances to practise. Now your performance is real, in full view of the public. The show must go on!

Dying will be like that. Our lives are rehearsals for the moment when the curtain of our body is withdrawn and we are left face to face with God. There will be no more chances to practise, to go back to the beginning and start again. What we have become, we now are, for ever. ◆

DOROTHY H WELLS

62

Our Doubts are Traitors

Hope, along with faith and charity, is one of the three great virtues praised by St Paul. Loss of hope is surely one of the greatest setbacks that can befall a young person. This passage is an exhortation to hope, not doubt.

As you'll find out if you stay on at school to take A levels, the results are usually announced on a Thursday in the middle of August.

Even though it's the middle of the school holidays, you'll find that several of the staff come into school to see how well their pupils have done. But this is a story not about a member of staff but a sixth-former.

◆

ANDREW HAD BEEN studying English Literature for the last two years. He'd absolutely set his heart on getting to university – but he knew he hadn't done his best in the exam room. And yes, when the results were published, he'd failed: his grades wouldn't get him to university. He was sitting there in the school hall, looking incredibly depressed.

His tutor talked to him, and tried to cheer him up. She tried telling him it wasn't the end of the world; he could study in the evenings, re-sit the exams, it'll be different a second time. But in his disappointment, Andrew snapped at her, 'I'm a failure. Don't give me *hope*'.

Being hopeful, full of hope; trying to look on the bright side can seem pretty naive. It's much smarter to be cynical, to *expect* things to turn out badly. 'Being realistic' we sometimes call it. And yes, when we're really depressed, even close to complete ☞

despair, someone who comes along and chatters about things 'turning out all right in the end' can seem pretty unhelpful. So what practical use is 'hope'? What *is* hope?

For the Christian, it's one of the three great virtues. There's a famous passage in one of St Paul's letters [*I Corinthians 13:1-13*] when he talks about faith, hope and charity or (as some translations have it) faith, hope and love – and because Paul goes on to stress the importance of love, we sometimes forget he's also saying how important hope is.

After Andrew had left the school that afternoon, his tutor thought of all the things she could have said if only she'd thought of them at the right time. Like a couple of lines from one of the plays they'd been studying, Shakespeare's *Measure for Measure*.

In that play, a man called Claudio is imprisoned and sentenced to death by the harsh and scheming Angelo. But Claudio's been able to send a message to his sister, Isabella, asking her to go to Angelo to plead for his life. But Isabella knows the sort of man Angelo is. Her mind is full of doubts, doubts that she has any chance of succeeding and so she's afraid to go and plead her brother's cause. But someone points out to her that the doubts that often fill our minds are not our 'friends', they're more like enemies. As Shakespeare puts it:

Our doubts are traitors
And make us lose the good we oft might win
By fearing to attempt.

Whether it's something major or something comparatively trivial, it's easy to let our doubts put us off trying something new. 'Oh, it's not worth trying, someone else'll already have had that idea.' Or we'll hesitate to ask someone a favour. 'It's not worth it. They'll only say no.' ☞

And it's the same when we're wondering whether we might do something that could help a friend or neighbour or someone in the same year. 'Oh, they won't want me interfering,' we say to ourselves. But when you find yourself thinking like that, remember those words of Shakespeare:

Our doubts are traitors
And make us lose the good we oft might win
By fearing to attempt.

Shakespeare knew that doubt cripples, hope makes things possible. And we often might fail to do something good or helpful simply by 'fearing to attempt' it. ◆

63

Oh Well

This was written as a Christian prayer but it is one in which many believers can share: its hopes and petitions are ones we might all echo.

This reading is a prayer which Christians and indeed believers of other faiths might wish to make to God. Even if you don't believe, as you listen to it, you might still agree with the hopes that it expresses.

◆

Dear Lord,
help me to live in such a way
that I daily become more kind
to those around me.

I'm so glad
that all the things I've done wrong in the past
are put behind me, and You have
forgiven me, even if
everyone else keeps moaning.

Help me to concentrate
on getting my life right for today and
tomorrow. Give me the insight
to see where You are guiding me,
the perseverance to keep on going on
in the path You want me to go on.

Help me to love genuinely, even if
    I'm tired,
    or irritated,
    or out of patience.

☛

Help me to grow a little better
day by day,
and then perhaps one day I might
look back and have the confidence to think
'Well, Lord – at least today
I didn't get it too far wrong!' ◆

ROSALYN RUSHBROOK

64

Love is the Solution

This reading (like passage 3) was written by a Roman Catholic priest. It has two simple messages: don't judge by appearances; and love, in its all its senses, is the only solution to the problems of the world.

When you see a grubby, drunken tramp, it's easy to jump to certain conclusions about the sort of person he or she might be. This is a true story and it was written by a priest who got to know one particular tramp.

◆

DID I EVER tell you about Martin? Well, that is not his name but if he should happen to see this, he will know who I mean. Martin was a delightful and vast Irishman, full of gentle charm and blarney. His eyes would twinkle as he told you the next downright lie and he gazed fixedly at you until you felt ashamed at disbelieving him. He was equally charming, drunk or sober, and one almost looked forward to his (usually expensive) visits. Knowing full well that one was being taken for a ride, one yet parted with a week's rent, enough for a new pair of working boots, or the price of a cuppa. Martin drove a hard bargain, and although he normally got less than he asked, one always gave more than one had intended.

Martin could never – or would never – hold down a job, or anything else for that matter. I recall, vividly, going to his lodgings one evening to pay his landlady a week's rent in advance. Some time after midnight that same night he called me from my bed drunk (Martin, not me) to say farewell as he had decided to leave the town. He had talked the money back from his landlady and drunk it. She would not have him back and ☞

now he had the decency (I had another word for it) to come and say goodbye to me.

The next time I saw Martin – many months later – he was in a bad state. He was drunk again, but this time he was in a very nasty mood. By now he was far gone on meths and his physical condition was much deteriorated. But he was still a tall and strong man, not readily to be crossed. Being one of nature's cowards, I tried to pacify him, and at the same time refused him money to buy more drink. Offers of food were rudely swept aside. Moreover, Martin was inside the house and refused to leave. Any attempt to steer him towards the door was met with violence. Neither my father nor I could achieve anything.

It was then that my housekeeper offered to help. On the principle that fools step in where angels fear to tread, I accepted, but was horrified with the simplicity of her solution. She filled a large jug with cold water and advanced on Martin. I expected her to throw it at him and counselled less violent methods. Ignoring my bleating she advanced towards her quarry. She grabbed his belt, pulled his trousers forward and poured the water down the front. Martin's face went as ferocious as anything I'd ever seen and I realized the moment of violence had come. But no! Suddenly he began to laugh and laugh until he was helpless – and so were we all with sheer relief. He was then persuaded to take a bath, sober up, and after a rest and food went on his way. We were sad to see him go, for clearly he was at the end of the downward path and the next step would be prison or even death. Again we were to be surprised.

About a year later, a local holiday camp had a special week for severely handicapped people, and a 'phone call from Martin, in London, asked us to go and see a certain girl at the camp. She was in an advanced stage of disseminated sclerosis, and quite ☞

helpless in most ways. Martin had found her deserted by her family in London, befriended her and then fallen in love. He waited on her day and night, fought all the social agencies for her, changed his way of life and gave up drinking. At first they lived in some squalor – when I visited I was far too fastidious to sit down – but Martin got a job, improved himself, and they moved into a flat. He now devotes himself entirely to her: working all day, caring for her every need, lifting her in and out of bed, washing, cleaning, cooking.

It all sounds too good to be true. In fact, if I had not been involved myself I should not have believed it. The lesson, if any, is that we are never entitled to judge any man from his appearance, his works, or his behaviour until we know his true condition. All too often we jump at the superficial explanation or try to alleviate instead of treating the cause. No one approves of hatred or violence, laziness or dirt, but perhaps if every man and every nation could only fall in love much would stop. Love does not always choose the beautiful. It settles on all kinds of people and causes. Many of us will not believe that love is a solution. In fact, it is the only one. ◆

FR ROBERT MANLEY

65

Prayer for Today

This American prayer was the choice of the rock musician Rick Wakeman when he was interviewed for the BBC Radio 4 early Saturday morning Prayer for the Day *programme.*

Some of you may know the music of the rock keyboard player and composer Rick Wakeman who played with the bands Yes and The Strawbs and who recorded several solo albums. He's now a Christian and he was once interviewed on a radio programme where he was asked to choose his favourite prayer. This is what he said.

◆

'I DISCOVERED THIS prayer by accident. I was doing some recording which required some devotional lyrics and which meant I had to choose some prayers, so I got the old *Book of Common Prayer* out and another book just called *Famous Prayers*, and I thought to myself, "This won't take me too long, a swift evening having a look through those ... ." Unbelievable! I went through them hunting for weeks!'

What he found was a prayer he describes as wonderfully pertinent to his own situation, as he begins to look back over his 25 years as a leading rock musician. For a moment he looks away and smiles a little as he remembers the success and failure of his early career:

'Way back in the '70s, I was given wealth. But I was also given the "talent" – call it what you like! – to get rid of it very quickly, and at the end of the day I sit here now a wiser and a happier man. I wouldn't say I craved to have lots of money (and I

☞

haven't got it any more), it just appeared, and I was totally unprepared for it and didn't know what to do with it, just like some women are given beauty and don't know what to do with that.

'We should all be satisfied with our lot, grateful for whatever gift we've been given, however tiny and however small, and sometimes we can be given something, or sent something, that we think, "Oh, this is desperately unfair, I don't want this." But if you look into it, there is a meaning, and that's what makes this prayer so clever for me.'

We carry on talking for a while, straying from the subject a bit, to talk about his family life, the way his life has changed, and about the music he's playing on his six-week British tour. It all leads him back to the prayer.

'I genuinely do feel that I am much cared for and, for me, certainly my unspoken prayers are answered. When you accept the Lord into your life, and you accept Christianity whole-heartedly, that is the initial stage of tuning in, and that is when you start to understand a lot more things. That is when people's lives open up an awful lot more.'

RICK WAKEMAN
interviewed by James Whitbourn

I asked for strength that I might achieve:
I was made weak that I might learn humbly to obey.

I asked for health that I might do greater things:
I was given infirmity that I might do better things.

I asked for riches that I might be happy:
I was given poverty that I might be wise.

I asked for power that I might have the praise of men:
I was given weakness that I might feel the need of God.

I asked for all things that I might enjoy life:
I was given life, that I might enjoy all things.

I got nothing I had asked for
but everything that I had hoped for.

Almost despite myself
my unspoken prayers were answered.

I am, amongst all men,
most richly blessed. ◆

ANONYMOUS CONFEDERATE SOLDIER
DURING THE AMERICAN
CIVIL WAR

66

What a Piece of Work

This reading is another meditation on the theme of optimism or, in Christian terminology, hope.

If I say the word *Hamlet* to you, the chances are you'll immediately picture something. It may be a small cigar – it may be something to do with Shakespeare's play about the moody Prince of Denmark. In that play, Hamlet learns from a ghost that his father has been murdered by his uncle. Hamlet is unsure whether he should take revenge on his uncle. This is a story about the play, not a small cigar.

◆

ONCE UPON A time, not so long ago, a man called Arnold went to see a production of *Hamlet*. It wasn't actually a brilliant production: what was special was the fact that Arnold had never seen the play before; he knew nothing at all about the plot, but he was absolutely hooked, fascinated by Hamlet's doubts; then by Hamlet's scheming and later by his uncle's intrigues against him. And there was something else. As Arnold said when the play was over, he'd been amazed how full of quotations it was. How many sayings in the English language actually began life in Shakespeare's play. 'To be, or not to be … ' 'Alas, poor Yorick!', 'Brevity is the soul of wit', 'More in sorrow than in anger'. There are hundreds of them.

Perhaps that's why it's a great play. Many would say the greatest ever written. And perhaps that's because Shakespeare really seems to have understood people: what makes them happy, sad, jealous, eager, competitive and, yes, sexy. He does seem to have had a profound insight into not just human nature but into our relationship with God.

And nowhere is this clearer than in some lines in *Hamlet*. At one point in the play, Prince Hamlet is in the deepest despair, overcome with profound gloom. As he says, 'I have lost all my mirth.' No wonder. He's learned that his father was murdered, his mother has hastily married his uncle – and, he's also just learned, it was that uncle who murdered his father. And in this deep, deep depression he begins to think of suicide.

The Earth, the sky, the heavens, the people around him seem to hold no attraction for him. And yet ... even in that despair, he can still see what is wondrous about a human being; about our mental and physical capabilities. And this is what he says:

> What a piece of work is a man, how noble in reason, how infinite in faculties, in form and moving, how express and admirable; in action, how like an angel; in apprehension, how like a god: the beauty of the world; the paragon of animals.

The paragon, the perfection of all the animal kingdom, that is what he realises humans are. It may be hard to believe this on days when the news is full of stories about war and suffering, about cruelty and thoughtlessness – but as Hamlet (or rather, Shakespeare) suggests, people can come close to being like the angels.

When we're young, we tend to prefer films and plays to end unhappily because tragedies seem more lifelike. As we get older, we prefer happy endings because we're wise enough to see what's possible. We dare to hope for the best.

Hoping for the best is not just some form of escapism. In the Bible, St Paul taught that one of the three great Christian ☛

virtues is hope – and Christian hope isn't just a matter of wishing good luck'll come our way. It's a 'sure and certain hope' in the next life; and it's a matter of expecting, of believing that even in this world we can be just a little like the angels. ◆

67

Meditations

Marcus Aurelius was Emperor of Rome from 161 until his death in 180 CE. Born into an aristocratic Spanish family, he was highly educated and a philosopher of the Stoic school. The Stoics taught that nature is controlled by divine reason and that human reason is a spark of the divine 'fire'. It is our duty to live in harmony and reason, indifferent to pain and other setbacks.

Stoicism has been attacked by some Christian writers (e.g. by Milton and T S Eliot) as being the reverse of Christian humility and it can seem a cold philosophy. Nevertheless there is a humanity and attractiveness about what are always called The Meditations of Marcus Aurelius (which he simply titled 'To Himself'). They were written in Greek in various army camps as he struggled to preserve his empire from invasion on the Danube front, war with Parthia, internal rebellions and plagues.

It is suggested that just one or two meditations be read on any one occasion.

These are the thoughts of a Roman Emperor called Marcus Aurelius. They were written over 1800 years ago. Do you think they're still true?

◆

THINK OF YOUR many years of procrastination; how the gods have repeatedly granted you further periods of grace, of which you have taken no advantage. It is time now to realize the nature of the universe to which you belong, and of that controlling Power whose offspring you are; and to understand that your time has a limit set to it. Use it, then, to advance your enlightenment; or it will be gone, and never in your power again.

Hour by hour resolve firmly to do what comes to hand with correct and natural dignity, and with humanity, independence, ☛

and justice. Allow your mind freedom from all other consid-erations. This you can do, if you will approach each action as though it were your last, dismissing the wayward thought, the emotional recoil from the commands of reason, the desire to create an impression, the admiration of self, the discontent with your lot. See how little a man needs to master, for his days to flow on in quietness and piety: he has but to observe these few counsels, and the gods will ask nothing more.

Be like the headland against which the waves break and break: it stands firm, until presently the watery tumult around it sub-sides once more to rest. 'How unlucky I am, that this should have happened to me!' By no means; say rather, 'How lucky I am that it has left me with no bitterness; unshaken by the present, and undismayed by the future.' The thing could have happened to anyone, but not everyone would have emerged unembittered. So why put the one down to misfortune, rather than the other to good fortune? Can a man call anything at all a misfortune, if it is not a contravention of his nature; and can it be a contravention of his nature if it is not against that na-ture's will? Well, then: you have learnt to know that will. Does this thing which has happened hinder you from being just, magnanimous, temperate, judicious, discreet, truthful, self-respecting, independent, and all else by which a man's nature comes to its fulfilment? So here is a rule to remember in future, when anything tempts you to feel bitter: not, 'This is a misfor-tune,' but 'To bear this worthily is good fortune.'

At day's first light have in readiness, against disinclination to leave your bed, the thought that 'I am rising for the work of man'. Must I grumble at setting out to do what I was born for, and for the sake of which I have been brought into the world? ☛

Is this the purpose of my creation, to lie here under the blankets and keep myself warm? 'Ah, but it is a great deal more pleasant!' Was it for pleasure, then, that you were born, and not for work, not for effort? Look at the plants, the sparrows, ants, spiders, bees, all busy at their own tasks, each doing his part towards a coherent world-order; and will you refuse man's share of the work, instead of being prompt to carry out Nature's bidding? 'Yes, but one must have some repose as well.' Granted; but repose has its limits set by nature, in the same way as food and drink have; and you overstep these limits, you go beyond the point of sufficiency; while on the other hand, when action is in question, you stop short of what you could well achieve.

You have no real love for yourself; if you had, you would love your nature, and your nature's will. Craftsmen who love their trade will spend themselves to the utmost in labouring at it, even going unwashed and unfed; but you hold your nature in less regard than the engraver does his engraving, the dancer his dancing, the miser his heap of silver, or the vainglorious man his moment of glory. These men, when their heart is in it, are ready to sacrifice food and sleep to the advancement of their chosen pursuit. Is the service of the community of less worth in your eyes, and does it merit less devotion?

There is a type of person who, if he renders you a service, has no hesitation in claiming the credit for it. Another, though not prepared to go so far as that, will nevertheless secretly regard you as in his debt and be fully conscious of what he has done. But there is also the man who, one might say, has no consciousness at all of what he has done, like the vine which produces a cluster of grapes and then, having yielded its rightful fruit, looks for no more thanks than a horse that has run his ☞

race, a hound that has traced his quarry, or a bee that has hived her honey. Like them, the man who has done one good action does not cry it aloud, but passes straight on to a second, as the vine passes on to the bearing of another summer's grapes.

Never let the future disturb you. You will meet it, if you have to, with the same weapons of reason which today arm you against the present. ◆

MARCUS AURELIUS

68

The Incomplete World

This 'Thought for the Day' was one of Rabbi Lionel Blue's talks on the BBC Radio 4 Today programme and is obviously suitable for most Monday mornings.

Have you ever felt God isn't making a very good job of running the world? Have you ever thought as you wake up on a Monday morning that it's all too much? You just don't want to get up and face the world? This is the answer of a Jewish rabbi (or teacher).

◆

YOU WAKE UP on a Monday morning, pick up the newspaper, switch on the radio, and wonder what sort of world you're in. You've got your own personal problems – there's the tax form falling through the letter box and an awkward interview with your boss, and there's no marge left in the fridge. You feel gruff and growly already. And when you turn on the radio, you shoot bolt upright and whimper because there's been another plane disaster – this time on a route you've flown on many times – death is very close. You need a cup of tea fast.

Some people say God is everywhere and in everything, so evil doesn't really exist. It's just good in disguise. We can't see it, that's all. I once tried to see the world that way and it made me cross-eyed. Neither concentration camps nor plane disasters are good in disguise. Dead bodies, weeping relatives are never good.

Some people take the opposite line and say if hell exists, then this is it. But that doesn't fit the facts either. I meet too much

☛

goodness and love in this world for that – too much charity, too much kindness.

I think things go wrong and disasters happen because the world is an incomplete sort of place. Like you and me, it's struggling towards its own perfection, but it hasn't got there. It's still going through its birth pangs.

So what's our place in it? Well I once sat in a church not far from a concentration camp, and thought about all the tragedies that had happened there. 'Why, God, didn't you take a hand in it?' I cried. Then I thought – how can God have hands? – He's pure spirit. But if He hasn't got hands, is He any use? Then suddenly it hit me. We're God's hands in the world and He works through us to complete His creation.

So don't dive back under your duvet as you read the news. Religion means facing facts not fleeing from them. Get up quickly, have your cup of tea, and work out what you can do. Can you comfort someone on the plane, or give something to a disaster fund? Monday morning can be dreadful – that's true, but that's why you're here. You might look and feel a mess but you're God's representative – His hands on earth, working to complete His creation.

It's what we were created for. So let's get up, and get on with it. ◆

RABBI LIONEL BLUE

69

Keeping an Open Mind

The two anecdotes within this passage encourage us to keep an open mind. They also hint at the fact that our inability to imagine the next life is not an automatic reason for disbelief.

Passages 69–75 may be used as a sequence of readings.

You can open and shut your eyes – but can you open and shut your mind? How much of the time is it shut to new ideas? Too often we're not prepared to *change* our minds, despite what we're told. This reading starts with a story about people we often call Eskimos but who actually prefer to be known as the Inuit people.

◆

ONCE UPON A time, a certain Greenland Inuit worked as a guide on one of the United States Polar expeditions. Later, as a reward for his help, he was taken to New York City for a short visit. He was filled with amazement at all he saw there: the skyscrapers, buses, motorway bridges and so on.

When he returned to his own village, he told his neighbours about the houses that reached into the clouds, about the smaller houses that moved along the trail, with people sitting in them as they moved; and about the tracks that left the ground and soared high over the river. Indeed he told them about all the wonders of the city in the best way he could – for there were no Inuit words for many of the things he had seen.

His neighbours looked at him as if he was mad and walked away. And ever afterwards, throughout the whole village he was known as Sagdluk, a name which means The Liar: his proper name was completely forgotten. ☞

Now it happened some years later that another explorer (called Knud Rasmussen) made a trek from Greenland right across the northern snowfields to Alaska – and he too employed an Inuit guide. This man was called Mitek (which is Inuit for Eider Duck).

After this Arctic journey had been completed, he too was given the reward of a holiday – this time in both Copenhagen in Denmark and New York. In both cities, like Sagdluk, he saw many things for the first time and was impressed. But he knew what had happened to Sagdluk and was determined he should not become known as a liar. So, on his return home, he decided not to tell the truth. Instead, he told his neighbours things they would understand.

He told them how he and Rasmussen travelled by kayak along a great river and how, each morning, they went out hunting. They had seen plenty of ducks, geese and seals and had enjoyed their travels very much. And he was much admired by his friends and neighbours for his courage and his honesty.

There is another story about an Oriental prince who, long ago, was told by a traveller that in Europe, when it became very cold, the water in the canals became solid; so solid that it could bear the weight of an elephant. The prince replied that until then he had believed what the traveller had told him, but now he knew that he was a liar and he immediately had him banished from his court.

And the point of both these stories is that people who tell us new things are not always popular. Jesus was crucified for what he said. One of his first followers, Stephen, was stoned to death for saying the same things. The prophet Muhammad was unpopular with the people of Makkah (Mecca). And when Galileo discovered that the Earth revolved around the Sun and ☛

not the Sun around the Earth, he was forced to deny his discovery.

The moral is, we need to be ready to think about new ideas. They may not be true – but then again they just might.

And a second moral we can learn is that, just as the Inuit people once had no idea what New York was really like and just as the Oriental prince could not imagine a severe frost, so we cannot imagine what the next life will be like. And not being able to imagine it doesn't prove it doesn't exist. ◆

70

The Incredible Exploits of Nothing

This passage, by a Christian writer, challenges the non-believer's view of creation as an 'accident'. Some readers may prefer to omit the last paragraph: it is then a slightly more cryptic reading.

So how did the universe come into being? There are various scientific theories but many people believe it 'just happened'. But did 'Nothing' gradually grow, all of its own accord, into the vast complicated 'Something' that we call the universe? Without anyone being in charge? Is this what you believe?

◆

IN THE BEGINNING there was Nothing. No world, no universe, no Ronald MacDonald, no humans and no Sumo wrestlers. Absolutely Nothing.

After several million years Nothing got bored and decided to become Something. And it wasn't long before Something got lonely and decided to split into two. (Just by chance he found he had the ability to do this.) Each of Something's two halves joined the trend and they divided. There were then four Somethings.

Eventually there were so many Somethings that they decided to join together into groups and form into galaxies of planets. Just by chance they all found that they could float around without bumping into each other too much.

Just by chance on one little planet – called 'Earth' because most of its surface was covered by water – there were lots of terrible thunder storms and, just by chance one day, in a particularly vicious one, a bolt of lightning hit a muddy puddle, which just happened to have the right chemicals in it to make Life. ☞

The heat of the lightning caused these chemicals to join together and, just by chance, the first little Living Something had been created.

Living Something like his Grandad, Nothing, got bored and lonely, and decided to grow up. After a long time Living Something just by chance found that he had grown up into a fish.

Living Something Fish would occasionally look out on all the air and land, and get quite dissatisfied with his watery living conditions.

Eventually one particular Living Something Fish made a decision which was to affect the whole of the rest of history – he decided to grow wings and become a bird.

Fortunately for Living Something Bird he found there was just enough oxygen for him to breath and enough things for him to eat (all just by chance, of course).

Zillions more years passed by and, just by chance, birds became animals, and animals eventually summoned up all their energy and put together all their best ideas and became Human Being Somethings.

Human Being Somethings looked at the world and the universe and said how clever it was of Nothing to become Something and wasn't it incredible that, just by chance, the world was such a beautiful place.

Human Being Somethings just by chance got really clever – far more clever than any of their ancestors – and they found out a lot about the world they lived in. They found out that the earth was round and spinning, yet no one had ever fallen off. They discovered that if conditions on earth were just a little different – a bit more oxygen, a little less gravity, half as much forest ☞

or a bit more ocean – it would be impossible for Human Being Somethings to live on Earth at all!

Humans looked at all this incredible evidence about their world and saw what a complicated place it was. They began to see how well-made it was and how each part seemed to have its own job to do. They saw all that Nothing had made and they said it was very good.

One or two humans began to ask sticky questions like, 'If our world is so wonderful – almost like it has been cleverly put together – wouldn't it be more sensible to assume that it started with a Someone, an Incredible Inventor, who planned things to be like this, rather than believing in hundreds of miracles making everything just happen by lucky chance?' But everyone laughed at the idea that there was a Someone involved in making the earth so beautiful and complicated. Instead they went on trying to discover how No One had got hold of Nothing and made Everything.

Of course not everyone believes in Nothing being quite so intelligent and powerful! Millions of Christians, for example, find that the Bible's account of an intelligent God making our well-designed world makes far more sense of the facts. This point is well demonstrated by a story told about the famous scientist, Sir Isaac Newton.

Sir Isaac Newton was a Christian. He discovered a lot about the way the earth works. In his study he had a big model of the planets in their different orbits. It was very impressive. One day another scientist (who did not believe in God) came to visit Sir Isaac for the first time and asked him who had made the model for him because he would like one the same. Sir Isaac said, 'No one made it!' His friend looked at him as though he was mad and repeated the question.

'Who made the model of the universe?'

'No one!'

'You're trying to tell me that this complicated working model just appeared in your study with no help from anyone at all?'

Sir Isaac said, 'Well, you tell me that the entire universe just happened all by itself with no help from anyone. So surely you can believe that this little model could have just happened.'

Of course his friend had no answer. However, the Bible does have an answer for how such a complicated and beautiful world came to exist. The Bible says that there was Someone involved in making the world. It's not all just one enormous lucky chance, but instead has been planned by the greatest, most powerful Someone imaginable – God. ◆

DAVID LAWRENCE

71

One God

This passage, known as the 'Mool Mantra' was the first hymn composed by Guru Nanak, the founder of Sikhism (see passage 45). It is, in one sense, the Creed of Sikhism but could serve as a summary of many believers' understanding of God.

When Christians go to church, they often say the Creed; a statement of what they actually believe. This poem is a statement of what Sikhs believe about God. It was written by the founder of Sikhism, a man called Guru (or 'teacher') Nanak.

◆

There is one God

1
There is one God.
His name is Truth.
He is the creator,
He is without fear or hate.
He is beyond time immortal,
His spirit pervades the universe.
He is not born,
Nor does He die to be reborn,
He is self-existent.
By *Guru's* grace shalt thou worship Him.

2
Never forget Him
    by whose grace thou art a noble creation.
Sing His glory, Nanak,
    by whose grace thou art honoured.

3

His praises are endless,
   endless are words of His glory,
His deeds are endless,
   endless are His gifts.
His vision is endless,
   endless is His power,
His purpose is endless,
   endless is His realization.

4

The fools are those
   who eat and drink
      but don't think of the Giver,
and those who suffer
   from hunger, pain and misery
      are also the gifts of the Lord.

5

He is the creator of the universe.
   He shall remain
      even if the worlds be ruined;
The King of Kings,
   the supreme Lord He is,
O Nanak, we abide by His will. ◆

GURU NANAK

translated by Pranap Bandyapadhyay

72

Accident or Purpose?

One of the basic questions with which philosophy concerns itself is 'Does God exist?' Resulting from that are the connected questions: 'Is the universe an accident or has it been designed?' and 'Does life have a purpose?' This passage raises these questions and could follow the reading of passage 70.

What is 'the big question'? The question which, if we only knew the answer, would make sense of everything? That question has to be the one religion tries to answer. Is there a God? And then there are the questions that follow from that one. Is the universe part of a great plan or is it just an accident? And what are we supposed to do about it? Do we have a purpose?

◆

SUPPOSE A BANK manager were to arrive at his office one morning and find it in a state of chaos – papers strewn about the floor, the safe door open and its valuable contents gone, the lock forced by the use of some explosive and clear evidence that a drill had been at work. If someone were to suggest that all this 'just happened' and that there was nothing to account for the damage, the manager would not be amused. His reason would be insulted by any such suggestion. Our reason and common sense insist that things do not 'just happen' by themselves. Every happening has a cause. Could the wreckage in that office conceivably have been produced by accident without human intervention?

How then will you explain this vast and wonderful universe, so simple and yet so orderly? So simple that the whole physical universe is made up of only about a hundred chemical elements. So orderly that it seems as if mind made it and so mind can understand it. Is this universe the result of an accident or is there a better explanation?

Geology shows us that somehow – through the explosion of a star, or the concentration of a dense cloud of gas – the earth was born. As its surface cooled, life appeared – first as the lowest form of vegetation, developing eventually into tropical forests. Animal life followed – first small, but later giant creatures with little brains. Then mind developed until man appeared – physically insignificant but mentally superior to all other life on earth; able to control it to serve him. Is all that just pointless?

History and archaeology outline man's past – from primitive man to his discovery of fire, the use of tools and the growing of crops. This development brought men together into families, tribes, kingdoms and eventually cities, with new evils of inequality, tyranny and dictatorship. But man also has nobler aims – love of beauty, goodness and truth. Is this development meaningless?

Religion tells us that men have always asked 'Why am I here?' Some have seen life as a punishment but most have believed that it has meaning. The Old Testament tells of the quest of the Hebrew people for the purpose of life, and the New Testament tells of the Christians rejoicing in finding the answer in Christ. Is there a purpose in life?

Geology, science, history and archaeology can't provide proof. The best that people who follow a religion can say is 'Well, I can't prove it but I still believe. It makes sense to me.' Belief has to be what we call 'intuitive': you just feel it must be so.

☞

247

You cannot prove – or disprove – the existence of God by scientific means. Science deals with the created world, and by definition, believers say, God is not part of that world; He is its creator. Neither is belief in God arrived at by argument alone. It begins as an intuitive leap in response to certain experiences, events, persons which seem to have about them something deep and profound. But although belief in God seems to begin as an intuitive response to experience, it is not necessarily an irrational belief. ◆

SCHOOLS COUNCIL

73

The Gambler's *Argument*

*One famous answer to the question 'Should we believe in God?' is that
expressed by the seventeenth-century scientist and theologian, Blaise
Pascal. It is known as 'Pascal's Wager' or 'The Gambler's Argument'.*
   *This passage follows on from the previous one: to believe may be
rational.*

How much would you bet that God exists? Some people say
God must exist because the universe is so cleverly made.
Some say he must exist because 'something' must have
started off the process of creation. And others say he
doesn't exist because the world is in such a mess, or he can't
exist because we can't see him. But nobody can prove
scientifically that he exists. So would you bet on God being
real? A very famous scientist and philosopher called Pascal
believed it *was* worth betting on his being real.

   His theory is known as the Gambler's Argument. You
may or may not agree it's worth placing the bet.

◆

THE GAMBLER'S ARGUMENT, which is derived from the
writings of the philosopher and mathematician, Blaise Pascal
(1623-1662), and is usually known as 'Pascal's Wager', does
not aim to provide proof, but rather to show that a sensible
gambler would be well-advised to 'bet' that God exists.

It begins from the position of an agnostic, that is, someone
who believes that there is not enough evidence to decide
whether or not God exists. An agnostic believes that there is a
genuine possibility that God exists, but that there is insuffi-
cient evidence to decide the issue with certainty. An atheist, in

contrast, typically believes that there is conclusive evidence that God does not exist.

The Gambler's Argument proceeds as follows. Since we do not know whether or not God exists, we are in much the same position as a gambler before a race has been run or a card turned. We must then calculate the odds. But to the agnostic it may seem just as likely that God exists as that he or she doesn't. The agnostic's course of action is to sit on the fence, not making a decision either way. The Gambler's Argument, however, says that the most rational thing to do is to aim to have a chance of winning as great a prize as possible, whilst keeping our chance of losing as small as possible: in other words, we should maximise our possible winnings, and mini-mise our possible losses. According to the Gambler's Argument, the best way to do this is to believe in God.

There are four possible outcomes. If we bet on the existence of God and win (i.e. if God does exist), then we gain eternal life – a great prize. What we lose if we bet on this option and it turns out that God doesn't exist is not great when compared with the possibility of eternal life: we may miss out on certain worldly pleasures, waste many hours praying, and live our lives under an illusion. However, if we choose to bet on the option that God doesn't exist, and we win (i.e. if God doesn't exist), then we live a life without illusion (at least in this respect), and feel free to indulge in the pleasures of this life without fear of divine punishment. But if we bet on this option and lose (i.e. if God does exist), then we at least miss the chance of eternal life, and may even run the risk of eternal damnation.

Pascal argued that, as gamblers faced with these options, the most rational course of action for us is to believe that God does exist. This way, if we are correct, we stand to win eternal life. If we gamble that God exists and are wrong we do not stand to ☞

lose so much as if we choose to believe that God doesn't exist and are wrong. So, if we want to maximize our possible gains and minimize our possible losses, then we ought to believe in God's existence. ◆

NIGEL WARBURTON

74

The First Mover

Of the three great philosophers of Ancient Greece (Socrates, Plato and Aristotle), Aristotle (384–322 BCE) was the last and arguably the greatest. He was also the first great European biologist.

A surprise bestseller of the early nineties was Jostein Gaarder's introduction to philosophy, Sophie's World. *This excerpt from it may be used in conjunction with the preceding passages.*

One way of explaining what a philosopher is, is to say that he or she is person who tries to understand and explain the meaning of life; they try to answer the question 'What's it all about?'

One of the greatest philosophers was a Greek who lived over 2000 years ago, called Aristotle. So what did he have to say about God – and whether God is real?

◆

ARISTOTLE ... FIRST OF all points out that everything in the natural world can be divided into two main categories. On the one hand there are *nonliving things*, such as stones, drops of water, or clumps of soil. These things have no potentiality for change. According to Aristotle, nonliving things can only change through external influence. Only *living things* have the potentiality for change.

Aristotle divides 'living things' into two different categories. One comprises *plants*, and the other *creatures*. Finally, these 'creatures' can also be divided into two subcategories, namely *animals* and *humans*.

You have to admit that Aristotle's categories are clear and simple. There is a decisive difference between a living and a ☞

nonliving thing, for example a rose and a stone, just as there is a decisive difference between a plant and an animal, for example a rose and a horse. I would also claim that there definitely is a difference between a horse and a man. But what exactly does this difference consist of?

When Aristotle divides natural phenomena into various categories, his criterion is the object's characteristics, or more specifically what it *can do* or what it *does*.

All living things (plants, animals, humans) have the ability to absorb nourishment, to grow, and to propagate. All 'living creatures' (animals and humans) have in addition the ability to perceive the world around them and to move about. Moreover, all humans have the ability to think – or otherwise to order their perceptions into various categories and classes.

So there are in reality no sharp boundaries in the natural world. We observe a gradual transition from simple growths to more complicated plants, from simple animals to more complicated animals. At the top of this 'scale' is man – who according to Aristotle lives the whole life of nature. Man grows and absorbs nourishment like plants, he has feelings and the ability to move like animals, but he also has a specific characteristic peculiar to humans, and that is the ability to think rationally.

Therefore, man has a spark of divine reason. Yes, I did say divine. From time to time Aristotle reminds us that there must be a God who started all movement in the natural world. Therefore God must be at the very top of nature's scale.

Aristotle imagined the movement of the stars and the planets guiding all movement on Earth. But there had to be something causing the heavenly bodies to move. Aristotle called this the 'first mover,' or 'God.' The 'first mover' is itself at rest, but it ☞

is the 'formal cause' of the movement of the heavenly bodies, and thus of all movement in nature. ◆

JOSTEIN GAARDER

translated by PAULETTE MOLLER

75

Something In It?

This passage looks at the question 'Does God exist?' from a Christian perspective.

Is it *reasonable* to say you believe in God? Even though there is no proof? Can belief be rational? Christians, like the followers of other religions, say that belief (or faith) *is* sensible.

◆

A SENTENCE FROM [*Alice*] *Through the Looking Glass* states the problem most clearly. 'With a little bit of practice it is possible to believe six impossible things before breakfast.' To have faith in anything, even in God, does not imply of itself that what is believed in is absolutely true. It may not be. The whole problem of faith is that the key element in it is uncertainty. If a thing was absolutely known for certain, then the question of having faith in it would not arise. To have faith does not mean that you are supposed to believe in what you know is not true – but to believe in something when you can never prove that it is true.

Faith requires a commitment to something, whether it is God, or another person, or a course of action. When we get married, we have faith in another person – we believe that we will be able to get on with that person and live happily together, for better or for worse, until the parting at death, or even beyond death. It may not work out like that, as we know – but getting married is an act of faith.

When we climb aboard a plane to go abroad, we have faith that

☞

the pilot will get us there safely. He may not, but we trust that he will, so we get in the plane and we go. When we buy a house, it is an act of faith. We take out a mortgage for 20 years, without having the least idea of whether or not the house will still be standing then! When a jury decides a man is guilty and puts him away for years, it is also an act of faith. They did not actually see him murder his rival, but they believe that he did strongly enough to condemn him. The faith is really in our judgement.

We cannot have scientific proof about the existence of God, just as it is highly unlikely that we could have a film record of our criminal committing murder, or foreknowledge as to whether our house will be bombed down or burnt or survive. All we can do is have a good look at such evidence as is available, make a decision, and act on it.

Either the Christianity based on the life, death and resurrection of Jesus is the most outrageous and evil mass hoax; or the whole edifice is the product of ridiculously stupid and gullible people suffering from mass delusion and hysteria; or there just could be something in it. ◆

ROSALYN A KENDRICK

76

Bronze Heads

This passage is based on a widespread medieval legend that certain brazen (or bronze) heads had the ability to speak. The reading is intended to encourage a proper use of time.

One of the strangest things that people believed in the past was that certain strange, wonderful heads made of brass were able to speak. These legends existed in many countries but one such story is told about an Englishman called Roger Bacon.

◆

ROGER BACON WAS a monk who lived in the thirteenth century. He studied at Oxford University and was said to be so wise he knew everything. He was, in fact, a very clever, early scientist. Among other things, he is often credited with inventing the magnifying glass.

Less likely to be true is the legend that he made one of these brazen or bronze heads. But, so the story goes, he did, and (also according to the story) he believed that if he ever heard it speak, he'd be successful in all his scientific experiments. If not, he would fail.

He got his assistant (who was called Miles) to watch the head at all times. And when Bacon was asleep, it did speak. 'Time is' it said. Nothing else – until half an hour later it said 'Time was.'

It was silent for another half hour. Then it spoke a third time. 'Time's past' it said. And it fell from where it was and broke into tiny atoms.

Whatever else that legend teaches is the fact that we can't cheat ☛

time. Time is the one dimension along which all traffic passes in the same direction. There's no going back. And there's no stopping the march of time – the march of Old Father Time.

When we picture this imaginary character it's often as a bald old man who carries a sharp-edged scythe, ready to cut us down 'when the time comes'. Indeed, he's sometimes presented as being the same character as Death, the Grim Reaper.

And throughout history, he's been shown in art as being bald – except for one lock of hair at the front of his head. The reason for this is that his baldness shows there's no going back to our youth. But never mind time future. Time present is what matters. Time present may be wasted – or it may be used well. As we say in one idiom, time may be 'seized by the forelock'.

If we do seize time by the forelock, then there's the question of how to use it wisely. Perhaps in the service of others or indeed of ourselves, by taking the occasional moment to catch our breath, to pause and think *how* we're using (or wasting) our lives.

But the problem with time is that it is so very elastic. It seems to move at different speeds. This is expressed quite neatly on a clock in the cathedral at Chester. On the clock are inscribed these lines:

When, as a child, I laughed and wept,
    Time crept.
When, as a youth, I dreamt and talked,
    Time walked.
When I became a full-grown man,
    Time ran.
When older still I daily grew,
    Time flew.
Soon I shall find on travelling on –

Time gone.
O Christ, wilt Thou have saved me then?
Amen.

Once upon a time, when we were very young, there seemed to be too much time. As we get older, time seems to move more rapidly – and before we know where we are, it's going so fast that ... well, none of us knows what the future will bring – or when! Because we can't *control* time! Like Bacon's brazen head, it may well find a way of defeating our plans and endeavours: we may have plenty of time to do all we want to; we may not.

In his letter to the Christians at Rome, St Paul wrote: 'The night is far gone, the day is at hand.' In other words: You've not got all day. Yes, we need time to play, to enjoy ourselves, as well as to study and to work. But time *wasted* is time lost for ever. Remember, there's no stopping Old Father Time: the Grim Reaper is always on the move. So think before you waste any more time! ◆

77

No Pain, No Death

Would a world without pain and death be desirable or unbearable? This passage describes one justification of the 'necessity' of pain and death. It is not suggested that it is necessarily suitable at a time of bereavement or mourning but it may perhaps be used at an anniversary or a time when it seems appropriate to consider, and come to terms with, the fact of death. (See also passages 78, 80 and 100.)

Just how much would you like the world to be altered if only you had the power? Suppose you could remove pain and death from the world. Would you do so?

◆

IMAGINE A WORLD in which there was no physical pain. At first it seems a blissful idea. But think for a moment.

Without pain, we'd have no early warning system that something was going wrong with our bodies. No headaches to warn us of stress or tension. No toothache to warn of an abscess. No pain in our stomachs to warn of over-indulgence or more serious internal problems. No hangovers to teach us we'd overdone it the previous night. And pain brings another 'benefit': it can force us to rest so that a part of the body will heal itself. Pain can, in fact, be quite useful.

Furthermore, pain can be a deterrent – stopping us from carrying out a physical activity that could damage our bodies. Through pain, we learn the danger of fire, of sharp knives, falling rocks and other hard objects. We learn how to take care of our fleshy, vulnerable bodies in a world full of very much harder objects.

Pain can be more than useful. It can be necessary. So, after all, ☞

perhaps we *don't* want a world without pain. But suppose we could alter creation on a much bigger scale. How do you fancy living in one of these worlds?

World number one

A world with birth but with no death, a world in which we all lived for ever; a world which would inevitably get more and more crowded.

World number two

A world without death but with no more births, a world with a set number of people; a world in which we all lived for ever, getting older and older and weaker and weaker.

World number three

A world without death but with no more births, a world with a set number of people; a world in which we all lived for ever, staying precisely the same age we are at the moment.

World number four

A world with birth and death, a world in which things can go right and things can go wrong; a world in which things change.

So which do you fancy?

Most people will want to rule out World Number One: a world with birth but with no death, a world in which we all lived for ever and which would get more and more crowded. Eventually, even quite quickly, life in that world would become unbearable.

After a bit of thought, most people will also want to rule out World Number Two. Do you actually want to live in a world without death but with no more births, a world with a set number of people; a world in which we all lived for ever, getting older and older and weaker and weaker? A world with no ☞

young people? A world in which we should all eventually be old and have no one younger to look after us?

So what about World Number Three? 'A world without death but with no more births, a world with a set number of people; a world in which we all lived for ever, staying precisely the same age we are at the moment.' If you're feeling really great at the moment, perhaps you *would* like to stay your present age for ever. But wouldn't envy and boredom set in at some time?

People your age would never get a chance to be in control of things: the older generations would make sure they always remained in charge.

There would be another problem in a world without death. Bullies could inflict unlimited suffering, world without end, on their victims. Victims of the world (whether they were victims of bullies or terrorists or armies; whether they were the hungry or the ill) might have to suffer for ever. There would be no way out of really terrible suffering.

So, in the end, do you want to live in a world where death is a part of existence? Do we settle for World Number Four, including the fact of death? ◆

78

Sure and Certain Hope

This is a second reading on the theme of death. This passage concentrates on the actual funeral service – an event from which children are typically 'protected' and which can then be traumatic if tragedy strikes and they 'have to' attend.

Death is not a subject people like to talk about. We find ways of avoiding even mentioning the word. We say someone has 'passed on' or 'breathed his last' or even 'kicked the bucket', anything but 'she's died'. Yet the fact that each of us will die one day is perhaps the one certain thing about our future. So why is death so difficult to talk about? And what does happen when a person dies?

◆

WHEN SOMEONE DIES, there are two particular problems: the disposal of the body and how to comfort the surviving relatives and friends.

Traditionally, there are four ways of disposing of the body: by earth, fire, air and water.

Some Tibetans leave the bodies of the dead on the ground to be worn away by exposure. There is good reason for this: in parts of Tibet in winter, the ground is too hard to dig (so burial is impossible) and there is little firewood available, so cremation is not easy.

Burial at sea is practised by some islanders around the world and is also given to those who die at sea. However, the major world faiths normally dispose of the body either by cremation or burial.

☛

The funeral service of the Church of England can be very short and quiet with only a few members of the family present, or it can be an occasion of great solemnity with music and hymns and a packed church. Whether it is held in a parish church or a crematorium chapel, it is usually either the plain funeral service from the *Book of Common Prayer* or the *Alternative Service Book*, and it can have the addition of hymns, favourite prayers and readings, and a talk or sermon. But, whatever the pattern of service, the words and actions all speak of a loving God and the preciousness to him of every individual human being.

When the body is to be buried in a graveyard, then the 'committal' of the coffin into the grave is the most solemn moment of the funeral service. What should happen is stated in the *Book of Common Prayer*:

> '*When they come to the Grave, while the Corpse is made ready to be laid into the earth, the Priest shall say, or the Priest and Clerks shall sing:* Man that is born of a woman hath but a short time to live, and is full of misery. He cometh up, and is cut down, like a flower; he fleeth as it were a shadow, and never continueth in one stay ... *Then, while the earth shall be cast upon the Body by some standing by, the Priest shall say:* Forasmuch as it hath pleased Almighty God of his great mercy to take unto himself the soul of our dear *brother* here departed, we therefore commit *his* body to the ground; earth to earth, ashes to ashes, dust to dust.'

On their own, these words can sound depressing, gloomy. But for every 100 people who have heard and recognize those words, there are probably fewer than 20 who know what words come next: 'Earth to earth, ashes to ashes, dust to dust in sure and certain hope of the Resurrection to eternal life through Our Lord Jesus Christ.'

The main belief of Christianity is that, through Jesus Christ, we shall be able to share in a new life in a new world. And as the Prayer Book says, for the Christian, that's 'a sure and certain hope'.

But is it a contradiction to say hope can be certain? When we say we *hope* something will happen, surely it's because we don't know if it'll happen or not? Not quite. The dictionary reminds us that 'to hope' means to expect, to trust, to have confidence.

For Christians (and indeed for the followers of most religions), when they say they hope for a new life after death, they are not just hoping: they are *expecting* it to happen. ◆

79

Doomsday

This passage provides an opportunity for speculation on that ever-interesting topic, the end of the world. Believers maintain it will happen in God's good time (unless we do the job for him before then). Others believe it will be just because of a cosmic accident.

If you knew when the end of the world was going to happen, how would you use your time until then?

Many people expected the end of the world to occur in the year 1000 CE. Different people have predicted it will happen on other dates – such as the year 2000. But one date for which there seemed quite good scientific evidence is 21 August, 2126.

◆

The date: August 21, 2126. Doomsday.

The place: Earth. Across the planet a despairing population attempts to hide. For billions there is nowhere to go. Some people flee deep under ground, desperately seeking out caves and disused mine shafts, or take to the sea in submarines. Others go on the rampage, murderous and uncaring. Most just sit, sullen and bemused, waiting for the end.

High in the sky, a huge shaft of light is etched into the fabric of the heavens. What began as a slender pencil of softly radiating nebulosity has swollen day by day to form a maelstrom of gas boiling into the vacuum of space. At the apex of a vapour trail lies a dark, misshapen, menacing lump. The diminutive head of the comet belies its enormous destructive power. It is closing on planet Earth at a staggering 40,000 miles per hour, ten miles every second – a trillion tons of ice and rock, destined to strike at 70 times the speed of sound.

Mankind can only watch and wait. The scientists, who have long since abandoned their telescopes in the face of the inevitable, quietly shut down the computers. The endless simulations of disaster are still too uncertain, and their conclusions are too alarming to release to the public anyway. Some scientists have prepared elaborate survival strategies, using their technical knowledge to gain advantage over their fellow citizens. Others plan to observe the cataclysm as carefully as possible, maintaining their role as true scientists to the very end, transmitting data to time capsules buried deep in the earth. For posterity ... .

The moment of impact approaches. All over the world, millions of people nervously check their watches. The last three minutes.

Directly above ground zero, the sky splits open. A thousand cubic miles of air are blasted aside. A finger of searing flame wider than a city arcs groundward and fifteen seconds later lances the Earth. The planet shudders with the force of 10,000 earthquakes. A shockwave of displaced air sweeps over the surface of the globe, flattening all structures, pulverizing everything in its path. The flat terrain around the impact site rises in a ring of liquid mountains several miles high, exposing the bowels of the Earth in a crater 100 miles across. The wall of molten rock ripples outward, tossing the landscape about like a blanket flicked in slow motion.

Within the crater itself, trillions of tons of rock are vaporized. Much more is splashed aloft, some of it flung out into space. Still more is pitched across half a continent to rain down hundreds or even thousands of miles away, wreaking massive destruction on all beneath. Some of the molten ejecta falls into the ocean, raising huge tsunamis [tidal waves] that add to the spreading turmoil. A vast column of dusty debris fans out into the atmosphere, blotting out the Sun across the whole planet. Now the sunlight is replaced by the sinister, flickering glare of a billion meteors, roasting the ☛

ground below with their searing heat, as displaced material plunges back from space into the atmosphere.

The preceding scenario is based on the prediction that comet Swift-Tuttle will hit the earth on 21 August, 2126. If it were to, global devastation would undoubtedly follow, destroying human civilization. When this comet paid us a visit in 1993, early calculations suggested that a collision in 2126 was a distinct possibility. Since then, revised calculations indicate that the comet will in fact miss Earth by two weeks: a close shave, but we can breathe easily. However, the danger won't go away entirely. Sooner or later Swift-Tuttle, or an object like it, *will* hit the Earth. Estimates suggest that 10,000 objects half a kilometre or more in diameter move on Earth-intersecting orbits. These astronomical interlopers originate in the frigid outer reachers of the solar system. Some are the remains of comets that have become trapped by the gravitational fields of the planets, others come from the asteroid belt that lies between Mars and Jupiter. Orbital instability causes a continual traffic of these small but lethal bodies into and out of the inner solar system, constituting an ever-present menace to Earth and our sister planets.

Many of these objects are capable of causing more damage than all the world's nuclear weapons put together. It is only a matter of time before one strikes. When it does, it will be bad news for people. ◆

PAUL DAVIES

80

Something After Death?

Most religions maintain a belief in some sort of afterlife – be it an ultimate 'fusion' with the Divine (as Hinduism teaches) or a new life following death and judgement (as Christianity and Islam both maintain). To many non-believers this is just 'pie-in-the-sky'; merely wishful thinking. Interestingly, however, there are those psychologists who hold that such beliefs are physically and mentally beneficial.

The quotation in the middle of this passage is from the Old Testament Book of Job.

Because we don't like thinking about death, we don't often face up to the question, 'Is there anything after death?' But is there, in fact, a life after death?

◆

IN PRACTICALLY EVERY country, and every age, there has been a belief that death is not the end, that something survives the destruction of man's physical body. Is this belief in survival of death wishful thinking? Do men seem unable to envisage their own annihilation? It may be so, and the fact that men want to survive does not prove that they do so. But this belief has been held at all stages of human development, and not only by ignorant or shallow people. Survival has been argued by learned men all down the ages, and they have given many other reasons for this belief which we shall consider. Basic to most of them is a conviction that the human being is more than his body and that this 'more' is not limited by space or time.

Certainly something survives death, for there is change and re-creation. Every autumn brings decay, with death shown in beautiful colours; every spring brings new life. There is a cycle ☛

of life, going round and round, from life to death and back to life again. Job saw this, and looked beyond it:

> There is hope for a tree,
> if it is cut down,
> that it will sprout again … .
> But man dies and wastes away;
> Yes, man gives up the spirit,
> and where is he?

Trees and plants are renewed, but animal bodies decay and die. Yet they do not become nothing, they gradually change into something else. If men live in a hot dry country they see the dead soon becoming dust, and they say, 'ashes to ashes, dust to dust'. If the body is embalmed it may last for centuries or millenia, and the British Museum has preserved bodies that are 6000 years old, still with hair, teeth and skin. But whether decay comes quickly or slowly, nothing is totally destroyed. Scientists tell us that matter is indestructible, it may change its form but new forms appear in due course. Our bodies do not become nothing, even if they are cremated, they take a different form in the universal whole.

But from prehistoric times men have been convinced that they are more than bodies. Primitive men knew that the bodies they buried had been killed or died of disease. They realized that the weapons or cooking pots placed by corpses could not be used by those inert bodies. But they believed that some essence of the dead person could use the essence of the weapon, and live a new life in the happy hunting grounds, or the Elysian Fields where the Egyptians thought the dead continued their earthly occupations. Men have changed their ideas about the nature of life after death. But that something survives which is the true essence of a person has been held throughout the world. ☞

The psychologist Jung, from many years of experience, said that it was of great importance to believe in life after death, so that meaning and purpose will be given to action. For most people it means a great deal to assume that their lives will have an indefinite continuity beyond their present existence. They live more sensibly, feel better, and are more at peace ... In the majority of cases the question of immortality is so urgent, so immediate, and also so ineradicable that we must make an effort to form some sort of view about it. ◆

GEOFFREY PARRINDER

LOVE THY NEIGHBOUR AS THYSELF

'It is easy to forget a kindness, but one remembers unkindness'
INDIAN PROVERB

'Three helping one another will do as much as six men singly'
SPANISH PROVERB

81

Tiny Tim: a Terror

This warning may be used to prompt thoughts and discussion about the need for discipline and punishment and also about parenting. Pupils might be encouraged to wonder whether they themselves have been indulged in ways similar to Tiny Tim in the story or what his parents might have done to 'correct' his behaviour. (See also passage 86.)

When you were small, were you allowed to do exactly as you liked? Were you 'spoilt'?

Do you think it's right to be firm with young children or should they be allowed to have their own way? This is the story of one child called Tiny Tim – and it's told by the nurse (or midwife) who helped at his birth.

◆

DONE AT LAST! At butcher Smith's a boy had come into the world. The father was beside himself over the child, his boy Tiny Tim. Any child going past his shop was given a sausage.

Meanwhile the baby was yelling. From the first he was a little terror in the home. He wanted to sleep during the day, and at night he had to be carried from room to room to stop him bawling. I raised a protest.

'Bring your boy up sensibly. Get him used early on to being obedient and tidy. Do everything he wants and you'll bring the child up for the reformatory.'

The mother would have none of it. 'Once he's old enough to understand he'll stop his naughtiness. You have to give a child freedom to develop.'

After about a year Mrs Smith called me in as I was passing by. ☞

There was Tiny Tim sitting on his potty in the middle of the table. He had his mother's scissors in his hands and was sliding to and fro on his throne and cutting off the buds and leaves of the plants in the window.

'And then you eat off that table afterwards!' I couldn't help remarking.

'What can I do? He won't stay sitting if he can't get to the window ... '

I took the scissors from the little lad's hands. 'If he pokes his eye out with them, Mrs Smith ... '

So then the little rogue went scarlet in the face, clenched both fists, stamped his feet, shouted and raged.

'Yes' the father laughed, 'the boy has something in him. He's got guts and won't put up with anything.'

And the mother made excuses. 'He cries until he gets what he wants. What can you do ... I give it to him to keep him quiet. As soon as he's old enough to understand it will be different. He's still so small ... '

I had seized the little man somewhat vigorously by his woolly without saying anything and sat him on his throne on the ground. 'Either you're quiet and do your business ... ' and I glared at him. Struck dumb and rigid he crouched there ... did not dare utter a whimper at such unwonted treatment ... looked round to father and mother for help. But they were quite as floored as he and the mother found a way out: 'It's easy to see you have no children or you couldn't be like that with him. He's still so small and hasn't any sense yet ... '

What I would have liked to say to that was: 'Just like you.' But I held my tongue and went. All that for nothing! ☛

Once the family was sitting in the back room having a meal. 'Don't want it,' bawled Tiny Tim and slung his plate full of soup onto the floor. His father laughed: 'He's a terror, our little Tiny Tim.'

Oh yes he was a terror, and more so every day. All the children ran from him when he was in the street. Soon he was tormenting little chickens. 'Oh they're only animals,' said his father.

Tiny Tim went to school. He was a stubborn and deceitful playmate and no one was safe from his tricks. As he could not be openly nasty there he was all the more beastly on the sly. His teacher repeatedly tried to have him sent to a home for difficult children. But nobody wanted to upset Tiny Tim and it never came off.

One fine day father and son came to blows. After the thirteen-year old horror had already gone through the whole contents of the till in the morning he tried to take the safe key in the afternoon. That was too much for his old father. 'That belongs to me so long as I'm master here. Get it?' Thereupon the lad in a rage seized hold of a meatcleaver and struck out at his father. He missed. But Mr Smith stood there as though hit by lightning. Then all at once his eyes were opened. And at that moment ungovernable rage gripped him too. For the first time he took hold of the boy and gave him a hiding, with neither rhyme nor reason of course. He would certainly have beaten him to death if the mother and the apprentices had not come between them. The Smith household was shaken. Tiny Tim lay in bed for a week.

The father had made a thorough job of it. But it was too late. This sudden change-round only brought out in the lad the vengefulness, malice and brutality which had been lurking under the surface. And hate stepped in.

Some months later he really did strike his father with the cleaver. The place was in an uproar. Such a thing had never been seen in living memory. And yet ... and yet ... they all saw and felt it: the father and mother had brought disaster on themselves.

Many parents took account then that bringing up children is no easy task and an important undertaking, and that it is no good waiting until 'They are old enough to understand'. ◆

PIERRE LEFÈVRE

82

Temper, Temper

The author of this excerpt gave up a place at Oxford University to become a nun (which she still is). The passage is, however, about her childhood. Two lessons may be learned from it. One is that many young people are prey to dark moods and that these moods are not without a cause. The other is that we can all do something to help other people's 'self image' or self-esteem.

Very few of us get through life without having bad moods. Some of these come when things go seriously wrong. Other moods seem to start for very trivial reasons. The writer of this passage found that, when she was in her teens, it needed only a simple remark from her parents to put her in a terrible mood.

It's a story that also reminds us how easy it is to hurt other people – and how we can help others to feel better.

◆

AS I GREW into adolescence the difficulties of my temperament increased and I became a burden to myself and a trouble in the home. A very slight affront, a sharp word, an impatient gesture from my parents would throw me, without warning, into a black mood. Often I would fly into a violent rage and attack with my fists. I could never hurt. No matter how great my rage, my hand fell limp. The rage would be followed by days of sulking. Utterly miserable myself, I tended to make others miserable too. I would stay outside the family circle, morose and sullen. I longed to join in again but was too proud to yield. Sometimes I would refuse to go with the family on their Sunday outings, all the time hating myself because I saw how eagerly and tenderly Mother and Daddy prepared it for ☛

us. I hated myself and the more I hated myself the more sullen and depressed I became. I was extremely unhappy and I did not know what was the matter. The world seemed utterly black.

At times I wanted to die; I used to think out how I could run away. However, love of the family always restrained me. I could never have hurt Mother and Daddy to that extent. My father was one of the principal causes of my moods. I think it was because I felt he did not sufficiently recognize my value but looked down on me as he would on a child. And yet I loved him. Even at the time I was behaving so badly I loved him and I felt hateful for being so horrid to him. I found it impossible to come back to him as I did to Mother. If I was at odds with her I nearly always ran back when I had taken but a few steps from the house on my way to school, to kiss her goodbye. I remember the occasions when I had gone off in high dudgeon without being reconciled with Mother. I lived in anguish for the rest of the day fearing Mother might die while I was away and I would not be able to tell her I was sorry and show her that I loved her. I think I was about fifteen when it came home to me how selfish I was; how I was upsetting the family and grieving my mother. I made up my mind to try to hide my feelings or at least, not let everyone else suffer from them. Then began the struggle which has gone on to this day. There were many, many lapses for my moods were tyrannical.

When I question myself as to the basic cause of this depression, sadness and bitter frustration, it is not easy to point to one particular thing. I have said sufficient of my earlier years to show that to a great extent it was inherent in my make-up. Intermingled with this was, I think, a religious problem, as I will tell, but I would suspect that underlying the grief was the ugly self-image. The slightest affront or criticism brought me face to face with it. I hated myself, rejected myself and shut out ☞

love. And the more I shut out love, the more I saw myself being bad, the more frustrated and hateful I seemed.

Many, many years later, I witnessed an incident which demonstrated how I might have been helped in this extremely difficult dilemma. My brother brought his little family to the parlour. Without warning, the eldest went to the back of the room and hid her face in the cushion. Some little remark had wounded her. I knew just what she felt like and the sheer knowledge that already she had gone so far as to disgrace herself before Aunty made the situation all the more hopeless. My brother, with tremendous understanding, went over to her quietly, gathered her up in his arms and cuddled her. Her face was flaming with shame and he buried it in his breast. After a little while he brought her over to us, remarking on her lovely plaits. Apparently she was very conscious of her straight hair. She thought it ugly. I was deeply moved by James' understanding and perfect handling of the child. As for the child, I identified with her completely. Alas, no one in my really loving home grasped the inner loneliness of the difficult child that was me. I think if Mother or Father had come over to me and put their arms round me I would have burst into helpless tears that would have been my healing. I was not scolded. I was just left to get over it. The family circle was always wide open and at the first sign I was welcomed, but I had to make the first move and it was this which was so appallingly hard. This trouble is with me still. I still have to resist the feeling of panic which arises when I am in any way criticized or found to be at fault. ◆

RUTH BURROWS

83

Too Tall or Too Short?

Many teenagers (if not all) worry about their appearance. These answers from an 'agony aunt' may be light-hearted but they still contain wise advice. Pupils might be encouraged to think how they could be adapted to help those who worry about other 'uncontrollable' physical features.

Do you worry about your height? Do you think you are too tall? Or too short? Is there something else about your appearance you'd like to alter? Here is a selection of letters from worried teenagers – and answers from Agony Aunt Chere Vainer.

◆

I HAVE THE problem of being too small. It first came to prominence two years ago when I was thirteen. I am very keen on sport and tried for the school football team. My favourite position is central defence because I like tackling players, but I wasn't picked for the first few matches. The rest of the team got at me for being too small and causing us to lose our training matches because the ball was being lobbed over my head. I was dropped, but then the player who replaced me was so terrible that I got my place back.

Answer: **As you've discovered, like many things in life, it's not your size that matters, it's the way that you use it.**

I am too tall for my age. Some people think I'm eighteen and call me 'lanky'.

Answer: **Teenagers grow at different times, according to when they start and finish going through puberty. Soon all your friends will grow too, and you may want to be even taller!**

☞

My mother took me to see the doctor because I'm very small. He said that in my case it is because all my family are small. I've always been small and people call me 'shrimpy' and 'half-pint'. People say smoking stunts your growth but I don't smoke. I've tried putting on high heels, but they make me look stupid and are just uncomfortable. It gets on my nerves when I'm buying clothes and when I buy trousers I end up by cutting off half the legs.

Answer: **Think of the advantages. You will save money when you're older as you'll be able to buy children's clothes and pay no tax on them. Think how much better being half-pint is than being quarter-pint. It's all comparative.**

I think I am too tall and get depressed about it when people call me a beanpole. When I was eleven I was short, but now I've shot up and don't even fit properly into my bed. I don't like being tall, but my dad wants me to become a policeman, and if I was short they wouldn't have me. I suppose there are some advantages. At football you can see over everyone, and having long arms helps me to play basketball.

Answer: **Get your parents to buy you a double bed so that you can fit your feet in. It'll come in useful later in life.**

I'm called 'titch' and 'midget', and I think I'm small because I was born prematurely. When I came to secondary school we were shown around the first day and had a woodwork lesson, and I was embarrassed because I couldn't see over the top of the bench. Because I'm small in height it makes me feel small in character. I tend to be quiet, so people say I haven't got much confidence in myself. I always find it much easier talking to someone the same size as me.

Answer: **Be patient, as most people who are born prematurely will end up a perfectly normal height. Concentrate** ☞

on all your good points and this will make you feel more confident. Being more confident will make you *feel* bigger. Just because people are big doesn't mean that they are better.

I am so small that some people have suggested that I make a career of being a garden gnome.

Answer: Well don't – make a career out of being you, instead. Many of my friends who consider themselves 'small' develop a devastating list of cutting replies to this kind of remark. Try making some up, ready for next time.

I'm too small and I've had this problem since I was five. I get teased and bullied, and cannot get into a '15' film without my birth certificate. When I'm in crowds, people look down on me and joke about it – even people I don't know. I laugh, but inside I get really upset. People think that I'm younger than I am and I don't like that. I read about some children being small because they lack something called 'growth hormone'. Could this be my problem?

Answer: Growth hormone deficiency causes smallness in about one in 4000 children. If you're worried I would suggest you see your family doctor and discuss it. ◆

AIDAN MACFARLANE AND ANN MCPHERSON

84

You're Just Immature ...

Adolescence is the road to maturity and it is not always a well signposted road. One thing about the journey is certain: most young people on that journey are criticized at some time for not being mature. This passage aims to help young people understand or recognize their destination by defining maturity.

How many times has someone said to you, 'Oh, do grow up' – when that is exactly what you are doing, as quickly as you can? And one of the insults adults throw at people your age is, of course, 'You! You're so immature.'

But what does it mean to be grown up? To be mature? What are the signs of a really mature person?

◆

MATURE PERSONS KNOW something about themselves. They possess something of the gift for seeing themselves as others see them. They are also able to laugh at themselves; they have a sense of humour.

In a world of social relationships personal insights must be accompanied by social insights too. The mature person is sensitive to the world of his fellows, able to see their point of view, and accept their right to hold opinions. Such insights are more than toleration. Social understanding, as well as social toleration, is necessary for the effective handling of human affairs.

A mature person is interested in many things. A cultured person has been described as one who can talk for an hour without revealing his occupation. He has a wide capacity for enjoyment.

☞

The cultivation of interests enriches our 'world' and widens our horizons. It also adds to our stability. In times of trouble the many-sided person has more to fall back upon as well as more to look forward to. Small worlds not infrequently collapse.

The mature person is an active participant. Insights and interests by themselves are not enough. There must be a capacity to 'lose oneself' in group participation. Indeed much of our self-discovery and many of our social insights arise, and can only arise, out of our participation and rôle-playing.

The mature adult is expected to participate in the important sectors of social life – as worker in the economic field, as husband or wife in the domestic field, as student in the educational field, as intelligent voter in the political field, as devotee and crusader in the religious field, as companion and enthusiast in the field of recreation and sport.

Not everyone, of course, will be equally active in all areas of life. There will be the bachelor and the person who dislikes sport. There are those who, somehow, cannot become interested in politics or religion. We must respect eccentricity and idiosyncrasy.

Mature persons have their emotional life well under control. They are not subject to excessive moods or undue outbursts of emotion.

A feature of the grown-up is his cool but persistent courage. Courage is needed in a wide variety of forms. Courage in the face of physical danger is by no means the only, or by any means the most important, form. We need moral courage in the field of values, social courage in the everyday give and take with our fellows, intellectual courage in the field of ideas, and spiritual courage to face ourselves and life.

None of these marks of maturity, however, operate in isolation. The mature person is a harmonious whole. All strands of his activity and thought come together in his personal working philosophy of life, his 'frame of orientation and devotion', which, in practice, almost always becomes religious in character. ◆

V C CHAMBERLAIN

85

Streetwise

This is another of Rabbi Lionel Blue's BBC Radio 4 Thought for the Day talks. Principally it is a warning that the barrier between 'respectability' and criminality is one that is all too easy to cross – accidentally or deliberately.

If you've never been in trouble with the law, you may feel quite smug. Or you may feel simply that you're not that sort of person: you're not a criminal. This is a warning that it's all too easy to slip into wrong-doing – or to be tempted into it by others. It's written by a man who's now a Jewish rabbi (or teacher) and he's remembering his childhood in the East End of London.

◆

IN 1936 THE economic depression lifted and both my parents found work. They left home before seven in the morning and came back, worn out but grateful, after eight, to get me my supper and put me to bed. We no longer had to hide from the rent man.

They paid the grocer, for my tea, and told me to pass the time till they came home, at the play centre or Hebrew classes. I did neither. I discovered the street instead.

As the gasman lit the street lamps, I watched other children through curtain chinks, sitting round their tea tables with their families. I must have felt lonely and resentful, because I remember tying a crying boy to a lamp post. He mustn't go home either. He must stay and play with me. I discovered I could be a bully.

I became streetwise quickly. I learnt to get into the cinema ☞

without paying – slipping past the usherette, changing seats constantly and escaping through the skylight in the gents. I could also wheedle chocolate out of strange grown-ups, by putting on childish charm.

At first, I thought the street was empty, but then I bumped into other children, who also wouldn't or couldn't go home and roamed the streets like me. They coalesced into gangs who fought like modern nation-states. I was allowed into one on probation because of my age and inexperience. But being not quite seven and small had its advantages. It was easier to steal for the gang at Woolworths, while the bigger boys and girls created a diversion.

It all ended in tears. One day my parents came home early to give me a treat. But I wasn't there. I was roving the London docks with my gang.

There was a colossal row, so serious I couldn't comprehend it. Some of the gang were taken into care, and some were sent to Borstal. I wasn't a juvenile delinquent, just an infantile one, so I escaped and ended up in religion, not in a reformatory.

Even nice people harbour a criminal inside them. Some call him the evil inclination and some original sin. I remember a charming lady at a party. 'I would murder or steal to help my family get on,' she said. Everybody laughed but I felt uncomfortable. Was it a figure of speech or did she mean it?

When you see gangsters and criminals at the cinema or on TV, it's like looking at animals in the zoo. They're inside the cage and you're outside it. You don't belong to the same species. But don't fool yourself – you do! Never take respectability for granted but thank God on your knees for it every day because only an accident or knife-edge separates you from them. I ☞

learnt that lesson before I was seven. If you haven't learnt it yet, you could do a lot of damage and be very dangerous, so take care! ◆

RABBI LIONEL BLUE

86

Childhood 100 Years Ago

Faith Osgerby was born in 1890 at Beverley, East Yorkshire and was the third of seven children. Her father was a stonemason who also kept a few cows. Her unpublished autobiography (from which this excerpt is taken) was written when she was 70. It is a useful reminder of how childhood has changed during the last 100 years and may provoke (possibly in conjunction with passage 81) useful discussion about parenthood and family discipline.

You may think life is tough at times. For most people of your age, it's pretty soft compared with the way things were 100 years ago. As you listen to this description of what it was like to be a young girl around the year 1900, you might think about whether children have a *right* to be happy – and also what makes a good parent. Is a little bit of strictness a good thing or not? You might also think what it was like to grow up in a family that was not very well off when there was no family planning.

◆

I WAS THE third child in a family of seven, and I can just remember the house where I was born. I remember my elder sister Ella who was five years older than I, and my brother Albert who was three years older. My elder sister was a victim of polio and she could only creep around, having lost the use of both legs. Later she had a wheelchair.

I think I respected and admired my father very much in spite of his narrow ideas. He certainly was strict with us but I can't remember ever seeing him inflict any physical punishment on us. That was always done by my mother, and truly she was very capable at the job … ☞

I remember how differently children were dressed. The dresses were longer than grown-ups wear today. If we showed our knees we were in trouble. We always wore white pinafores and our dresses (made by Granny) always had a pocket at the side. We wore horrors called 'open drawers'. They would be judged quite indecent today. The two legs were made quite separately and only joined at the top with a topband which we fasted round the waist with a button and buttonhole. Thus, little girls' bottoms were so very accessible, and mine was smacked so very often sometimes for such small faults, such as a sulky look when asked to perform some task, or for answering back (we didn't dare do this often) or maybe a childish argument (frequent in a family of seven) when my mother would step in and punish *both* – to make sure she got the right one, she said. And if any of us cried for some reason she was not aware of, we got a smacked bottom so that she *would* know what we were crying for. Many times I have gone to school with her finger marks on my poor little seat, and even sometimes on my cheek – and girls would ask what I had done to my face. I used to make up a story (as I went to school trying to hide my tears) about having a fall or running into a door, etc. I must have been a terrible little liar sometimes.

When I was three years old we moved into Eastgate, just before my brother George was born. Babies were not welcomed in our family. I have heard my mother say on more than one occasion in her middle age that if she had to live her life again and knew as much as she did then she wouldn't have had one of us. She told me she even took gunpowder to get rid of *me*, mixing it to a paste in a soapdish on her washstand every night. I hope she didn't hold it against me that I refused to budge. When I was born the doctor called me a very strong healthy child, so much so that he used *me* to vaccinate six other chil- ☛

dren from. This seems horrifying nowadays but it was the usual thing then, to take serum from one child to another. Mother even knew the names of some of the six who went to school with me.

Well, as I have said none of us had an enthusiastic welcome. I can never remember in all my life being cuddled or kissed or 'loved' as we love our babies today. I think all this gave me an inferiority complex which has last all my life. Even today I feel most unwilling to enter a room full of people. I always feel I have no right to be there, and if everyone turns to look at me I wish I could drop through the floor. I always feel even now that I must give place to others. For instance, we were never allowed to sit in either of the two armchairs with cushions which were on each side of the fireplace. One was for Dad and the other for my mother. Of course we *did* sit in them if they were empty, but if Dad or mother came we jumped out very quickly and sat on a hard wooden chair. Well, this must have got into my bones, because *even now* if anyone walks in I immediately vacate my easy chair. I just can't help it. I'm *forced* to do it. Parents were very much above us – people to be obeyed on the instant with no ifs or buts.

All my life has been ruled by fear I think. It must have been the first emotion I ever felt, fear of swift punishment. I seem to be painting an awful picture of my mother. I don't really mean to do that because I do realize she must have had a great deal to put up with all the time. Seven children to clothe and feed and little enough money to do it. Also my elder sister being an invalid from infancy must have been a very great trouble to her. Doctors had to be paid for their services, and I am quite sure my sister had everything done for her that could be done in those days. I remember two doctors coming to the house to operate on her legs and feet. It seems strange to think it had to ☞

be done at home. How surgery has progressed since then! My sister had to have no food for 24 hours before the operation but it did no good whatever. Also I remember my mother taking her into Hull every week to be (as she said) 'galvanized', which I imagine was some kind of electric treatment. However, nothing ever did any good, and she lived in a wheel-chair for the rest of her life. She was very useful to my mother in the house. She could push her chair around all over the house. She went to a private school for a little while. I believe the fees were one shilling a week. Susannah [my grandmother] took her there each day and she learned to read and also to write a little with her left hand. When the school closed down after about a year my sister's education was finished. She did learn to play the piano and also she had a very good voice, so could amuse herself (and us) quite well. We often had sing-songs.

Well, I believe life must have been pretty tough for my mother, and I excuse her harshness to me although I used to say to myself that if I ever got married and had children, I would love them dearly, and do everything I could to give them a happy childhood. ◆

FAITH OSGERBY

293

87

Why Do We Go to School?

*Born in southern India, Krishnamurti was brought to England by a
woman called Annie Besant who believed he was a new Messiah. At the
age of 32 he disbanded the organization that had proclaimed him as its
leader, and announced that he did not want any disciples. Since then he
has travelled around the world, teaching that peace and harmony in
society can come about only through individual understanding.*

*This excerpt from his writings may help older students to develop a
sense of idealism and of purpose. Although not narrowly 'religious', it is
in many ways a spiritual passage.*

Well, you've been doing it for several years now: going to
school. So why do it – apart from the fact that you'll be in
trouble if you don't? What is the point of education? This is
one answer to that question.

◆

I WONDER IF we have ever asked ourselves what education
means. Why do we go to school, why do we learn various
subjects, why do we pass examinations and compete with each
other for better grades? What does this so-called education
mean, and what is it all about? This is really a very important
question, not only for the students, but also for the parents,
for the teachers, and for everyone who loves this earth. Why
do we go through the struggle to be educated? Is it merely in
order to pass some examinations and get a job? Or is it the
function of education to prepare us while we are young to
understand the whole process of life? Having a job and earning
one's livelihood is necessary – but is that all? Are we being
educated only for that? Surely, life is not merely a job, an
occupation; life is something extraordinarily wide and pro-

found, it is a great mystery, a vast realm in which we function as human beings. If we merely prepare ourselves to earn a livelihood, we shall miss the whole point of life; and to understand life is much more important than merely to prepare for examinations and become very proficient in mathematics, physics, or what you will.

So, whether we are teachers or students, is it not important to ask ourselves why we are educating or being educated? And what does life mean? Is not life an extraordinary thing? The birds, the flowers, the flourishing trees, the heavens, the stars, the rivers and the fish therein – all this is life. Life is the poor and the rich; life is the constant battle between groups, races and nations; life is meditation; life is what we call religion, and it is also the subtle, hidden things of the mind – the envies, the ambitions, the passions, the fears, fulfilments and anxieties. All this and much more is life. But we generally prepare ourselves to understand only one small corner of it. We pass certain examinations, find a job, get married, have children, and then become more and more like machines. We remain fearful, anxious, frightened of life. So, is it the function of education to help us understand the whole process of life, or is it merely to prepare us for a vocation, for the best job we can get?

What is going to happen to all of us when we grow to be men and women? Have you ever asked yourselves what you are going to do when you grow up? In all likelihood you will get married, and before you know where you are you will be mothers and fathers; and you will then be tied to a job, or to the kitchen, in which you will gradually wither away. Is that all that *your* life is going to be? Have you ever asked yourselves this question? Should you not ask it? If your family is wealthy you may have a fairly good position already assured, your father may give you a comfortable job, or you may get richly married; but there also you will decay, deteriorate.

Surely, education has no meaning unless it helps you to understand the vast expanse of life with all its subtleties, with its extraordinary beauty, its sorrows and joys. You may win degrees, you may have a series of letters after your name and land a very good job; but then what? What is the point of it all if in the process your mind becomes dull, weary, stupid? So, while you are young, must you not seek to find out what life is all about? And is it not the true function of education to cultivate in you the intelligence which will try to find the answer to all these problems? Do you know what intelligence is? It is the capacity, surely, to think freely, without fear, without a formula, so that you begin to discover for yourself what is real, what is true; but if you are frightened you will never be intelligent. Any form of ambition, spiritual or mundane, breeds anxiety, fear; therefore ambition does not help to bring about a mind that is clear, simple, direct, and hence intelligent.

You know, it is really very important while you are young to live in an environment in which there is no fear. Most of us, as we grow older, become frightened; we are afraid of living, afraid of losing a job, afraid of tradition, afraid of what the neighbours, or what the wife or husband will say, afraid of death. Most of us have fear in one form or another; and where there is fear there is no intelligence. And is it not possible for all of us, while we are young, to be in an environment where there is no fear but rather an atmosphere of freedom – freedom, not just to do what we like, but to understand the whole process of living? Life is really very beautiful, it is not this ugly thing that we have made of it; and you can appreciate its richness, its depth, its extraordinary loveliness only when you revolt against everything – against tradition, against the present ☛

rotten society – so that you as a human being find out for yourself what is true. Not to imitate but to discover – *that* is education, is it not? It is very easy to conform to what your society or your parents and teachers tell you. That is a safe and easy way of existing; but that is not living, because in it there is fear, decay, death. To live is to find out for yourself what is true, and you can do this only when there is freedom, when there is continuous revolution inwardly, within yourself. ◆

JIDDU KRISHNAMURTI

88

The Problem with Food

Another passage intended to give an understanding of the past and to develop a sense of gratitude for the conveniences of modern life.

From 1909 to 1913, the Fabian Women's Group recorded the daily budgets and lifestyles of 30 families living in south London. Their record, which became a classic text, was published under the title Round About a Pound a Week.

Supermarkets, fridges, freezers ... there is so much we take for granted these days. It wasn't the same in the past and it isn't the same in many countries. What would life be like without the machines and food storage we now take for granted? This is a description of how a housewife managed in the year 1910 on the housekeeping allowance her husband gave her of round about a pound a week.

◆

THE PLACE WHERE food is bought is important. How it is bought and when are also important questions. The usual plan for a Lambeth housekeeper is to make her great purchase on Saturday evening when she gets her allowance. She probably buys the soap, wood, oil, tea, sugar, margarine, tinned milk, and perhaps jam, for the week. To these she adds the Sunday dinner, which means a joint or part of a joint, greens and potatoes. The bread she gets daily, also the rasher, fish, or other relish, for her husband's special use. Further purchases of meat are made, if they are made, about Wednesday, while potatoes and pot herbs, as well as fish, often come round on barrows, and are usually bought as required. When she has put aside the rent, the insurance, the boot-club money, and spent the Saturday night's five or six shillings, she keeps the pennies for the ☞

gas-meter and the money for the little extras in some kind of purse or private receptacle which lives within reach of her hand. A woman, during the time she is laid up at her confinement, will sleep with her purse in her hand or under the pillow, and during the daytime she doles out with an anxious heart the pennies for gas or the twopences for father's relish. She generally complains bitterly that the neighbour who is 'doing' for her has a heavy hand with the margarine, and no conscience with the tea or sugar.

The regular shopping is monotonous. The order at the grocer's shop is nearly always the same, as is also that at the oilman's. The Sunday dinner requires thought, but tends to repeat itself with the more methodical housewife, who has perhaps a leaning towards neck of mutton as the most interesting of the cheaper joints, or towards a half-shoulder as cutting to better advantage. It is often the same dinner week after week – one course of meat with greens and potatoes. Some women indulge in flights of fancy, and treat the family to a few pounds of fat bacon at sixpence per pound, a quality which is not to be recommended, or even to the extravagance of a rabbit and onions for a change. These women would be likely to vary the vegetables too; and in their accounts tomatoes, when tomatoes are cheap, may appear. It is only in the budgets of the very small family, however, that such extravagant luxuries would creep in.

In households where there is but one room there may be no storage space at all. Coal may be kept in the one cupboard on the floor beside the fireplace; or there may be such hoards of mice in the walls that no place is safe for food but a basin with a plate over it. One woman when lying in bed early in the morning unravelled a mystery which had puzzled her for weeks. She had not been able to find out how the food she kept ☛

on a high shelf of the dresser was being got at by mice. On the morning in question her eye was caught by movements which appeared to her to be in the air above her head. To her surprise, she realized that a long procession of mice was making use of her clothes-line to cross the room and climb down the loose end on to the high dresser shelf. They would, when satisfied, doubtless have returned by the same route had she not roused her husband. 'But 'e ony terrified 'em,' she said sadly, ' 'e never caught one.' In such cases it is necessary for the housekeeper to buy all provisions other than tinned milk, perhaps, day by day. She probably finds this more extravagant – even to the extent of paying more for the article. Tea, butter, and sugar, by the ounce may actually cost more, and they seldom go so far.

Another reason for buying all necessaries daily is that many men, though in a perfectly regular job (such as some kinds of carting), are paid daily, as though they were casuals. The amounts vary, moreover. One day they bring home four shillings and sixpence, another three shillings. The housewife is never sure what she will have to spend, and as the family needs are, so she must supply necessaries out of the irregular daily sum handed to her. ◆

MAUD PEMBER REEVES

89

A Counter-blast to Tobacco

A reminder of the dangers of smoking – and a possible answer to those who say that smoking-induced cancer is God's fault rather than the smoker's.

Often, we're tempted to blame God for a lot of the suffering in the world – but much of it isn't his fault. We start wars, he doesn't.

But what about those 'accidents' that we haven't got the wit to prevent? Not the sort of accident that's caused by the machines we make and misuse, like high-speed cars in built-up areas, nor the sort of accident that's caused by our carelessness or drunkenness, but an 'accident' such as illness? Surely God could have arranged things so that we don't suffer such terrible diseases as cancer?

◆

WE DON'T YET understand the cause of all cancers but nowadays it's surely our fault (and not God's) if we persist in smoking when there's a warning on every pack of cigarettes and there's so much health education material around. But what about the people who died before the connection between smoking and cancer was properly understood? Whose fault was that?

One answer is that the first warning about the dangers of smoking came very early on. It's generally agreed that smoking was made popular in Britain by Sir Walter Raleigh (and others) around 1585. Only 20 years later, no less a person than the King (King James I) was issuing a stern, and very accurate,

☞

warning about the dangers of smoking, and the dangers of passive smoking. If only his advice had been followed …

And for the vanities committed in this filthy custom, is it not both great vanity and uncleanness, that at the table, a place of respect, of cleanliness, of modesty, men should not be ashamed to sit tossing of tobacco pipes, and puffing of the smoke of tobacco one to another, making the filthy smoke and stink thereof to exhale athwart the dishes, and infect the air, when very often men that abhor it are at their repast? Surely smoke becomes a kitchen far better than a dining chamber, and yet it makes a kitchen also oftentimes in the inward parts of men, soiling and infecting them, with an unctuous and oily kind of soot, as hath been found in some great tobacco takers, that after their death were opened.

And is it not a great vanity, that a man cannot heartily welcome his friend now, but straight they must be in hand with tobacco? No, it is become in place of a cure a point of good fellowship, and he that will refuse to take a pipe of tobacco among his fellows (though by his own election he would rather feel the savour of a sink), is accounted peevish and no good company, even as they do with tippling in the cold eastern countries. Yea the mistress cannot in a more mannerly kind entertain her servant, than by giving him out of her fair hand a pipe of tobacco. But herein is not only a great vanity, but a great contempt of God's good gifts, that the sweetness of man's breath, being a good gift of God, should be wilfully corrupted by this stinking smoke, wherein I must confess, it hath too strong a virtue: and so that which is an ornament of nature, and can neither by any artifice be at the first acquired, nor once lost, be recovered again, shall be filthily corrupted with an incurable stink, which vile quality is as directly con- ☛

trary to that wrong opinion which is holden of the wholesomeness thereof, as the venom of putrefaction is contrary to the virtue preservative.

Moreover, which is a great iniquity and against all humanity, the husband shall not be ashamed to reduce thereby his delicate, wholesome, and clean complexioned wife to that extremity, that either she must also corrupt her sweet breath therewith, or else resolve to live in a perpetual stinking torment.

Have you not reason then to be ashamed, and to forbear this filthy novelty, so basely grounded, so foolishly received and so grossly mistaken in the right use thereof? In your abuse thereof sinning against God, harming yourself both in persons and goods, and taking also thereby the marks and notes of vanity upon you: by the custom thereof making yourselves to be wondered at by all foreign civil nations, and by all strangers that come among you, to be scorned and condemned. A custom loathsome to the eye, hateful to the nose, harmful to the brain, dangerous to the lungs, and in the black stinking fume thereof nearest resembling the horrible Stygian smoke of the pit that is bottomless. ◆

KING JAMES I (AND VI OF SCOTLAND)

90

Position Vacant

This 'advertisement' is for the 'post' of a parent responsible for running a home and family. Traditionally the post would have been a 'mother and housewife' (or 'working mother and housewife'). In that light, it may be a suitable reading for use as Mothering Sunday approaches or to encourage respect and admiration for parents on other occasions. The reader may choose not to announce in advance what post the advertisement is for.

Today's reading is a job advertisement. As you listen, decide whether it's a job you're capable of doing and whether it's one you fancy. My hunch is that quite a few of you will end up doing this job.

◆

APPLICATIONS ARE INVITED for the position of manager of a lively team of four demanding individuals of differing needs and personalities. The successful applicant will be required to perform and co-ordinate the following functions: companion, counsellor, financial manager, buying officer, teacher, nurse, chef, nutritionist, decorator, cleaner, driver, child-care supervisor, social secretary and recreation officer.

Qualifications: Applicants must have unlimited drive and the strongest sense of responsibility if they are to succeed in this job. They must be independent and self-motivated, and be able to work in isolation and without supervision. They must be skilled in the management of people of all ages. They must be able to work under stress, for long periods of time if necessary. They must have flexibility to perform a number of conflicting tasks at the same time without tiring. They must have the

☞

adaptability to handle all new developments in the life of the team, including emergencies and serious crises. They must be able to communicate on a range of issues with people of all ages, including public servants, school teachers, doctors, dentists, tradespeople, businesspeople, teenagers and children. They must be competent in the practical skills listed above. They must be healthy, creative, active and outgoing, to encourage the physical and social development of the team members. They must have imagination, sensitivity, warmth, love and understanding, since they are responsible for the mental and emotional wellbeing of the team.

Hours of work: All waking hours and a 24-hour shift when necessary.

Pay: No salary or wage. Allowances by arrangement, from time to time, with the income-earning member of the team. The successful applicant may be required to hold a second job, in addition to the one advertised here.

Benefits: No guaranteed holidays. No guaranteed sick leave, maternity leave or long-service leave. No guaranteed life or accident insurance. No worker's compensation. No superannuation. ◆

ANON

91

The Bad Samaritan

Most people like to think that they would be like the Good Samaritan in the Gospel story and would assist a victim of, say, a mugging rather than 'passing by on the other side'. This passage could be used in conjunction with the well-known parable of the Good Samaritan (Luke 10 ; 29–37).

In some circumstances, it may be necessary to warn listeners of the dangers of 'having a go' personally: the answer is to summon help rather than to put themselves at risk.

Would you help the victim of a mugging? Not if you were the only witness and there was a gang of attackers who could outdo any help you might offer, but if it was taking place in a busy street?

The Bible teaches us to be 'good Samaritans'; to go to the help of such victims. But are we more likely to be 'bad Samaritans'? And whom do we choose to help?

◆

ONE OF THE recurring images of our time is that of someone being attacked and screaming for help in the middle of a large, impersonal city, his or her cries going unheard, and the onlookers doing absolutely nothing except mind their own business. This apparent apathy has been used as evidence of the alienated and uncaring attitude which modern cities induce in most of their inhabitants.

There have certainly been many real-life incidents that seem to fit this gloomy picture. A famous example was the case of Kitty Genovese, who was stabbed to death in the Queens area of New York City as she returned home from work at three o'clock in the morning. Yet there were 38 witnesses who not ☞

merely saw but *watched* the murder from the windows of their apartments, and none of them intervened. Only one person took the relatively modest step of calling the police, and even that action was only taken after he had sought the advice of a friend in another part of the city.

In another incident in New York, this time in the Bronx, an eighteen-year old switchboard operator was raped and beaten while alone in her office. She escaped briefly from her attacker, and ran naked and bleeding into the street, screaming for help. Approximately 40 people gathered and watched in broad daylight as the rapist tried to drag her back upstairs. Not one of them came to her rescue despite her screams. She was finally rescued by two policemen who happened to be passing.

Then there was the case of Andrew Mormille, a seventeen-year old boy who was stabbed in the stomach as he went home by train at Manhattan. Although his attackers promptly left the compartment, not one of the other eleven people in the compartment tried to help the boy as he bled to death.

John Darley and Bibb Lantané of New York University were intrigued by the Kitty Genovese case. Was the apparent apathy displayed by the witnesses quite what it seemed? They pointed out that although it seems sensible to suppose that the greater the number of people who witness an incident the more likely the victim is to receive assistance, this proved shockingly untrue in the Genovese case. With so many witnesses to the murder, surely someone should have gone to the girl's assistance?

Darley and Latané argued that, paradoxically, a victim may be in a more fortunate position with just one bystander than with several. In such a situation, responsibility for helping the victim falls firmly on to one person rather than being spread ☞

among many. In other words, when there are many observers of a crime or an emergency there is a diffusion of responsibility. Potential blame for failing to help is also distributed. Each person bears a small portion of the guilt, rather than the full weight of it.

As a general rule, we have more sympathy for victims we believe to be blameless than for the victims who appear to have 'asked for it'. The drunken bully in the bar who boasts of his great strength and then gets knocked out is left on the floor.

[Another researcher,] Irving Piliavin and his associates investigated this phenomenon by staging a number of incidents in the subway in New York. A male 'victim' staggered forward and collapsed on the floor, lying face up. Sometimes he carried a black cane and appeared sober, and sometimes he smelled of alcohol and carried a bottle of liquor wrapped in a brown paper bag. Less assistance was given when he was 'drunk' than when he was 'ill', probably because drunks are seen as responsible for their own plight, and because helping a smelly drunk who may vomit or become abusive involves greater 'cost'. However, provided there was one Good Samaritan who offered assistance, several more helpers were usually quick to materialize, irrespective it seemed of whether the victim was ill or drunk.

In an emergency, bystanders have to act rapidly on the basis of fairly meagre evidence. However, one fact about the victim that is immediately obvious is his or her race, and it is reasonable to assume that this plays a part in whether bystanders help or turn a blind eye. Samuel Gaertner of the University of Delaware put forward the interesting theory that most whites in the United States would prefer not to think of themselves as the sort of people who would ignore a black victim's cries for assistance if the responsibility for helping was clearly theirs ☞

alone. However, he argued, if the situation allowed them to rationalize their prejudice, then prejudice would operate, but in a fairly subtle manner.

Gaertner investigated this hypothesis by arranging for a series of white female bystanders to witness a stack of chairs falling on a screaming girl, who was either black or white. The bystanders were either alone or with a calm, impassive confederate of the experimenter. All the bystanders who witnessed the incident on their own went to the assistance of the injured victim. Her race did not affect their action. However, 90 per cent of those who were with the impassive confederate lent a helping hand to the white victim but only 30 per cent of them helped the black victim. In the latter situation, it was possible for them to rationalize their prejudice against the black victim simply by arguing that the incident was not serious or that it was not their particular responsibility to act. Incidentally, both in this study and in others, people who expressed unprejudiced views in questionnaires acted in just as biased a way as those who admitted they were prejudiced. ◆

HANS AND MICHAEL EYSENCK

92

Human Rights

<hr>

'Freedom' is something naturally sought by young, and indeed older, people: the freedom to do as we wish. This passage sets out to demonstrate that freedom and rights must inevitably be balanced by obligations and justice.

<hr>

'I want to be free to do what I like.' Many of us may have said or felt that at one time or another. But just how free can we be? What would happen if we were always able to do just as we want?

◆

AN OLD LADY in her seventies was strolling through a London park on a quiet Winter afternoon. Three lads were strolling too and as the old lady approached they stood under a tree where a bird was singing. The lady stopped and listened with them and chatted, then turned to go on her way. In a flash the boys leapt forward, one jerked the handbag from her hand and the three raced like lightning through the park gates.

Well, what's special about that, you may say. This and much worse happens daily in our towns and cities. What does it matter if one old lady loses her pension, her door key, and her precious handbag? What does it matter if she was shocked and her peace of mind was disturbed for a long time afterwards?

The boys may have thought they were free to snatch the old lady's handbag. But were they? Were they really free to do as they liked? Are any of us free to act on a sudden impulse?

The boys broke the law. This is a fact which nothing can change. If caught, they would be liable for conviction and punishment. But there is far more to the action than this. A principle was violated: the right which every one of us has to go about our daily business in security and freedom from molestation. By their action the boys have not only transgressed the law. They played a part in undermining that which keeps society together.

They broke down mutual trust and they generated fear. In future the old lady will always regard youths sauntering in the park with fear and mistrust instead of friendliness. And what about the people who heard about it? Their mistrust was increased too. They were angry. Some said: 'The boys ought to be thrashed! It's time the birch was restored'. So the action aroused mistrust, fear and a desire for revenge.

The rule of law did not suddenly come into being. It has taken hundreds of years to establish and become a part of the life of civlized men. Long before laws were made, personal revenge was taken for granted. It was the only kind of justice. If a man injured or murdered or stole from another, someone from the family or tribe would retaliate. It was a tremendous advance in civilization when laws were established to promote justice between people, and outlaw personal revenge.

Thousands of years ago people learned that it was essential for man to honour and obey the law. When the Ten Commandments were written down a unified society became possible. And the old story in the Bible tells us that Moses received the tablets of stone on which the laws were inscribed from the Lord God Himself at the top of a high mountain, a holy place. This impressed upon the people the sacredness of the law and convinced them that it was the will of God that they should obey it. The people also felt that the laws were written 'in their inmost hearts'. They knew it is not only the law acting from outside that makes men just, but also the law within. ☞

311

Those people today who disregard the outer and inner law, who, as we say, 'take the law into their own hands' are going back on centuries of human progress. They may say they have a righteous cause to justify their acts of violence, murder and destruction. In these actions they are not bringing justice to birth. They are repudiating it. It is a contradiction clear to everyone that we cannot achieve justice by murder and destruction.

We need to ask what is our own attitude when we hear of such things. Are we ready to stand up and be counted in the cause of justice and human rights? What are the human rights which belong to all men and women irrespective of their nation, their colour, their class, or their religion?

These were clearly stated for the first time in the western world in the American Declaration of Independence which became the foundation of the constitution of the United States. This is the Declaration made on 4 July 1776:

'We hold these truths to be self-evident: that all men are created equal; that they are endowed by their creator with certain unalienable rights; that among these are life, liberty and the pursuit of happiness; that to secure these rights, governments are instituted among men, deriving their just powers from the consent of the governed; that whenever any form of government becomes destructive of these ends, it is the right of the people to alter or abolish it and to institute new government, laying its foundation on such principles, and organizing its powers in such form, as to them shall seem most likely to effect their safety and happiness.' ◆

CATHERINE FLETCHER

93

The Automotive Nightmare

Are motorists a favoured group? Are they allowed to infringe the rights of others by not being treated, when guilty of serious offences, as criminals? This polemic may initiate further thoughts about the freedom of the individual when balanced against those of the community.

Do you believe everyone should be punished equally if they commit a certain crime? Should killing and wounding always bring the same severe penalties – or doesn't it count if you're a motorist?

◆

EACH YEAR, ONE group of people rob the country of twice as much as all other criminals combined. They seriously wound five times as many people, and kill at least twenty times as many. Yet these destroyers, maimers and killers are uniquely privileged. When they wound, they are given a small fine, though others usually go to jail for at least a year. Even if they kill, they are less likely to be sent to prison than convicted prostitutes. When they merely wreck and damage, they almost always get off scot-free.

The reason for this leniency is simple: these are the criminal drivers, who in the UK are found guilty of a million crimes a year. In practice, this means that any driver, over a period, is more likely to be convicted than to remain guiltless. The convicted include those who make laws, those who administer them, those who talk about them and form opinion about them, those who lead and govern ... The probability of conviction hangs over most electors. When the convicted criminals outnumber the innocent, is it surprising that the guilty are ☞

exceptionally favoured? Or that eminently respectable theo-rists sometimes almost manage to explain away the bloody havoc wrought by motorists as an accident of nature?

One favourite theory at the moment is that motorists who crash or hit people are the victims of uncertain risks and haz-ards which simply can't be avoided. Once motorists enter their car – so the theory goes – they surrender control over their movements to an imperfect machine. They become part of a compelling mechanical mythology, as 'bio-robots' – curious mechanical centaurs whose behaviour is such an elevated mys-tery that it needs the canons of an entirely new science to interpret.

Blandly, the high priests of the car cult go to amazing lengths to absolve criminal motorists from all blame, by pinning their guilt on the most unlikely scapegoat. One distinguished road engineer, understandably very popular with the motoring magazines, has even managed to argue that 'the law is probably the largest single factor in accident causation. It even teaches bad driving; obviously, if the driver is always at fault no one else need take any care and the young who start their road careers on foot or on bicycles are then taught by the full maj-esty of the law that their safety depends on others. If they then carry that idea with them to the wheel when they start driving who can blame them?'

The law's failing is not that it pins too *much* guilt on the driver, but that it treats with reckless leniency people who wound and kill on the roads. ◆

ALISDAIR AIRD

94
Death Penalty

This excerpt is a famous passage from Dostoyevsky's religious novel, The Brothers Karamazov. *At this point, Ivan is talking to his younger brother, Alyosha, who is a novice monk. Ivan is trying to understand why there should be so much suffering in the world. It is included here partly to bring Dostoyevsky's name to attention but also to allow time for thought about the death penalty: what, if anything, does it achieve?*

What do you think about the death penalty? Should a proven murderer lose his or her own life? Some might think so – but what does the death penalty achieve? This story comes from one of the greatest novels ever written. It's by the Russian writer, Fyodor Dostoyevsky, and it's an example of terrible cruelty. What do you think would be the right punishment for the murderer in this case?

◆

THERE WAS AT the beginning of the century a General, a very rich landowner with the highest aristocratic connections, but one of those (even then, it is true, rather an exception) who, after retiring from the army, are almost convinced that their service to the State has given them the power of life and death over their 'subjects'. There were such people in those days. Well, so the General went to live on his estate with its two thousand serfs, imagining himself to be God knows how big a fellow and treating his poorer neighbours as though they were his hangers-on and clowns. He had hundreds of hounds in his kennels and nearly a hundred whips – all mounted and wearing uniforms. One day, a serf-boy, a little boy of eight, threw a stone in play and hurt the paw of the General's favourite hound. 'Why is my favourite dog lame?' ☞

He was told that the boy had thrown a stone at it and hurt its paw. 'Oh, so it's you, is it?' said the General, looking him up and down. 'Take him!' They took him. They took him away from his mother, and he spent the night in the lock-up. Early next morning the General, in full dress, went out hunting. He mounted his horse, surrounded by his hangers-on, his whips, and his huntsmen, all mounted. His house-serfs were all mustered to teach them a lesson, and in front of them all stood the child's mother. The boy was brought out of the lock-up. It was a bleak, cold, misty autumn day, a perfect day for hunting. The General ordered the boy to be undressed. The little boy was stripped naked. He shivered, panic-stricken and not daring to utter a sound. 'Make him run!' ordered the General. 'Run, run!' the whips shouted at him. The boy ran. 'Sick him!' bawled the General, and set the whole pack of borzoi hounds on him. They hunted the child down before the eyes of his mother, and the hounds tore him to pieces! I believe the General was afterwards deprived of the right to administer his estates. Well, what was one to do with him? Shoot him? Shoot him for the satisfaction of our moral feelings? Tell me, Alyosha!' ◆

FYODOR DOSTOYEVSKY

translated by David Magarshack

95

Belsen: a Glimpse into Hell

Appreciation of humanity's potential for evil is one way of controlling it. This reading may help to develop a proper revulsion at such cruelty 'lest we forget'; develop a sympathy for those who suffered, and for all persecuted minorities, and nurture convictions that such evil must neither be tolerated nor repeated. (See also passages 53 and 54.)

During World War II, the German Nazis imprisoned thousands of Jews, Poles, homosexuals, gypsies and others in concentration camps where they were treated most terribly. Towards the end of the war, Allied troops (that is, the Americans, British, French, Russians and those fighting on their side) entered the camps. This is how a newspaper might have reported what they discovered.

◆

THE ALLIES HAVE known of the existence of concentration camps for years, but no one could have guessed at the extent of the horror being unfolded today, as more and more camps are liberated by shocked soldiers. What is emerging is the awful truth about a cold-blooded and systematic attempt by the Nazis to destroy an entire section of the human race.

For millions of Jews, Poles and other victims, rescue has come too late. In one camp alone, near a village called Belsen, British soldiers found 40,000 prisoners, many of them beyond human help, suffering from starvation, typhus, typhoid and tuberculosis. Great heaps of naked rotting corpses testify to the callousness of the SS guards. One such heap of unclothed women prisoners measured 80 yards in length, 30 yards in width and 4 feet in height. Children played near this pile and close to gutters filled with dead. ☞

Almost all the living and the dead are grossly emaciated, stick-like figures, their skin pulled so tight to their skulls that they are hardly recognizable as human beings. Despite every effort, more than 600 are being buried daily.

A senior medical officer described Belsen as 'the most horrible, frightful place I have ever seen. I am told that 30,000 prisoners died in the last few months. I can well believe the figure.'

As British troops entered the camp, the German guards were shooting prisoners trying to take potatoes from a pit in the camp. Several guards, including women, have been shot trying to escape; others have committed suicide.

At the Buchenwald concentration camp, American forces are fighting to save the lives of 20,000 prisoners, although 2,500 of these are so close to death that there is little hope for them. They include 900 boys under 14, their parents either dead or among the millions of homeless refugees wandering Europe today. American doctors are feeding them with every drop of milk available until they can begin to digest solid foods.

It will be months, possibly years, before the dreadful balance sheet of death is completed, but already proven stories of unbelievable cruelty are emerging. At Buchenwald, the victorious army preserved the portable scaffold from which prisoners were hanged publicly, a lampshade made from tattooed human skin for the camp commandant's wife, brass-studded leather lashes, even shrunken heads.

Many prisoners have even been used as medical 'guinea pigs' and subjected to operations without anaesthetics. ◆

CHRONICLE OF THE TWENTIETH CENTURY

96

Hiroshima

Having invented nuclear weapons, it is impossible to uninvent them. Each generation needs to be aware of the reality of their effect. To understand, to empathize, and perhaps to pray that they are never used again, could be said to be a necessary aspect of 'being religious'.

World War II ended in Europe in May 1945. It continued in the Far East against Japan until August that year when two atom bombs were dropped on the Japanese cities of Hiroshima and Nagasaki. This is how a newspaper of the time might have reported the event.

◆

9 AUGUST. FOR the second time an atomic bomb fell upon Japan today, obliterating Nagasaki, the ship-building centre on the Japanese island of Kyushu. Smoke and dust clouds completely covered the town and rose five miles high in a giant mushroom-shaped cloud. Japan claims that 70,000 perished and more are dying daily.

The world's first atomic bomb, with 2000 times the blast power of the 'Grand Slam' British bomb yet only a tenth of the size, destroyed Hiroshima three days ago. Both raids were carried out by the US Army Air Corps' Super-Fortress aircraft. President Truman delivered a fresh warning. 'If Japan does not surrender, atomic bombs will be dropped on her war industries.' He had already threatened 'a rain of ruin from the air, the like of which has never been seen on this earth'.

The plane that carried the Hiroshima bomb was named *Enola Gay* after the mother of the pilot, Colonel Paul W Tibbets.

☛

Also on board was Captain William Parsons, US Navy, who described the flash of the explosion as being as brilliant as the Sun. Concussion from the burst struck the plane ten miles away with the force of a near-miss by flak. Reconnaissance planes have reported that, four hours after the explosion, nothing could be seen of the city but a pall of smoke and fires round the outskirts.

The wonder weapon, created by British and American scientists, is described as the greatest scientific discovery in history. They worked round the clock to have it ready for action.

Mr Churchill (Britain's Prime Minister) said: 'By God's mercy British and American science outpaced all German efforts. The possession of these powers by the Germans at any time might have altered the result of the war and profound anxiety was felt by those who were informed.'

10 August. A secret project, which involved 100,000 workers and took years to bring completion, lay behind the atomic bomb dropped on Hiroshima in Japan. Central to this Manhattan Project was the new city of Los Alamos in the New Mexico desert, which grew until it had 70,000 inhabitants. Here an international team of scientists, under the direction of Dr Robert Oppenheimer of the University of California, carried out the basic research for the bomb, and designed and built it. Two gigantic factories, one at Oak Ridge in Tennessee, the other at Hanford, Washington, produced materials for the bomb. Their exact nature has not been revealed, but is known that uranium is involved.

Shortly before the war the German scientist Otto Hahn discovered that atoms of a form of uranium called uranium-235 would undergo fission, that is, splitting into two roughly equal halves, with the release of energy in a chain reaction, which ☛

could provide the basis of an atomic bomb. However, uranium-235 forms less than 1 per cent of natural uranium and, as it has identical chemical properties to the other 99 per cent, separating it is a very formidable task. This is presumably one of the tasks undertaken at the big Manhattan Project factories.

According to a statement by Mr Winston Churchill, British scientists played a major part in the early days of the research, before the US came into the war. However, when the vast scale of the enterprise became clear, all work was transferred to the United States.

14 August. Japan has surrendered unconditionally to the Allies. The announcement was made simultaneously tonight by Mr Attlee and President Truman. Emperor Hirohito of Japan will order all his military, naval and air commanders to cease active resistance and surrender their arms. So ends the war which, for Britain, has lasted only a few days short of six years. The return of peace is to be celebrated in this country by two days of public holiday. ◆

CHRONICLE OF THE TWENTIETH CENTURY

97

Urgent: Crisis in Africa

Famine relief appeals can encourage whole-hearted responses from young people – but such appeals can, tragically, also become 'mundane'. A suspicion can also develop that the aid doesn't get through. This description of an incident in the life of a field worker for a relief agency may help dispel such feelings.

We've seen the adverts. We've seen the pictures on television. Another famine, another drought hits one of the poorest parts of the world. But can anything we give really help? And what is it like being a field worker for one of the charities? Musa is a victim of a famine; Miles O'Shea works for one of the relief agencies.

◆

MUSA WINDS ALONG a path across a field of withered sorghum [a cereal belonging to the grass family]. Even if the rain comes, he cannot wait the two months until harvest. By then he and Rahila, his six-year old daughter, will have died of starvation. On his head is a bundle tied in a blanket. Rahila is barefoot, wearing only a mottled blue dress. On her head is a five-litre can of water. Musa turns and takes a last look at the huts that have been his home for fifteen years. With the help of friends, he built them and thatched them. His five children were born there. His wife and four of them are buried there.

He is now taking Rahila over scorched hills and plains to the safety of the town 80 miles away. He has heard that the brothers at the mission are giving away food. Walking is an effort for both himself and Rahila. Two years ago, he could carry a sack of grain to the village market fifteen miles away and then walk

back the same evening. His limbs were sturdy. Now, they re-
semble the branch he is using as a staff. Rahila, too, was once
strong and healthy. Now, her cheeks are hollow and her eyes
sunken. A distance of 80 miles is a long way without food but,
perhaps, someone will take pity on the way.

Miles O'Shea puts down his knife and fork. As the waiter
collects the plate, Miles says, 'Those pancakes were delicious.'
His gratitude belies the fact that he had pancakes for breakfast
and pancakes last night when he arrived. He is the only guest
in the town's only guest house – a town and a guest house
almost out of food.

This morning, Miles went to the military headquarters and
then to see the brothers at the mission. He is a field worker
with a relief organization and is here to ascertain the need
caused by the drought. He puts on his white cotton cap and
makes his way on foot to the northern edge of the town. He
follows the pot-holed ribbon of tarmac that is the main street.
There are people about but no traffic apart from the odd bicy-
cle and military vehicle. On either side of the street are mud
and breeze block stores. There are no shop windows, just
doorways with wooden and enamel placards above them advertising 'Pepsi', 'Tate and Lyle', 'Sunlight', and 'Persil'. Few
of the stores have provisions left, though one of them has slabs
of washing soap on a trestle table outside. Further along, a
woman is cooking over an open fire. Miles is tempted to buy
from her but changes his mind. A metal tray is resting on the
embers with pancakes cooking on it.

He reaches the edge of the town. Tents made of plastic sheet-
ing and cardboard stretch a quarter of a mile towards the sparse
savannah. A hot wind blows from the north raising the dust
and rattling the plastic of the makeshift homes. The breeze is
like the draught from an oven though the smell is not so pleas-

ing. A gust whips up a cloud of grit and sweeps it like a burst of rain across the hovels. It is the wet season but that is the nearest thing they have had to a drenching.

There are neither chickens, goats, dogs nor donkeys, just forlorn people. Men in long white robes sit on their heels under a tree. Women are tending fires in the manner they used to when there was food to cook. Small children are lying on a grass mat shaded by green bin liners tied together and supported by poles. Older children are queuing at the water tank – a six-foot cube of sheet metal with an opening in the top and a tap on the side. The army comes each morning to fill it. Once a day, brothers from the mission bring gruel but their supplies are almost out and the number of people to be fed grows daily.

Miles is soon surrounded by hands held out for food. A man with a wound under his eye asks for medicine. A naked boy of five, with a running nose and skin white with dust, holds out his hands for bread. A woman carrying a sick toddler asks for milk. People press in on every side. All are so thin and sickly that they look near to death. He tries to brush them away but the more steps he takes the more people he gathers. Then, in the distance, 30 people emerge from the bush. They trundle towards the makeshift tents and then weave between them asking where to find water. They look too thin to stand but they are carrying babies, straw mats and bundles. Among them is Rahila, the little girl with the mottled blue dress and sunken eyes. Musa, her father, did not make it.

Miles turns to make his way back to the town but cannot move for the crowd. Then, a burst of automatic gunfire sends the throng shrieking away. Some throw themselves to the ground. Others stumble as they try to run. Miles dives behind a cardboard hovel and then hears raucous male laughter. 'Englishman', shouts a voice, 'come here!' There is an open-backed lorry on the edge of the camp. On it is a handful of soldiers.

They had seen Miles' predicament and had fired in the air to disperse the crowd.

At four o'clock in the afternoon, as previously arranged with the military, Miles goes to their local headquarters in the centre of the town to radio a request for aid to his colleague in the capital. The walls of the radio room are bare mud. The only furniture is a desk and chair. On the desk is a transmitter in a dark green metal case. Above it, on the wall, is a poster of Michael Jackson. There are no windows. The only light comes from a desk lamp, leaving most of the room in darkness. A young major is seated, wearing headphones and speaking into the microphone. Moments later, Miles has taken his place and is radioing the request.

He vouches for the ability of the brothers at the mission to administer the aid and reads out a list of food and medical supplies. His colleague says, 'Subject to military clearance, one month's supplies will be on their way within 24 hours and should arrive in two-and-a-half days. Sorry, we can't send more at this stage. The picture we're building is of a catastrophe greater than we have seen. The crisis extends beyond this country. Unless the West makes a swift response, our regional food stocks will be depleted in weeks. And, Miles, drive to Bharga as arranged. The Finnish Lutherans are reporting an influx of refugees.'

At the relief organization's HQ in Britain, an appeal is orchestrated. An adequate response to the crisis would use up the organization's reserves three times over. A multi-pronged campaign has been devised. A TV crew is flying out. TV coverage will then be backed up with press advertising and a mail-shot to known supporters. The envelopes will have printed on them in red: 'Urgent! Crisis in Africa!' ◆

GEOFFREY HOWARD

98

Prisoner Abroad

This story of wrongful arrest for drug-trafficking may seem irrelevant to most pupils. It is included as a warning of the need to be absolutely 'clean' in this area – more than a few of those we teach may one day travel in areas where drugs are common currency – but also as a reminder that basic human rights do not exist in every country: the work of organizations such as Amnesty International is necessary.

There's no need to answer this now but have you ever been, as the law says, 'in possession' of drugs? And what's the worst that could happen if you were caught 'in possession'?

But suppose you were caught abroad, and in possession of a considerable amount of drugs? If you're innocent, do you get off?

◆

IT WAS AN unusual situation. A driver who had rented a unit to pull a trailer of oranges from Morocco had phoned the hire company with a plausible tale. He said his son had been injured in a motorcycle accident and he had to fly home. Someone was needed to finish the run. John Jones was asked by his boss and agreed, somewhat reluctantly, to fly out to Morocco.

'I flew down with all the documents to Rabat. The truck was empty, so I loaded up with oranges in Larache and drove to the dock. There they checked the whole vehicle and started to drill holes in everything. Then one of the customs men came up to me and said, "You've got a problem!" '

He had. They had found 1200 kilos of hashish in the roof of the trailer.

'I'd only been in the country eight hours, so they knew I couldn't have loaded the drugs. But they didn't believe me. They handcuffed me to a pole, sat me up on a chair, took my shoes and socks off, and beat my feet with a rubber hose. They beat me across the shoulders as well. They had to carry me back to the cells.'

Five days after being arrested, John was taken for trial. Morocco's legal system is a legacy of French rule, where defendants are assumed guilty and have to prove their innocence – which is rather difficult to do when you can't speak the language.

'I spent the six hours of the trial handcuffed to bars in the toilet, then they brought me out for about two minutes. But it was all in Arabic so I didn't understand what was going on.'

He was charged with customs evasion, drug trafficking and driving a truck loaded with hashish. The first two charges were eventually dropped, but the third earned him a five-year sentence, coupled with a £30,000 fine that adds another four years if unpaid. Disbelief at his predicament turned to despair once the realities of the sentence sank in.

'I kept thinking, "God, what am I doing here – I've done nothing wrong!" I'd never even had a parking ticket!'

John started his ordeal in Tangier prison, where there were 40 people to a room, sharing an open toilet. Later he was moved to the top-security prison at Rabat. Here the corruption that characterized Tangier was missing, but the regime was strict and life a lot harder. Prisoners were allowed out of their cells for just four hours a day. Like Tangier, many of the basics of life were hard to come by.

'After six weeks there they eventually gave us beds. There was ☞

no furniture – no chairs, no tables. You sat on the floor, ate on the floor. As for the food, all we got was carrots, carrots, carrots, carrots and carrots. Once a fortnight we got a small piece of beef.'

John's predicament was not unusual. In many prisons around the world, particularly in the poor countries, what we regard as the basics of life are highly-prized luxuries that have to be bought. [The charity,] Prisoners Abroad, used to send him a small but valued amount of cash to help him along.

'I used it to buy food – you could get soups, potato puree and fruit. My wife, Lynne, also used to send me vitamin tablets through the Consul. I shared these with a Dutchman I befriended and I'm sure they kept us healthy – all the other Europeans came up in scabs except us.'

Health was a constant worry – a Moroccan prison is no place to get sick. Fortunately, John was in good condition when he started his sentence and although he had lost three stone in weight by the end of his two years confinement, he managed to avoid serious illness. Others were less fortunate.

'A Colombian man next to me got so sick we had to carry him out. Two days late he was dead. Two guys had TB and walked around with tubes coming out of their chests that fed into jam jars. They died. A Dutchman got appendicitis and died. And there was the constant fear of AIDS because they reuse the syringes. One fellow from London had a raging toothache and needed an extraction, but wouldn't have an injection. They took the tooth out with an adjustable spanner from a motor-cycle toolkit.'

Whilst John was trying to come to terms with the harsh realities of prison life, there were others back home who were also suffering. In John's case, his wife Lynne had the emotional and ☛

financial support of their children, who helped fund her fourteen visits during John's ordeal. Yet when John was moved to Rabat, where the visiting rules were ridiculously strict, they had just four minutes together after a long journey that had cost over £300.

But the contact and the hope it brought were vital. John's family, at first devastated by the news of his imprisonment, were keeping up the fight to secure his release, and had the support of his local MP and Prisoners Abroad. The British Consul was also eventually convinced of his innocence, though their natural assumption at first was that he was a drug smuggler who got caught. But as the facts of his case came to light, it was clear that the real guilty party was the man who had hired the unit.

The turning point came when this man was traced to Dublin and caught. Further diplomatic pressure followed, and eventually, almost two years after being imprisoned, John received a pardon from the King. He flew home to a family that are still coming to terms with the lost years. His biggest fear was whether their separation would affect his relationship with Lynne.

'We thought we would feel awkward with each other, but we fell right back into it. We've always had a very close relationship.'

Back home, John has to readjust to freedom and reassemble a normal life. For the moment, his travelling days are on hold.

'I love travelling – but I don't want to go anywhere right now.' ◆

REPRODUCED WITH PERMISSION FROM

WANDERLUST MAGAZINE

99

Facts of Life

These simple statistics present a picture of a sorry society. They are intended to instil not gloom but idealism; not despair but responsibility.

You have only to look at the newspapers to see how many things go wrong each day: unwanted pregnancies, shootings, drug abuse, divorce ... But what are the figures for these tragedies – many of them preventable if only people behaved sensibly?

◆

In the United States of America in the 1990s, in any one day:

2795	teenage girls get pregnant
372	teenage girls miscarry
1106	teenage girls have an abortion
67	babies die before one month of life
105	children die from poverty
10	children are killed by guns
30	children are wounded by guns
135,000	children bring a gun to school
6	teenagers commit suicide
7742	teenagers become sexually active
623	teenagers get syphilis or gonorrhea
211	children are arrested for drug abuse
437	children are arrested for drinking or drunken driving
1512	children drop out of school
1849	children are abused or neglected
3288	children run away from home
1629	children are in adult jails
2556	children are born out of wedlock

2989   children see their parents divorced
34,285   people lose their jobs

America is of course a bigger country than ours: its population is getting on for five times the size of Britain's. And it's easy to think the problems are too big to solve. But one way of starting is to do all we can to ensure that neither we, nor those we know, become part of those statistics.

And there is one other problem nearer home that needs to be thought about. What can be done about homelessness?

An article in *The Independent* newspaper in December 1992 quoted the following statistics.

'More than 600 homeless people died on the streets of England and Wales in 1991 ... Based on coroners' records, it shows death rates among homeless people are three times higher than for the rest of the population. The homeless are also:

- 150 times more likely to be killed in an assault;

- 34 times more likely to kill themselves;

- 8 times more likely to die of an accident;

- 3 times more likely to die of pneumonia.

... The average age of death was 47, compared with an average life expectancy in Britain of 73 for men and 79 for women.' ◆

100

Dying ... and Death

One reason some young people seem to undervalue the gift of life and fail to be aware of the finality of death may be because we have taken so much trouble to shield the young from the reality of death. Elderly relatives are 'put away'. Funerals and cremations are thought to be unsuitable for young children (see passage 78). This passage is included to help pupils to come to terms with bereavement and death – still taboo subjects in many circles. (See also passage 80.)

It is natural to be sad at someone's death. But there is such a thing as a 'good death'. Some old people are lucky enough to die comfortably at home. Their grown-up children are able to look after them till the end and then death comes gently and easily as they slip away from this life. Some people are not so lucky. The death of some old people, and some young people as well, can involve a period of suffering. Because they cannot be cured, there is no point their going into hospital. So they may be sent to a place called a hospice.

◆

IT HAS BEEN my privilege to work as a hospice doctor. But what is a hospice?

The patients are in the advanced stage of progressive incurable illness such as cancer, and when they arrive at the hospice they are often frightened, anxious, and most are already aware that their life expectancy is weeks rather than months. Many are suffering severe pain or in great discomfort from other distressing symptoms. Our first duty is to gain the patient's confidence and trust by providing appropriate treatment to alleviate the physical suffering. This does not include extraordinary or excessive measures which would be quite wrong for a patient who is dying. It does require medications and nursing skills which when correctly applied will relieve physical distress while not reducing mental alertness. Fortunately, such treatment is available and is extremely effective.

Other causes of suffering must then be considered – social, emotional, spiritual. A dying patient is still a living person and the hospice aim is to enable patients to *live* until they die, and to use the remaining precious weeks to good purpose. They are frail, dependent, vulnerable and in need of that security which can only be demonstrated by love and kindness. And the most valuable thing we can give them is our time; their time is rapidly running out.

As the patient's life disintegrates, the life of the family may also fall apart and be in need of support. Even before the patient dies the anguish of grief will be evident. Grief is the price we pay for loving someone and there is no shortcut through it. It is however a particular aspect of suffering for which a firm religious faith will give great solace.

DR J F HANRATTY

For those people who have a sure belief in a future life, death is not final. It may be sad. It is, after all, like saying goodbye for a long time. But for believers, it is not saying goodbye for ever. This is what one Christian was able to say about his own death.

Death is nothing at all ... I have only slipped away into the next room ... I am I and you are you ... Call me by my old familiar name, speak to me in the easy way which you always used. Put no difference into your tone; wear no forced air of solemnity ☞

or sorrow. Laugh as we always laughed at the little jokes we enjoyed together. Play, smile, think of me, pray for me. Let my name be ever the household word that it always was. Let it be spoken without an effort, without the ghost of a shadow on it. Life means all that it ever meant. It is the same as it ever was. Why should I be out of mind because I am out of sight? I am but waiting for you. For an interval, somewhere very near just around the corner … All is well. ◆

CANON HENRY SCOTT HOLLAND

Calendar

		Passage no:
29 Sept.	Michaelmas	1
Oct/Nov.	Divali	2
24 Oct.	United Nations Day	92
1–2 Nov.	All Saints' and All Souls'	3, 80, 100
11 Nov.	Remembrance	4, 95
Nov. (fourth Thursday) Thanksgiving		5
Late Nov.	Guru Nanak's birthday	45, 71
Nov/Dec.	Hanukkah	6
Dec.	Christmas	7, 8, 15
6 Jan.	Epiphany	9
Jan. (third Monday) Martin Luther King day		10
31 Jan.	Feast of St John Bosco	49
Feb/March	Mardi Gras/Shrove Tuesday	11
	Lent	12
	Holi	13
17 March	St Patrick's Day	14
March (mid-Lent Sunday) Mothering Sunday		60, 90
25 March	The Annunciation	15
March/April	Holy Week and Easter	16, 42
	Wesak	17
24 May	John Wesley	46
29 May	Everest climbed, 1953	56
May/June	Whitsun/Pentecost	18
24 June	Midsummer	19
June (third Sunday) Fathers' Day		60
4 July	American Independence Day	92
Variable	Ramadan and Id-ul-Fitr	20

Author/Source Index Passage No:

Adams, Richard	29
Aird, Alisdair	93
Aurelius, Marcus	67
Bagry, Sanjit Kaur	37
Ball, Bobby	58
Barclay, William	42
Blue, Rabbi Lionel	68, 85
Book of Common Prayer	78
Burgess, Alan	52
Burrows, Ruth	82
Chamberlain, V. C.	84
Chaundler, Christine	14
Children's Encyclopedia	46, 48
Chronicle of the Twentieth Century	95, 96
Church, Richard	39
Davidson, Margaret	11
Davies, Paul	79
Dekel, Sheila Cohn	54
Dickens, Charles	23
Dostoyevsky, Fyodor	94
Eysenck, Hans and Michael	91
Fletcher, Catherine	92
Gaarder, Jostein	74
Garfield, Leon	27
Gaukroger, Stephen	33
Giono, Jean	31
Goudsblom, Johan	19

Hanks, Geoffrey 5, 50
Hanratty, Doctor J. F. 100
Hartman, Bob 15
Hayter, John 53
Herodotus 22
Holland, Canon Henry Scott 100
Howard, Geoffrey 97
Hughes, Erica 1, 19

Independent, The 99

Jackman, Stuart 16
Jaffrey, Madhur 13
James I (and VI of Scotland) 89

Kendrick, Rosalyn A. 42, 75
Kenneth, Brother, CGA 14
King, Martin Luther 10
Kossoff, David 24
Krishnamurti, Jiddu 87

Lagnado, Lucette Matalon 54
L'Anselme, Jean 34
Lawrence, David 70
Lefèvre, Pierre 35, 49, 81
Lennon, Frances 18
Longfellow, Henry Wadsworth 9

Macfarlane, Aidan 83
Mais, Roger 36
Manley, Father Robert 3, 64
McLeish, Kenneth 21
McPherson, Ann 83
Mercer, Nick 33
Mitchell, Adrian 60

Nanak, Guru 71

O'Connor, Bernard, OSA 12
Osgerby, Faith 86
Ouaknin, Marc-Alain 26

Owen, Wilfred   4

Parrinder, Geoffrey   80
Pascal, Blaise (*see Warburton, Nigel*)

Reeves, Maud Pember   88
Rice, Judith   59
Rinaldi, Peter   49
Rotnemer, Dory   26
Rukaini, Abdul Rahman   7, 43, 44
Rushbrook, Rosalyn   63

Schools Council   32, 72
Self, David   2, 9, 18, 20, 25, 45, 55, 62, 66, 69, 76, 77, 78
Shah, Idries   28
Shakespeare, William   62, 66
Shin, John   47
Sparks, Allister   57
Stephenson, Michael   8, 9

Tenzing, Sherpa   56
Thurber, James   30

Ure, Jean   38

Wakeman, Rick   65
Wanderlust Publications   98
Wangu, Madhu Bezaz   17
Warburton, Nigel   73
Watkins, Peter   1, 19
Wells, Dorothy H.   61
Westall, Lilian   51
Wilson, A N.   41
Wilson, Bishop Leonard   53
Wood, Angela   6

Yevtushenko, Yevgeny   40

Motley Miscellaney by Father Robert Manley © The Estate of Father Robert Manley (pp. 10–12); Moonlight Publishing Ltd for 'The Baal Shem Tov' from *I'll Tell You A Story* (series: Tales of Heaven and Earth) by Marc-Alain Ouaknin and Dory Rornemer, translated by Sarah Matthews, published in the UK by Moonlight Publishing Ltd © Editions Gallimard, 1994, English text © 1995 by Moonlight Publishing (pp. 92–5); Oxford University Press for 'Too Tall or Too Short' from *Diary of A Teenage Health Freak* by Aidan Macfarlane and Anne McPherson, 1987 (pp. 281–3); for 'Remembrance' from *Wilfred Owen: Collected Letters* ed. Harold Owen and John Bell © Oxford University Press, 1967 (pp. 13– 14), and for 'The Road To Bethlehem' (pp. 26–8) and 'Epiphany' (pp. 29–30) taken from *The Christmas Almanac* by Michael Stevenson. All by permission of Oxford University Press; Pan Books for 'Auschwitz, 1944' from *Children of The Flames: Dr Joseph Mengele and the Untold Story of the Twins of Auschwitz* by Lucette Matalon Lagnado and Sheila Cohn Dekel (pp. 191–4); Professor E. G. Parrinder for 'Something After Death?' (pp. 269–71) from *Search for A Meaning* Book 2 - Something After Death? by E. G. Parrinder, published by Denholm House Press; Pavilion Books for 'Holi' from *Seasons of Splendour* by Madhur Jaffrey, reprinted by permission (pp. 43–5); Penguin Publishers for 'The Peacable Mongoose' from *Further Fables For Our Times* by James Thurber (pp. 108–9); for 'Meditations' from *Marcus Aurelius: Meditations* translated by Maxwell Staniforth (pp. 231–34); and for 'Death Penalty' from *The Brothers Karamazov* by Fyodor Dostoyevsky (pp. 315–16); Peters Fraser and Dunlop for 'The Automotive Nightmare' from *The Automotive Nightmare* by Alistair Aird © Alistair Aird, reprinted by permission of Peters Fraser and Dunlop (pp. 313–14); Phoenix House for 'The First Mover' from *Sophie's World* by Jostein Gaarder, translated by Pauletter Moller (pp. 252–4); Prion for 'The Bad Samaritan' from *Mindwatching* by Hans and Michael Eysenck, published by Prion at £5.99 paperback 1995 (pp. 306–9); Religious and Moral Education Press for 'Mardi Gras' from *Shrove Tuesday, Ash Wednesday and Mardi Gras* by Margaret Davidson (pp. 36–9); Routledge for 'Lilian Westall: Housemaid' by Lilian Westall (pp. 180–3); for 'Childhood 100 Years Ago' by Faith Osgerby (pp. 290–3); for 'No Schooling' by John Shinn (pp. 164–7), all from *Destiny Obscured*, edited by John Burnett; and for 'The Gambler's Argument' from *Philosophy - The Basics* by Nigel Warburton (pp. 249–51); SCM Press for 'Pontius Pilate' from *A New People's Life of Jesus* by William Barclay, SCM Press 1965, (pp. 147–50); Scripture Union for 'Learn The Lesson' from *Frogs 11* by Stephen Gaukroger and Nick Mercer © Stephen Gaukroger and Nick Mercer/Scripture Union, used by permission (pp. 117–18); and for 'Incredible Exploits of Nothing' from *The Superglue Sandwich* by David Lawrence © David Lawrence/Scripture Union, used by permission (pp. 240–3); Selesiana Publishers for 'Don Bosco' from *Man With A Dream* by Father Rinaldi. © Selesiana Publishers (pp. 172–3). Used by permission; Sheed and Ward Ltd, London for 'Temper, Temper' from *Before The Living God* by Ruth Burrows (pp. 278–80); Sinclair Stevenson Ltd for 'Legion and Jairus' from *Jesus* by A. N. Wilson, © 1992 A. N. Wilson (pp. 144–6); The Society For Promoting Christian Knowledge for 'Prayer for Today' from *A Prayer in the Life* by James Whitbourne, published by Triangle, an imprint of The Society for Promoting Christian Knowledge, 1993, used by permission (pp. 225–27); St Paul Publications (St Pauls), Slough for 'Don Bosco' (pp. 173–5), for 'Nothing To Be Done' (pp. 121–4), and for 'Tiny Tim: A Terror' (pp. 274–277), all from *One Hundred Stories to Change Your Life* by Paul Lefèvre; for 'When The Curtain Goes Up' from *The Way Home* by Dorothy H Wells (p. 216); for 'Oh Well' from *Where Did I Go Wrong?* by Rosalyn Rushbrook (pp. 220–1); and for 'Dying ... and Death' (pp. 332–3) from *A Hospice Doctor* by Dr J. F. Hanratty in *I Will See You In Heaven* ed. Father Michael Seed; *The Independent* for the extract on pp. 331; Wanderlust Publications Ltd for 'Prisoner Abroad' from *The Story of John Jones* (pp. 326–29); Ward Lock Educational Books for 'The Happiest Man In The World' from *Herodotus: The Histories*, quoted in *A Book For Assemblies* (in Secondary and Middle Schools) © Guy Williams, 1979 (pp. 80–2); Peter Watkins for 'Michaelmas' (pp. 2–4) and 'Midsummer Fire' (pp. 68–70) both from *Here's The Year* by Peter Watkins and Erica Hughes, published by Walker Books Limited; Weidenfield and Nicolson for 'Doomsday' from *The Last Three Minutes* by Paul Davies (pp. 266–8); Willow Publishing for 'Whitsun' from *A Trafford Childhood* by Frances Lennon (pp. 64–7) Writers House Inc. for the extract from *I Have A Dream* speech by Martin Luther King. Reprinted by arrangement with The Heirs to the Estate of Martin Luther King, Jr., c/o Writers House, Inc. as agents for the proprietor. Copyright 1963 by Martin Luther King, Jr., copyright renewed 1991 by Coretta Scott King (pp. 33–5)

The publishers have made every effort to trace copyright holders. However, if any material has been incorrectly acknowledged, we would be pleased to correct this at the earliest opportunity.

Acknowledgements

The publishers would like to thank the following for use of the passages in this book:
Andre Deutch for 'The Bricklayer' from *The Ring Around The World* by Jean L'Anselme, translated
by Michael Benedikt (pp. 119–20); A P Watt on behalf of Kenneth McLeish for 'The Gift of Fire'
from *Children of the Gods* by Kenneth McLeish published by Addison Wesley Longman (pp. 76–9);
A P Watt on behalf of Idries Shah for the parables entitled 'Astrology', 'The Legend of the Three
Men' and 'Feeling' from *Thinkers of the East* published by Jonathan Cape, 1971; Pranap
Bandyapadhyay for 'One God' from There Is One God by Guru Nanak in *Many People, Many
Voices* eds. Norman Hidden and Amy Hollins; B T Batsford Limited for 'Hanukkah' from *Judaism
(Dictionary of World Religions)* by Angela Wood (pp. 18–20); Rabbi Lionel Blue for 'The
Incomplete World' (pp. 235–6) and 'Streetwise' (pp. 287–9) from *How To Get Up When Life Gets
You Down* by Rabbi Lionel Blue and Dr Jonathan Magonet, published by HarperCollins *Publishers*,
copyright © 1992 Lionel Blue and Jonathan Magonet; Bloodaxe Books Ltd for 'Parents' from *My
Parents* in *Greatest Hits* by Adrian Mitchell published by Bloodaxe Books, 1991 (pp. 212–14).
Reprinted by permission; Bodley Head for 'A Walk In The Woods' from *A Proper Little Nooryef* by
Jean Ure (pp. 132–5); Cassell plc for 'St Patrick's Day' (first passage) by Christine Chaundler
(revised by Brother Kenneth CGA) published in *A Year Book Of Saints* (pp. 46–8); and for 'St
Patrick's Day' (second passage) by Brother Kenneth CGA published in *Every Man's Book of Saints*
(p. 48); V.C. Chamberlain for 'You're Just Immature' from *Adolescence to Maturity*, by V. C.
Chamberlain, published by Bodley Head (pp. 284–6); Christian Focus Publications for
'Thanksgiving' (pp. 15–17) and 'William Booth' (pp. 176–9) from *70 Great Christians* by Geoffrey
Hanks; The Conde Nast Publications Ltd for 'The Man Who Planted Trees' from *The Man Who
Planted Trees* by Jean Giono © Vogue, The Conde Nast Publications Ltd (pp. 110–14); Darton,
Longman and Todd for 'Urgent: Africa In Crisis' from *Weep Not For Me* by Geoffrey Howard.
Published and copyright 1993 by Darton, Longman and Todd, used by permission of the publishers
(pp. 322–5); David Higham Associates on behalf of Richard Adams for 'The Blessing of El-ahrairah'
from *Watership Down* by Richard Adams © Richard Adams. Reprinted by permission of David
Higham Associates (pp. 104–7); Dorling Kindersley for 'Belsen: A Glimpse Into Hell' (pp. 317–18)
and 'Hiroshima' (pp. 319–21) from *Chronicle of the Twentieth Century*; Eric Dobby Publishing Ltd.
for 'Sherpa Tenzing' from *Men of Everest* by Sherpa Tenzing with James Ramsay (pp. 199–201);
Faber and Faber Limited for 'Miss Mary Magdala' from *The Davidson Affair* by Stuart Jackman (pp.
55–60); Facts on File, New York for 'Wesak' (pp. 61–63) from *Buddhism* by Madhu Bazaz Wangu
published by Facts on Faile, 1993; Catherine Fletcher for 'Human Rights' from *Search for Meaning
Book 3 – Am I Free?* by Catherine Fletcher, published by Denholm House Press (pp. 310–12);
HarperCollins *Publishers* for 'The Problem With Food' (pp. 298–300) from *Roundabout A Pound A
Week* by Maud Pember Reeves; for 'The Small Woman' from *The Small Woman* by Alan Burgess
(pp. 184–6); for 'Take Up Thy Bed' from *The Book of Witnesses* by David Kossoff (pp. 86–8), for
'Red the Bully' from *A Precious Autobiography* by Yevgeny Yevtushenko (pp. 139–41), and 'The
Princess' from *New Testaments* by Judith Rice (pp. 209–11); Erica Hughes for 'Michaelmas' (pp.
2–4) and 'Midsummer Fire' (pp. 68–70) from *Here's The Year* by Peter Watkins and Erica Hughes,
published by Walker Books Limited; Hodder Headline for 'Rock On, Bobby' from *My Life* by
Bobby Ball (pp. 206–8); and for 'Jumbo Wilson and Changi Jail' from *John Leonard Wilson:
Confessor for the Faith* by Roy McKay (pp. 187–90); The Incorporated Catholic Truth Society for
'Lent' from *The Human Face of Jesus* by Bernard O'Connnor OSA (pp. 40–2); John Johnson
Limited on behalf of Leon Garfield for 'Bubblefoot' from *Apprentice Stories* by Leon Garfield ©
Leon Garfield (pp. 96–100); Just Seventeen Magazine for 'Being Accepted' by Sanjit Kaur Bagry.
Published by EMAPelan (pp. 128–131); Rosalyn Kendrick for 'Something In It?' from Some
Thoughts On Faith (pp. 255–6); and for 'Pontius Pilate' (pp. 147–50) both in *Setting The
Foundation*; Krishnamurti Foundation Trust Limited for 'Why Do We Go To School' from *The
Penguin Krishnamurti Reader* ed. Mary Lutyen, 1970, © Krishnamurti Writings Inc (pp. 294–7);
Laurence Pollinger Limited and The Estate of Richard Church for 'Four Eyes' from *Over The
Bridge* by Richard Church, published by Mulberry Books (pp. 136–8); Lion Publishing for 'The
Annunciation' from *Angels, Angels All Around* by Bob Hartman (pp. 49–54); Macmillan Press Ltd
for 'Maryam and the Miraculous Baby' from *Stories of the Prophets of Islam* -Vol. 7 (pp.21–5); for
'The Young Prophet' from *Stories of the Prophets of Islam* - Vol. 8 (pp. 151– 54); and for 'The
Prophet's Escape' from *Stories of the Prophets of Islam* Vol. 10 (pp. 155– 57) all by Abdul Rahman
Rukaini, used by permission of Macmillan Press Ltd; Roger Mais for 'Blackout' from the short story
of the same name in *West Indian Stories* ed. Andrew Salkey (pp. 125–27); Mandarin Books for
'Another Country: Nelson Mandela and Willem de Klerk' from *Tomorrow is Another Country* by
Alistair Sparks (pp. 202–5); The Estate of Father Robert Manley for 'All Saints' and All Souls' from